ALDEN 54

LOA: 54'1"
LWL: 40'4"
Beam: 14'4"
Draft: Shoal Keel: 6'8"
　　　　Deep Keel: 8'8"
Displacement: 46,500 lbs.
Ballast: 15,990 lbs.
Sail Area: 1,170 sq. ft.
Fuel: 50 gals.
Water: 100 gals.
Designer: John G. Alden Co.

PRINCIPLE DIMENSIONS

HULL	RIG
L.O.A: 54'-2"	I = 63'-0"
L.W.L: 40'-0"	P = 58'-0"
BEAM: 14'-4"	E = 20'-6"
DRAFT: 6'10"	J = 20'1"

DETAIL "A" SHOWING MAST RAKE

CARBON FIBER MAST SECTION
@ PARTNERS FROM GMT
SCALE 1:1

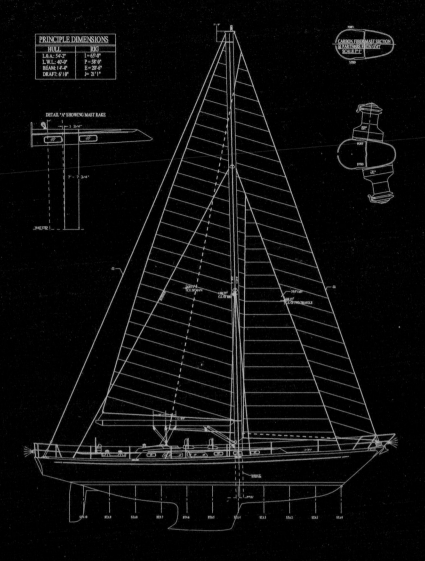

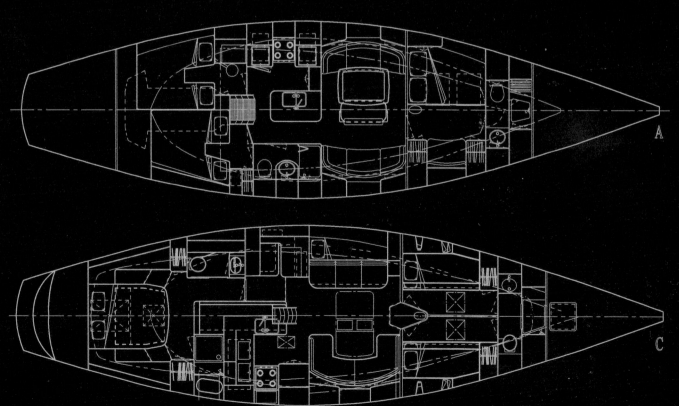

A

C

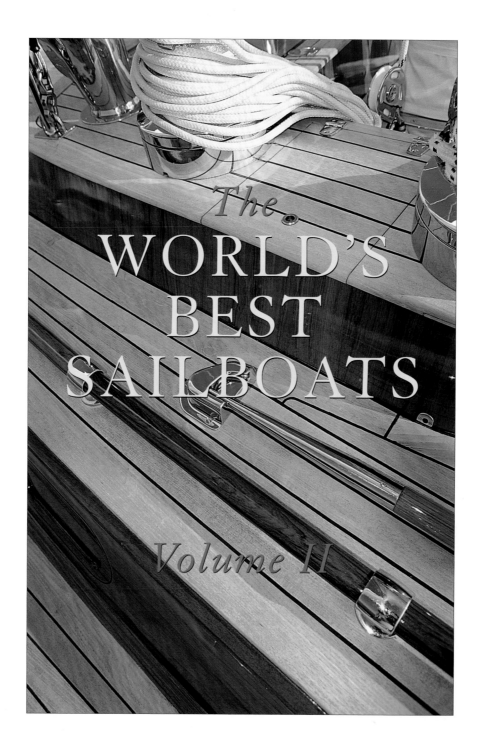

The
WORLD'S
BEST
SAILBOATS

Volume II

FERENC MÁTÉ

ALBATROSS

W.W. NORTON · 500 FIFTH AVENUE · NEW YORK 10110

OTHER BOOKS BY FERENC MÁTÉ

From a Bare Hull
Best Boats
The Finely Fitted Yacht
Shipshape
The World's Best Sailboats Volume I
Autumn, A New England Journey
A Reasonable Life
The Hills of Tuscany

Published by Albatross Books
ISBN 0-920256-44-9
Printed in Italy by A. Mondadori

10 9 8 7 6 5 4 3 2 1

CONTENTS

for Enrico Battei, my dear friend, and the world's best color consultant, without whose impeccable artistic sensibilities, insistence on perfecting the tiniest detail, and endless good humor, this book would not have been possible.

INTRODUCTION

Few things are as exhilarating in life as learning. When one can couple it with personal passions, such as sailing and travel, the exultation is all the greater. No wonder, then, that surveying the world's best sailboat yards throughout Europe and North America seemed to me like a series of strung-together Christmas mornings. The presents I found were all beautiful, most very creative, and some truly amazing and ingenious.

Vast changes have occurred to sailboats in the decade and a half since *Volume I* was published. Quality has soared. The technology has evolved so much that it often seems like a brand-new world. The designs have been refined—not just in hull shapes, underbodies, and their appendages, but also in the fastidiousness of details. The emphasis seems to be on 'comfort,' followed by 'ease of handling' and 'speed.'

You will find on these pages all the new boats—many dramatically different—of builders covered in the first book; I also warmly welcome the big group of 'new' builders. Some you will recognize as established names who have leapt to the forefront in both design and quality; others, more recent entries, but with

such fine achievements in a relatively short time that they cannot be overlooked.

One huge change, I'm rather sad to say, is size. Boats are becoming forever larger, grander, infinitely more complex—no longer the little magic carpets that could whisk us away from our accumulated burdens; instead, they seem to be the very embodiment of the burdens we tried so hard to leave behind.

I tried, as before, to achieve a balance. Apart from the ultra-moderns, I have included a few classics for the romantics among us. But, as in *Volume I*, I chose only builders who truly have their hearts and souls in sailboats, who continue to contribute and invent, while never losing sight of practicality, quality, and beauty; their works are ones you could safely and proudly pass down to your children.

But please remember that, just as *Volume I*, this book is not a shopping list, not a catalogue of a limited number of boats from which to choose. It is, as best as I could make it, a book of *best ideas*—a collection of ever-blossoming, ever-evolving design concepts and construction methods—all of them tried and true—most of which you would do well to remember when evaluating a sailboat of any kind, any make, any design.

Ferenc Máté, Tuscany, 2003

ALDEN
YACHTS

'When we build a boat, when we design whatever small thing into a boat, I always ask myself, What will people think when they look at this twenty years from now? Or even fifty years from now. Will they chuckle or will they say—Boy, that sure is a beautiful sailboat.'

David MacFarlane is one of those rare people with an unerring eye for beauty. His line of Alden Yachts sailboats, all designed by John G. Alden Company, with many details perfected by MacFarlane himself, are lasting works of nautical art. Each time I see one, a sense of great calm comes over me—the same calm that I feel when I see an old stone house here in Tuscany, with the shapes just right, the proportions so human, the beauty everlasting. It's almost a feeling of having lived before, as I cherish something people have loved for centuries; and perhaps it's even a glimpse of eternity, as it may still be loved long after I'm gone.

Apart from his good taste, MacFarlane is crazy. Not clinically, but in a pleasant way that not only makes him completely entertaining, first-class company, but that definitely makes you want him to build your next boat. He's obsessed. Obsessed with perfection. Of every detail. Even at lunch in a restaurant, he lines up the wine glasses just right, turns the flowers just so. Nothing wrong with that, you say; but at the next table?

He was the general manager at Alden Yachts when Tillotson-Pearson owned it, until seven years ago when he bought the company. In all, he has been building Aldens for twenty-five years, and while some builders have stayed with old designs, the Aldens have evolved—the new *45* is much broader aft than its predecessor, the *44*, with more power and much better stability numbers. They have also incorporated the most worthwhile developments in the evolution of keel forms and rudder profiles. But they have miraculously retained the beauty of their lines and their near-unique aura of an elegant gentleman's yacht. And they sail like a dream.

'Everyone who has ever crossed an ocean in one of our boats,' MacFarlane says, straightening my fork and knife, 'always asserts what terrific offshore boats they are. Especially in bad weather. It's easy to do well in anything, be it sailing or life, when you're not challenged. It's when you're challenged that you separate the good from the not-so-good.

'Our mentality in building sailboats hasn't changed at all. I still try to build a very conservative boat; good classic form, good offshore boat; haven't gone to superfine, plumb bows that will bury themselves. We still do longer overhangs because with that you pick up a lot more reserve buoyancy in big seas. Folks who just sail in the bay in flat water can have plumb bows, but it's not a good offshore feature. To gain more stability and better handling, we have gone to bulb keels and foil rudders. And we still build the boats of the best materials we can find.

'What has changed the most is that we're more heavily involved in technological advances, so we're building stronger and lighter boats.

'Take the laminations, for example—the type of glass we use has changed. Whereas before we used woven materials (that is where the weave went over and then under the warp), the new cloths are stitched with unbent flat runs of fiber so you don't have the fracturing of the bundles that you had in the woven. And we have switched from polyester to epoxy resin, not only because there are no VOCs—volatile organic chemicals—with their emissions, so epoxy is better environmentally, but also because it's stronger and lighter.

'We now have the capacity to do wet-preg epoxy for our hulls on premises. And we do it right—we post-cure it in a huge oven, which you have to do to get the best properties and strengths out of epoxy. With wet-preg, instead of laying up dry cloth that you wet out by spraying in the mold then rolling it all out, you have an impregnator that looks like an old-fashioned wringer washing machine with two rollers. It takes cloth through a bath of resin so you get total saturation. Then you wring it all out between the rollers, which gives you exactly the right cloth-to-resin ratio. With the old spray-and-roll system, it's humanly impossible to get that ratio perfectly constant; you tend to get some lean spots and some almost-invisible resin puddles.

'We wet-preg some pieces that are 54 inches wide and 50 feet long. It's hard to handle. Kind of like wrestling an anaconda on steroids. You have to pick it up and lay it in with a crane. So the people laying in can pull it in as they need it. We still roll it all to get the air out, but the resin stays constant. Then we vacuum-bag it half a hull at a time to get out any minute bubbles of air. We've been vacuum-bag molding for fifteen years.

'We vacuum-bag in three steps. First the outer skin, then we add the core and vacuum-bag that, then we lay in the inner skin and vacuum-bag that in. Then comes the best part: We post-cure the entire hull in a giant oven, a massive 60-foot-long-by-20-foot-wide insulated box inside our building. We can control the temperature in ten different areas with ten probes. It's a very sensitive operation. We want the heat in each area to rise at the same rate as we heat up to more than 150°F. And it has to be done at a slow rate, no more than 10 degrees of rise an hour. Then, when we arrive at the final temperature, we have to keep it there—evenly—for twelve hours. And afterward, we have to let it cool with just as much care—no more than 10 degrees per hour.

'We still core our hulls with balsa, as we have been doing for twenty-five years. We feel it's the strongest material in compression, considerably stronger than expanded-cell materials. The core is below the waterline as well, but it's solid anywhere there is a through-hull or the shaft hole.

'And we like coring for its thermal effects—a lot cooler in summer and much warmer in winter, and with no condensation.

'Our main bulkhead is also cored for weight-saving. And we use balsa for horizontal surfaces such as bunk tops, because it saves a bit of weight, it's good and strong, and again it prevents condensation from body heat so you're not always having to air your berth cushions.

'When we are asked to use something heavy, such as marble for countertops, we put a thin layer of the material over a very rigid but very light honeycomb panel to compensate.

'We work extremely closely with our owners. While all our sailboats are still being designed by John G. Alden, our in-house group does many of the details. We have three full-time engineers—one mechanical, one electrical, and one who has a degree in naval design. Now they may work together as a team in designing, but then one of them is assigned to a specific boat as project engineer—to coordinate, be in direct contact with the owner. So all the details are comprehended.

'During construction, we go through the boat every week with a digital camera and then download that into our computer files. So, say we want a special piece of hardware made; we can send the maker not only a blueprint but also a visual piece so that he can see what's to be done and how it should look when it's done. And of course we send photos to the owners so they can see how their boat is coming along. We still do a lot of sketching by hand when we're discussing things with them. First, it helps to communicate, and some people just like to have

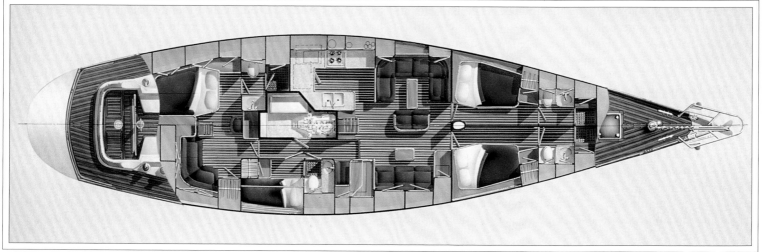

sketches for their albums. You know, they come and say, Well you sketched things out for so-and-so, how about doing it for me? But I enjoy doing perspective drawings; I was born with it, I guess. And I studied architecture.'

And he has been around boats all his life—racing them or building them—so his passion for perfection goes into every item, from the rod rigging to the carbon-fiber masts if people choose. But while his racing days have left him weight-conscious, it's never at the cost of beauty; the balsa-cored bulkheads are trimmed out in solid teak for that classic-yacht look.

And there are the details. He doesn't want you to scratch the beautifully finished cabinets when you lift the floorboards, so he creates a 1-inch solid-wood margin around the floorboards, to set them back from the face of the cabinetry. It's a lot of work, but when you want your boat to last a lifetime, what's a bit of effort? In the forepeak, an above-berth locker has a beautiful 3-inch-radius finishing piece, so you wake up to beautiful furniture.

'We want to build the highest quality we can without going beyond what I feel to be good taste and fine craftsmanship. I mean, I could inlay our counters with gold trim, but that's not the kind of stuff that I want to see in something that I am involved with.'

Blissfully, David MacFarlane speaks his mind freely about the boats he does like to be involved with, and most sailors would do well indeed to heed his wise words.

'Too many people choose boats like they do apartments; the more square feet, the better. So boats end up looking like a shoe box, and some sail like one. Sure, a bit fuller stern gives you more power off the wind, plus a bit more interior accommodation, and that's fine, but to me, aesthetics are extremely important. A boat has to be beautiful, but even more important, she has to sail and handle well offshore. I mean, your apartment doesn't have to be good at surfing under a storm jib down the face of a 20-foot wave; but your boat does. You have to consider these two factors first and then you can look and see what kind of accommodations are left. Not the other way around.'

His ideas have obviously pleased people over decades, for his twenty-five-year-old *Alden 44*s, which cost $160,000 when new, now sell for a quarter of a million.

He loves nice, wide side decks; a good, work-comfortable cockpit; and a simple boat that lets you sail with absolute confidence, in peace—not one that's a shipwright's and a small-appliance repairman's nightmare.

'I like the fixed keels. Some people would say, That's terrible, how do I go gunkholing? But with all the advances in keel-shape design, a fin keel with a big bulb gives you great stability, allows you to get into pretty shallow places. Perhaps not all the places that a centerboard would (you do give up a few inches), but then there is a sizable advantage that you can't deny—no moving parts. The simpler you can make things, the nicer they are.

'Now for my own boat—and I know this would fly in the face of what we do here 99 percent of the time—I wouldn't have even a portion of the gadgets people pack into their boats nowadays. I wouldn't even have a fridge or a freezer. First, they're a lot of weight, and second, a lot of maintenance. Now we have some pretty good aerospace technology that gives us amazing insulation, so you can have an icebox that makes a few blocks last a long, long time. You couldn't keep ice cream, but for all that maintenance, space, and weight saved, I wouldn't mind

going ashore for an ice-cream cone.

'I wouldn't have air-conditioning. A few well-placed hatches with good wind socks, and a couple of small fans for those calm days, would give you nice airflow and save you a lot of electro-mechanical systems, which means saving on space, weight, and things that break down.

'I think we have advanced to the point that we can design boats well enough that people wouldn't even miss the gadgets. Look at most people's homes in subtropical and tropical islands—well-thought-out, simple houses, thoughtfully placed windows for airflow. Almost no one lives on air-conditioning. You have to design things to work within their environment, intelligently, instead of just saying, Oh, well, let's just put in another system. You can literally save hundreds of thousands of dollars leaving these things out, and you'll gain a heck of a lot of peace of mind not having the constant worry of shutting things off and turning things on, charging and maintaining, servicing, and ultimately—and that's guaranteed—repairing.

'An autopilot I *would* have, but the navigation systems nowadays—good God—they are much too complicated. Having a good GPS is terrific, but when you have to interface six different pieces of equipment, and they all whir away talking to each other, having a meeting in your company that you're not invited to, and then they take action based on what *they* decide without telling you what they're doing, well, as a great mind once said, Not over my dead body!'

'Of course, I love a first-class compass, and in fog I love radar, but I don't need a system that turns the boat on its own, gets around on its own. Then I might as well stay at home. A couple of good instruments are great, but *isolated*, so that if one of them has a problem, I don't want it to carry over to several other systems in the boat. I think our boats are becoming imitations of our daily lives—far too complicated.

'I would not have a generator on a boat. If I don't have a refrigeration system or air-conditioning, I don't need a generator. A good alternator system is infinitely simpler.

'I would do a carbon-fiber rig to keep the weight down and the stability numbers up, probably with an in-boom furling; I'm not getting any younger.

'So, you see, I'm not one of those guys who like to navigate by their bunions or claw down the sail with their teeth, but if at all possible, I like to keep things simple. And this mentality, I think, is vital and shows in the entire construction, every step, of our boats—keep it simple, keep it reliable.

'But I do like the way our boats look—the classic, elegant yacht with just the right amount of wood on the outside. Some people would swear that a boat with, for example, teak toerails, requires more upkeep. Well, I would seriously challenge that, because with a yacht you have to think long term. In the short term, yes, you have to sand and varnish it, but then if you get a ding or a gouge in wood, you can always cut out the damage and replace it in a perfectly master-craftsman fashion. But if you put a good dent in an aluminum toerail, what do you do? You have to take off the whole thing. Then if your boat is ten years old, you might find your builder didn't own the dies for the rail, and whoever did, didn't keep them. Then you have to replace both sides. And pray to God your bolt holes match up, because if they don't—I'd rather not even think about it.

'Now all this long-term thinking might not interest most people. But we build boats for people who love their sailboats, who love the beauty of sailboats—that simple, eternal elegance.'

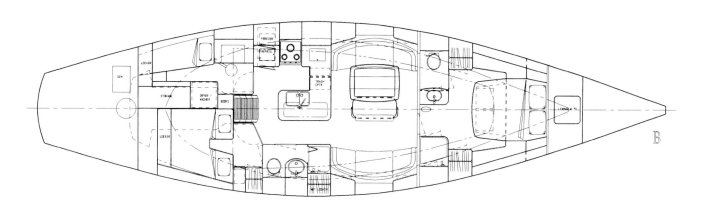

Few boatbuilders have managed to come up with perfectly designed boats as consistently as has Alden Yachts. Starting with the original 44-foot yawl (below right) up to their new 72-foot dual-cockpit sloop (above), they have maintained their hard-to-equal reputation as the classic 'Gentleman's Offshore Yacht.' The 44 has evolved into the new powerful 43/45 (see last page of chapter)—the first with traditional, the second with reverse transom. Right in the middle fall what, to many, are the 'perfect yachts,' the 50-foot sloop or cutter (below), and the 54 (top right). Not only

do they have spectacularly balanced proportions, great lines, and elegant detailing, but they also incorporate the best of the latest innovations, such as the retractable carbon-fiber bow-sprit, upon which foots one of God's great gifts to cruising sailors—the asymmetrical spinnaker. This poleless wonder not only takes the bear-wrestling out of downwind sailing, it also allows you keep flying on a reach. As for the 72, rarely has the center-cockpit solution been resolved so well—there is a smaller, working cockpit aft, from which one can see and feel the whole boat, and a large lounge of a center cockpit, with a great U-shaped settee and a fold-down dining table. And best of all, the profile has remained as sleek, uninterrupted and beautiful as all of their yachts.

The Alden Yachts interiors have an almost Zen-like purity of detail. They combine the very best of classic yacht joinery with modern practicalities, such as the curved laminates in the galley cabinet corner (small photo above) and that welcoming berth in the top corner of the opposite page. There is also a lot of hidden engineering, such as the Corian tops, which, if they were as solid as they seem, would weigh a ton. They are in fact just a quarter of an inch thick laid over a super-rigid, ultralight honey-comb board. A close look at the cabin sole in the photo bottom right shows the intricate, 1-inch-wide solid teak and holly relief around the base of the cabinets, which allows you to lift the floorboards without damaging the vertical faces. In the same photo, note the barely visible, super-elegant hood over the galley stove, and the inlaid, well-rounded saloon

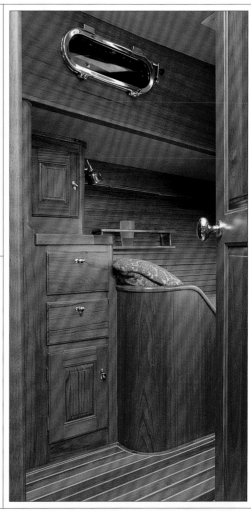

table with the subtly contoured searail. And it's nice to see bookshelves, nowadays too often displaced by the boob tube. For more classic yacht joinery, see the arched, raised-panel door in the small photo above. In the photo bottom left, you can just get a glimpse of the two super-comfortable armchairs. Note also the searails that encircle the counters in the galley. With the molded Corian tops, the searails become overhanging caprails, offering solid-grip handholds. There are even handholds at the foot of the double berth in the forward cabin. Alden Yacht interiors are second to none.

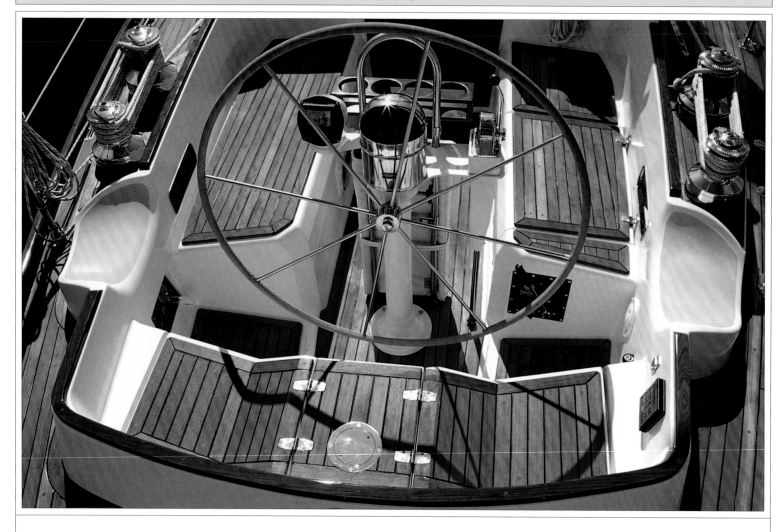

W hile some of the best builders rest on their laurels, Alden Yachts keeps making noteworthy improvements. The cockpit of the new *43*—arguably one of the very best all-round boats in the world—is an ergonomic wonder combined with elegant teak work. The small shell seats port and starboard are perfect for giving the helmsman a comfortable place from which to keep an eye on the headsail. Note that all the corners and edges of the cockpit seats are generously rounded and beveled, both for comfort and for visual elegance. The splendid fairlead with rollers in the small photo at top opposite, prevent those squeaky docklines in the night; and below it, the two small cavities in the excellent tooling under the portlight prevent pooling of dirt and water. In the cockpit photo of the 54-footer (top right-hand corner), note the shell seats that double as a locker;

the fixed jackline in the cockpit side for attaching lifelines; the perfect location for a life raft; and the teak cockpit coaming that would make a maker of grand pianos die of envy. The Dorade box in the lower right corner and the one-piece stainless steel bow fitting in the photo beside it are simply master-pieces. The large stainless door (oppo-site) is watertight, enabling one to iso-late the bow in case of damage; and last but not least, this is the only boat I know that has chrome plating on the bronze base of the marine head to prevent green streaks from condensa-tion. This is as best as the best gets.

'You know, when you look at an old Mercedes roadster, it has a certain essence that's kind of eternal. That's why I stay conservative; try to avoid whims. I like to design and build things that will stand the exacting test of time.'

BALTIC
YACHTS

I f you want to voyage into the future of yachtbuilding, PG Johansson of Baltic Yachts is, without doubt, your best and most entertaining guide. With him, it's not all just theory and conjecture, because at their yard, in northern Finland, the future has already arrived. It's as if somehow the best goodies always come to them first; but then maybe that's what you get for living so close to the North Pole.

J ust a few hours' drive from the Arctic Circle, in the town of Pietarsaari, Finland, they have been building boats since Michelangelo began chipping stone. It's a flat, watery, marshy land with long, long winters and long, long winter nights, so they have lots of time to sit around and figure out how to do things best. And at Baltic, where five mutineers from Nautor started on their own almost thirty years ago, they have managed to make an art of figuring out the best in both technology and innovation, most often a few years ahead of anybody else.

'We were always using the highest technology available,' PG begins in his quiet, thoughtful way. 'For me, the most exciting part of boatbuilding is learning how to do better what you have always done well. And it hasn't always been easy. When we started this company, we could not dial direct to our designers in Canada. I would have to wait half an hour before I was connected by the operator. Then, when we finally got telex—we were the first to get it—we were in heaven.

'The world has changed so much since then, with computers. Now we can collaborate with a designer in New York on almost anything right here on the screen, not to mention what we can do ourselves. In one way, it has made boatbuilding easier, having all these tools, but in other ways, people ask you to perform, respond—whether it's a price or a new layout for a client—much faster than you once did. In all, I would say it is tougher to build boats today. But it's more interesting. As long as you have the capability and interest to follow the new things, it's beautiful. But the day you lose interest, you'd better retire.

'We built mostly standard boats fifteen years ago, but as those clients wanted new boats, we began to change so many things for them that we slowly evolved into an almost purely custom boatyard. Our clients were always, I've felt, much more knowledgeable than the average boat buyer. They knew what technology was available and understood the advantages that it offered. We often start with a standard model as we talk with the clients, but by the time we finish, there is not very much left. Sometimes we even modify the hull—the length, even the beam. But it is easy for us because that is what we're set up to do.

'The most dramatic changes have come in the last ten years. We now commonly build in Pre-preg carbon—where the carbon fiber is pre-impregnated with resin—and Nomex sandwich, so the boat is about half the weight of a normal hull and deck of its size. And this is not just for racing boats, but also for cruising boats for very knowledgeable clients, many of whom have had one or more of our boats before and just like to do fast cruising.

Sometimes people go to designers first, then come to us with a finished design; others just come with a vague notion of size and style and ask us to come up with the whole concept. But in extreme building like ours, the yard should be involved right from the beginning. The biggest challenge with a boat is weight calculation—well, maybe not the biggest challenge, because there are many big challenges. If you build a conventional boat of medium to heavy displacement and you miss a little bit, well that's life. But if you do the extreme kind of construction that we do, where weight really matters, then your calculations become critical. Naval architects, even the best, have to have the yard involved. I mean, if you look at some of the panels we do now, we're doing things no one else can reach, because we have equipment and methods that are just a few steps ahead. So it's not just the weight, but also the position of the weight, the x, y, z coordi-

nates to determine the position, the height of center of gravity.

'This is not difficult to calculate for extreme racing boats that are empty—laminates are pretty simple to forecast accurately—but the interior, that's another thing. Our boats come out looking like they have solid wood interiors, but everything you see is done with Nomex core with a very thin carbon layer on each side, covered by thin veneer. We even do trim that looks like solid wood, but it's veneer-covered foam. For big bulkheads—you can imagine how big those are for a 147-foot boat—we invested in a giant hydraulic press, made especially for us. It has heated upper and lower metal tables—heated so we can do Pre-preg laminates of enormous size. And we can put in extra reinforcement where needed, whatever the size or shape—yet it all comes out totally flat, so we don't have to sand or fill anything; we just glue on a perfectly flat veneer.

'We got into epoxy and vacuum-bagging very early—in the early eighties for hulls and decks—but now almost all our boats are pre-impregnated carbon fiber. We get the Pre-pregged fibers frozen to minus-18 degrees centigrade; then, when we take them into a room-temperature situation, we have about five to six weeks' time to put them on the mold, drop on the vacuum bag, and get it all into the oven. We have giant ovens to cure the laminates, with computer-controlled temperatures at up to forty measurement points, so we can control every surface, every area. You have to bake the whole thing at once—the entire length of the hull, but not all the layers. First you do the inside skin. That's one curing. Then you glue in the coring—at room temperature on the small boats, but on the big ones we use a glue film, and that has to be baked. Then you do the outside skin, and that's another oven curing. You have five weeks to do

each skin with the pre-preg.

'Even the smaller boats that we wet-laminate and vacuum-bag, we post-cure in the oven. Most people don't do that. It's acceptable to cure at room temperature. But if you 'post-cure it' in the oven, you increase the properties quite a bit. We put everything together completely, so all the structurals are in—the bulkheads, the stringers—laminated into the hull; then we put it in the oven for about twenty hours at 50 to 55 degrees centigrade. With the pre-pregs, the sensors are critical—not just for the final temperature, but also because the *acceleration* of the temperature is critical. You can't go too fast or too slow; you first get to about 60 degrees and keep it there for about two hours. Then the epoxy starts to flow a bit so you give it time to even out the temperature. This gives you time to check your vacuum bags for leaks. Then you go over 80 degrees. How slowly or fast you get there depends on the thickness of the laminate. It's pretty tricky. Great fun.

'I honestly believe we're doing things no one else is doing. I mean, you look at our pulpits and stanchions and they look like stainless steel, but they're titanium. You save close to half the weight but it's very costly. We do some of the hydraulic systems in titanium. If you do a fancy laminate and construction, it's best to follow through with the little things, as well. All those little things add up to a lot of the weight-saving. Let's say a naval architect starts with a blank paper, or today a blank screen, having in mind a certain sail-area-to-displacement ratio and a certain ballast-to-displacement ratio; these are the main things you look at for a given length. Then you can say, We'll raise the technology in building and save a thousand kilos. For argument's sake, let's say you have a 50 percent ballast-to-dis-

placement ratio, so now you can trim a thousand kilos off your ballast. Then you look at your sail-area-to-displacement ratio and realize that, for the *new* weight, your mast is too high. Once you build a high-technology boat, very light, then you realize you can shorten your mast and still have ample power to drive the boat. So you save another few hundred kilos. Now, with the short rig, you don't need all that ballast, so you start the cycle again and trim off another few hundred kilos. Then, with the light keel, you don't need as heavy a hull construction to hold the keel, so around and around you go in a circle, reducing weight. I'm not saying the boat will finally disappear, but when you set out to save weight from the beginning, all sorts of possibilities arise.

'In our big boats we have the financial opportunity to do some new things that you could not afford to do on smaller boats. But eventually that new method or system gets down to the smaller boats—whether you meant it to or not. You learn things in a special way for the big boat, and then the next small boat will get done the same way, because people have pride in what they do; they need to do it to the best of their capabilities. You can't ask people to go backward. We value our workers and they value the chance to show what they can do. We are one hundred thirty-nine here, and growing slowly. You cannot grow fast and maintain the quality.'

As we talk, we end up in a huge shop where, instead of the color of pale fiberglass one saw years ago, now everything is black—hulls, decks, bulkheads, hollow floor beams, furniture; almost everything is carbon fiber. To spread the enormous loads the mast exerts at its base, a giant V of carbon fiber runs down one side of the main bulkhead, under the mast step and up,

spreading out and feathering on the other half of the bulkhead.

'We do our chainplates in carbon fiber and Kevlar technology; this way, they can be molded and baked together with the hull. We find this stronger than metal that's mechanically joined. We can easily lift the boat by them. This is not an extreme thing to do. I have always said you should never go to sea in a boat that you can't lift by the chainplates.

'The beauty of building custom boats is that, unlike serial production boats where the molds are needed for the next hull, we can leave ours in the mold until we set in all the bulkheads and interior, or even the deck. This guarantees perfect hull shape, no distortions. If you take a bare hull out of the mold without bulkheads or stringers or furniture to hold the hull shape, you have to have some pretty fancy and extremely accurate cradles to hold the hull shape while you install all those things.'

We stop at a piece of furniture that looks like it's built out of some heavy packing material. PG laughs. 'That's Nomex. A honeycomb board based on a cellulite fiber, like Kevlar. A 2-foot- by-2-foot hatch built with it and covered by the same carbon fiber we use in the hull and decks, weighs about 2 pounds.

'Carbon fiber is wonderful stuff, but like any material, it has certain negative aspects. The first negative aspect with carbon is cost. The other is that it is excellent for transferring noise. When your boat slams into a wave, it's almost as loud as if the wave slammed into your forehead. A Kevlar hull is more silent. Even with the coring in, there is still a noticeable difference. I don't think you can find any single material that solves all your problems, or one that has no negative aspects. And carbon is a bit difficult, because as you're wetting out, you cannot see what is wet and what isn't. You have to have experience; you have to

have good people.

'For the durability of the boat, the most important thing is not so much the fiber as a really good resin. If you use a bad resin, your boat's life will be short. What is especially good about epoxy is that it has elasticity; it can stretch 5.5 percent without cracking. Ortophtalic polyester can stretch only 1.5 to 1.6 percent and then it cracks. Normal glass can stretch 4.5 percent so it's pretty obvious that they are not working together in optimum harmony. From an engineering point of view, it is silly to have the fibers—made to take the load—stretch more than the resin, which has no strength and is only there to hold the fibers together. You are simply not using the fibers to their full potential. Because most laminates are overdimensioned, they will not fail immediately, but you will get micro-cracks, allowing water to penetrate, and then you have weakening.

'Keels have changed a lot in fifteen years. On our smaller boats, the keel is made in two pieces. The upper part, what we call the keel fin, is mainly cast in stainless steel, then computer milled by machine to the perfect shape. At the bottom of that is a lead bulb, which gives the stability to the boat. The reason for all this is to get the weight as far down as possible, with as short a chord—as shallow a keel—as possible. The other big advantage of this system is that, because stainless steel is so strong, we can have a large top cast into the stainless fin, which then spreads the load over a much larger area. You can't do that with lead, because it lacks the strength. So we have a keel connection to the hull that is stronger than that with a normal, all-lead keel. And we use titanium bolts from the airline industry. They're simply stronger. They're the best technology has to offer.

'We have done classic-looking boats and very modern-look-ing boats, but what they have had in common is the high technology. Even the classic boat designed by Bill Dixon, which looked like an old wooden boat, was built with a carbon hull and deck, and a hydraulic lifting keel for better performance.

A while ago, I saw one of our first boats, a thirty-year-old *Baltic 46*. I was actually shocked. Looking at it, I got really depressed. On one hand, I was happy because the owner was still thrilled with it; it still sailed well, looked new. But I looked at the design and thought, Did we really build such an old-fashioned boat? But then, during dinner that night, I remembered how that boat was developed: We did several hull models; we tank-tested; we did tests with different heeling angles, leeway angles; we got drag numbers—very scientific, especially for the times. For construction, we used high-tech sandwich, unidirectional fibers, rod rigging, plus many other things. So, as my dinner went on, I began to feel pretty comfortable because that boat—built in 1973—technology-wise and quality-wise, was so far ahead of the average boat built *today*. The next morning, when I went back to the marina, that boat didn't look so old anymore. I felt pretty proud of having had a part in developing her. Then, when I looked at the difference between that boat and what we do today, I thought of all that we have learned, all that we have achieved. I became even more proud to be a part of this gang at Baltic. We really have a beautiful bunch of people. Almost every morning when I get up, I can hardly wait to get to the yard—I always look forward to something interesting happening, something stimulating.'

I ask PG if he'll be here for *Volume III* ten years from now.

'Yes,' he says without a pause. 'You can never guarantee anything, but I'm having so much fun that, if it's up to me, yes.'

Wow! Certainly the most intriguing double page in this book. Starting with the photo to the left—this Bill Dixon-designed 70-foot cutter looks more classic than a classic but is super-light and super-stiff, made with carbon, epoxy, sandwich construction. It also sports a most unclassic lifting keel. Below is the granite-solid-looking 78 designed by Reichel/Pugh. Apart from its almost impossibly clean lines, it has such intriguing items as the opening transom inside which lives the inflated inflatable. The construction is high modulus carbon pre-preg, Nomex

honeycomb sandwich in hull, deck, and interior laminates; carbon rudder, mast, and steering pedestals. It sports a catapult-type anchor launcher, which allows the anchor to be stowed in a well 4 feet from the bow, keeping the end light. And a little something extra—it has a 'canting' keel system, which, when swung up to 35 degrees to windward, adds entire knots of speed and great stability. Almost forgot; it has ultralight, ultra-strong, and ultra-pricey titanium deck fittings. In the photo above is the 97-foot, in-house-designed double-headsail wonder that does 15 knots in a moderate breeze and, with a mix of captive and self-tailing winches, can be handled by a crew of three. Below is my favorite Baltic, the 52. With its double cockpit and arrow-graceful looks, it is unmistakable anywhere.

It is almost inconceivable that people who build the world's most technologically advanced, super-light-weight, super-strong, and super-fast yachts can also build some of the world's most stunning interiors, but that is exactly what Baltic Yachts has managed to do. Perhaps it's because of their six-hundred-year tradition of boatbuilding in Pietarsaari, Finland, or just because of their attitude of 'whatever you can do, we can do better,' they seem to be able to come up with yacht interi-

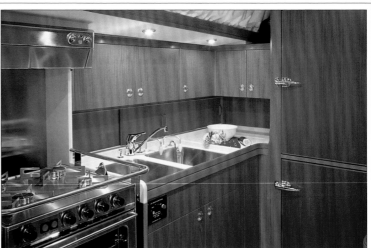

ors that literally take your breath away. And not only is their join-erwork stunning, even using a classic-boat scale, but the most amazing thing is that all the wood you see here weighs next to nothing. Much of it—including the large, curved corners and even some trim—is made of a honeycomb board called Nomex (see top three photos, page 30), combined with various rigid foams and carbon fiber, with a thick wood veneer over them. So whether they are doing the most advanced, almost minimalist European design—see the bottoms of both these pages—or the more classic joinery—tops of both pages—of raised-panel doors; solid, beveled drawers; turned posts; and the myriad wonderful small compartments (beyond the settee, top right), the final result is always in keeping with their original concept of 'fastest, lightest, strongest.' And you might as well add, 'very best.'

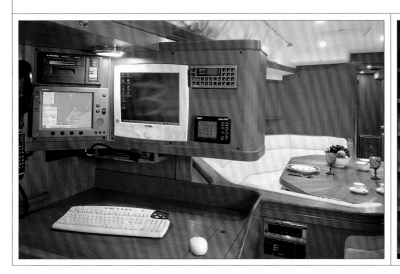

This is as technologically advanced as yachtbuilding gets. Top of opposite page— workers laying down carbon fiber to create an enormous bulkhead. Even the smallest piece of carbon fiber is engineered. Note in bottom corner of this page, the chalk sketches show how the next carbon layers are to be laid, to reinforce the corner of a cutout in the bulkhead. Once laid up, bulkhead laminates are 'pressure cooked'—in the giant press with heated tables (right-hand page, bottom). Baltic's advanced thinking can create masterpieces such as the enormous

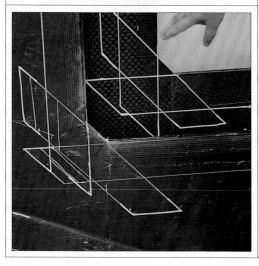

lifting-keel housing beside which PG Johansson justifiably grins from ear to ear. The chainplates, above that photo, are composite, made up of about ninety carbon layers. The three photos top left are of Baltic's 'solid wood cabinetry,' whose principal ingredient is air. The farthest left shows the Nomex honeycomb center with a rigid foam edge to enable finishing-out and trimming. They are held together and given structural integrity by the layers of carbon fiber. Over that comes a laminate of solid wood. The corners are also of foam, kerfed to enable bending. Their carbon-fiber boats are *all* carbon fiber, even the floors (center bottom, left page), and even the louvers for the engine vents, being made by the masked worker. The Baltic keels have stainless steel upper trunks with lead bulbs. The flat bottoms get the weight as low as possible. Simply the best of the best.

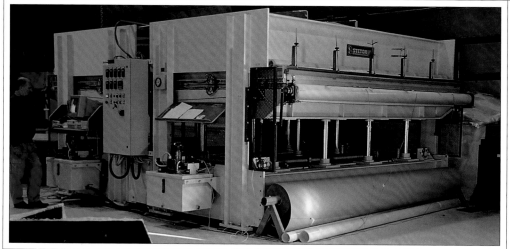

'We are looking at some metals for keels that are about 55 percent heavier than lead, based on Mallory, used mainly in radiation shields, or counterweights where you have limited space. It could reduce the size, hence the resistance, of the keel quite a bit. We're not using it yet, but we're investigating. It's pretty exciting. Great fun.'

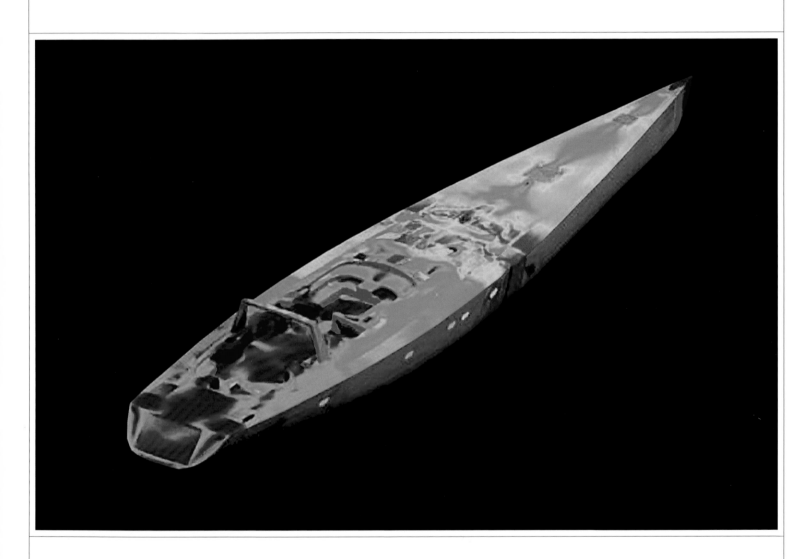

CABO
RICO

'I had twenty-nine boats in Hatchet Bay—including five Cabo Ricos— when Hurricane Andrew's 230 mph winds blew us apart. Only my Cabo Ricos were able to return to charter service.'

I t is fair to say that not a boat in this book would exist were it not for the passion and dedication—the kind that borders on obsession—of a few people to whom the ultimate in quality is a natural reflex, to whom everything worth doing is worth doing best. Fraser and Edi Smith of Cabo Rico are two of the blessedly obsessed.

As you near a Cabo Rico, what strikes you first is the impeccable workmanship, the quality. Even before you notice the romantic bow, or the pretty house or the feisty sheer, the first things that jump out at you are the elegant but robust teak caprails, jewel-like chainplates, and creatively useful Dorade boxes. Only after that do the classic lines of that magician of naval architects, Bill Crealock, or the self-assured proportions of Chuck Paine's designs, catch your eye.

The next thing you notice is the clipper bow. Now some, yours truly included, used to think clipper bows an affectation, a new boat trying to look like a classic. I was made to see the light after sailing a cold-molded wooden ketch designed by Bruce King for his wife and himself. The thing flew. We bought it after the third tack. Even with a modest genny, we still continually sail past nasty and aggressive-looking modern things built uncompromisingly for speed.

A fine technical/historical explanation of this was given to me by Scott Steward, a Naval Academy graduate who is cruising aboard his third Cabo Rico, which he singlehanded up and down the east coast on a maiden run of 4,500 miles. No slouch he. In his five years of cruising, he has been through much of what the sea can dish out, including a voyage in a *CR45* down the west coast from Seattle to San Francisco in up to 50 K winds, doing 13 knots under triple-reefed main and staysail. He calls Cabo Ricos, 'Fabulous offshore boats that sail happily in big winds.' And he adds, 'Partly from the clipper bow, partly from the hull shape, they have a smooth, powerful gliding motion. They're not boats that scare the hell out of you, unlike some light boats I have sailed that terrify the owners, where exhilaration soon becomes high anxiety.'

'The boats have a true compound-curve clipper bow, attesting to Bill Crealock's long personal experience offshore. He designed the boats for serious blue-water sailors. The true clipper bow has a very fine entry—remarkably close in the lower parts of the first two sections to Grand Prix racers—but flares, to what amounts to good reserve buoyancy, which is vital in keeping the boat from submarining when driving into waves.

'The clipper ships that evolved in the mid-nineteenth century have set and kept nearly all ocean-passage records. The only boat ever to beat *Flying Cloud*'s record from New York to San Francisco via Cape Horn was a racing catamaran. No monohull has ever beaten a *cargo vessel* that sailed the seas in 1850. Until that time, cargo ships were touted for their load-carrying capacity, not their speed; but with the opening of the American West, and particularly the gold rush, it became very profitable to get people and cargo out there in a hurry. This meant a long trip around Cape Horn, as well as crossing the calms of the inter-tropical conversion zone twice, with every wind and sea condition known to man. Records suddenly became money. The fastest ships could charge a premium.

'At this point, the masters of vessels began to be asked for input on how to make the boats go faster. So boats became sleeker, longer, lower to the water, with taller rigs. The compound-curved clipper bows thus were born to part the waves in

a very smooth fashion. Once it parts the waves, the flare in the bow keeps it up, and the boat glides powerfully on. I have been in seas taller than the spreaders and never buried the bowsprit. The medium displacement gives the boat enough mass, enough momentum—which is a product of its mass and its velocity—to keep driving on through.'

One *Cabo Rico 38* owner is a rear admiral of the British fleet, a naval architect and head government marine surveyor—one of the group that put together the first Whitbread Round the World Race. He sailed his *38* back to England and wrote a letter saying it was the driest sailboat he has ever been on. And one of the fastest cruisers.

Now it's true that if you want to race and don't give a damn about your crew, you can go through steep waves and end up a bit faster, but a heck of a lot wetter. That might be fun for an hour or two, but it gets old very fast on an offshore cruise. As Scott adds, 'The boats are so stable underway that it's easy to let go the wheel and walk around. The motion is very predictable.' And when you're out there on a vast, capricious ocean with the family you dearly love, that's exactly the kind of boat you want.

Perhaps the secret of Bill Crealock's enduring designs is his firm belief that, 'The best human design usually follows nature.' So it's no accident that the Cabo Rico underbodies bear an uncanny resemblance to the shapes and curves of a dolphin—a design perfected over a few million years and a few billion sea miles. What makes a body move well through water simply has not changed since bodies and water began. Perhaps what finally has changed is our comprehension of them.

As Fraser says in his friendly drawl, 'Pushing high-tech boats to racing rules often results in limited boats like those in the America's Cup, which, once barely past their bow parameters, break up and go to bottom. I think you'd want better margins than that on a cruising boat. The farther you get from clipper-ship bow parameters, the worse a boat behaves.'

And Fraser builds the boats to such perfection that if the unplanned-for does happen, the boat can take it. As one circumnavigating sailor in his sixties—for whom his *Cabo Rico 34* was his first-ever sailboat—wrote from somewhere in the Coral Sea: 'When Typhoon Lisa caught us, the autopilot surrendered, shearing its pin. My wind gauge melted at 120 knots, so I went below and had a cup of tea. My Cabo Rico was a perfect lady through it all.'

So Fraser builds solid glass hulls. 'Then, inside, we put a half-inch of balsa with a layer of mat and roving over it. But that core is not structural; it's insulation. I think a boat that plans to go anywhere should have a dry, mildew-free interior. We also build using Core-Cell, the newest-generation linear polymer foam, vacuum-bagged into the hulls and decks as a structural core on our more recent 40-foot-and-over boats. But the solid hulls that we insulated with balsa have withstood things that amaze even me. They have been thrown ashore in hurricanes.' He shows me a photograph of five of them in a pile, and not one has a hole in the hull.

'We use Vinylester resin on outer layers because it is not susceptible to osmosis blistering. The rest of the laminate uses GP resin, because it is stronger than Vinylester. Next to the less-porous ISO NPG gelcoat, we put our own mat. The problem with off-the-shelf mats is that their thickness is inconsistent and the fibers are held together by starch, which is hydroscopic, attracts moisture, and can lead to blistering. The laminates we use are a mixture of unidirectional and biaxial S-glass or

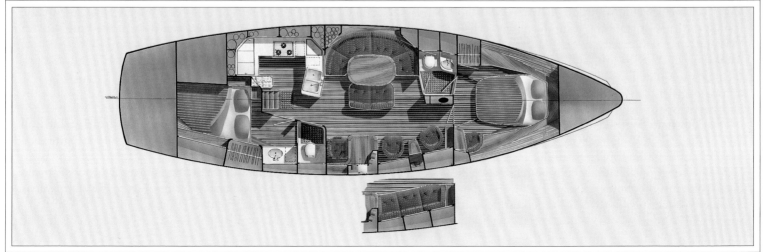

E-glass—all laid roving stitched to mat. We make the hulls in one piece. They have hit containers at 7 knots. Divers found only small scrapes. The first layer after the mat is a 1708, which has elliptical bundles of fibers instead of the normal roving, which is round. The rest of the laminates are stitched 1808 cloth. I don't like going heavier than 18-ounce cloth, because it gets difficult to get the resin into all the fibers without ending up with a lot of excess resin. It simply tends to hold more, and is much harder to squeegee out to perfection. So while it's more work to put in more thin layers than fewer thick ones, we get much better fiber-to-resin ratios our way, and that of course is where we get our strength. The beauty of building in Costa Rica is that we can afford to put in more time. And we can afford such luxuries as three engineers on staff.

'I know it sounds like I'm bragging, but I have one of the best construction crews in the world. My head of production has been there twenty-seven years. He has a chemical engineering degree from Louisiana State. But everyone on the crew is Costa Rican, no gringos. It works much better. There is no friction because of cultural differences. It's a wonderful country—the literacy rate is 93 percent; there's no army, because they think it a waste of money; and the people are amazingly honest and hard-working. We literally have no turnover at the plant. Some of our people—we have eighty of them—have been with the company since the day it was formed thirty-seven years ago by John and Nora Schoffield. My wife and I bought it in 1987; we're only the second family to own and operate Cabo Rico.

'Our goals are extremely specific—we want to produce sailing yachts that one or two people can handle. Across the bay or across any ocean, our boats will take care of you. They have to be safe, comfortable, easy to handle, and as fast as those parameters will let us go.

'I don't like accepting things either from naval architects or engineers until I work them through. I just feel better if I do. For example, Chuck Paine, whom I greatly respect—he did our *42* and our new 56-footer—kept pushing for external ballast to lower the center of gravity. His reasoning was that since our hull is 1 1/2 inches thick down there, putting the ballast on the outside of that would naturally lower our CG. Now that 1 1/2 inches may sound a trifle but when you consider the ballast is only 24 inches high, it's a nice percentage. But then I calculated that you would lose all that space down there for your tanks, because you sure as hell can't put tanks over keel bolts, and ending up with tanks up high somewhere, full of stuff that weighs 8 pounds per gallon, you would lose a lot more in your CG than you've gained. Chuck worked it out and said, 'You're right.'

'I like to be sure my boats last a long time. I don't put any wood below the cabin sole—the floors are all solid fiberglass. It's not the kind of place you want to give rot a chance.

'We put our tanks in the bilge. They're of ISO NPG gelcoat backed up by Vinylester resin, built in a mold outside the hull then pressure-tested for a week at 3 PSI. Then they are glassed to the hull.' And in typical Fraser-the-Perfectionist fashion, the tanks come with a gauge *and* a dipstick—just in case.

'Detailing to us does not mean buffing up the teak searails,' he says smiling when I laugh at some of his typical overkill and call him crazy. 'Detailing means making sure everything is perfect—electrical installations, plumbing, mechanical—every detail. Not just the showy ones.'

'Quality control is extremely important to me. When we spend a lot of time and effort doing something beautifully, there is no sense saving a few hours here and there with workmanship that isn't perfect. This is not just a personal thing. It makes good business sense, too, because it doesn't cost me that much to do something perfectly in Costa Rica, but it costs me sixty-five dollars an hour to fix it here in the U.S.'

All such perfection takes time—14,000 man-hours to build a 45-footer, but then the boat is flawless. The glasswork is flawless. The hidden floor timbers are laid up and detailed almost as flawlessly as the main hatch hood. Their fabricated pieces—they have their own metal shop so they do stanchions, Dorade guards, chainplates, and pulpits all of 316 L stainless—have welds so beautifully finished that the pieces seem to be cast. The classic raised-panel bulkheads are standard. And the woodwork is jewel-box quality. It must be a pleasure to wake up on a CR, with little cabinets everywhere; the tiniest spaces have a locker or drawer. And of course, beside the bed are little teak drink-holders for your morning mimosa.

'All our doors are louvered, with the louvers identical inside and out,' he says almost apologetically, knowing full well that it takes a lot more time. 'I just don't like our owners to feel they're looking at the back of a door when they open a locker.'

On his boats, practicality is constantly combined with beauty. The six opening hatches and four gargantuan cowl vents tell you that these guys really care and know about airflow. All hatches are mosquito-screened, in elegantly bullnosed teak frames, and the companionway screens have their own varnished teak storage place in the lazarette when they are not in use. This beats our boat, where they get stuffed behind the laundry bag.

Every angle of the cockpit is thoughtfully ergonomic; the curved seats, even without cushions, are nearly as comfortable as a couch. This is vital on any serious cruiser, not just for sipping rum punches in port but also for sitting comfortably on any heel during those seemingly endless tacks on which cruising boats often find themselves. The dodger extends well aft so you can sit protected while the autopilot slaves away. And of course the grand-piano-quality teak cockpit table has 'CR' inlaid in ash just to remind you where all this fine work came from.

The engineering is as impressive as the woodwork. The hull-to-deck joint is as good as it gets, with a heavy flange and through-bolts. Its 'U'-channel-shaped bulwark provides tremendous stiffness to the vessel and safety underfoot on a heel as well. The exhaust tube is solid, last-forever fiberglass bonded to the hull. But what is most intelligent is that the tube tapers, getting wider as it distances itself from the through-hull, so that if water is forced in, it will fan out and slow. This markedly cuts down on the possibility of a flooded engine. Just to be sure, there is also an anti-waterlock. Then there is the little fuel-lift pump for when you change filters or run out of one tank and get air into the system. Instead of having to bleed it all, you just turn on the pump until it's full, and *voilà*.

Down below, the quantity of wood seems enough to sink the *Titanic*, but looks are deceiving. It is very intelligently made to look twice as thick as it really is. On a boat of 35,000 pounds, all the solid wood that you see weighs only 600 pounds. Not much of a penalty for all that beauty.

Even the emergency tiller is locked onto its own wooden rack. And there is a teak fishing-rod locker next to the companionway. That does it; I just died of jealousy.

All the Cabo Ricos reflect the unique sensibility of two of the world's very best boat designers—Bill Crealock and Chuck Paine. The first of the fleet was the Crealock-designed *38*, in the two photos on the opposite page. With its true clipper bow, moderate overhangs, and mod-est beam, it is about as seakindly a boat as you can get. Note the beautifully drawn and eminently comfortable cockpit coamings, molded dodger base, and guaranteed leakproof sea hood over the main hatch. The foredeck is ample and uncluttered, with a rode locker that will easily accommo-

date 200 feet of rope. This makes coiling the anchor rode a pleasant one-man job, instead of the normal two-man horror show of stuffing rope belowdecks through a tiny hole in the deck. The top photo on the left and on page 44 is of the new Chuck Paine-designed 45. Note the moderate

beam brought well aft for good power. Just look at the wake she's leaving with only a staysail forward. Note that the staysail has no boom—you may lose the self-tacking, but it sure makes for a safer foredeck. If you look closely, you can see the flap in the stern that opens down into a landing platform.

The bottom photo on the left page and the small photo above it show one of my favorite boats of all time, the *Cambria 44*, designed by David Walters. and now owned and built by Cabo Rico. Her proportions are perfect and her lines timeless.

For lovers of classic, all-solid-wood interiors, there is really nothing like a Cabo Rico. The overlay on the bulkheads and the faces of cabinetry can be solid V-grooved teak that appears structurally massive but is only about 1/4 inch thick. The joinerwork and detailing, as evidenced by the table above and the back of its center settee, is of jewel-box quality. Note also the three good hand grips in the trim. The settee is truly remarkable in that it slides outboard to provide access to the engine below the cabin sole. The utilization of even the smallest or shallowest of places for most practical cabinetry can be seen in the bottom left photo; note the suspended

cabinet above the bulkhead cutout, and the number of perfectly located doors and drawers behind the companionway steps. I like the intelligent corner cabinet in the galley (above) and the classic, shallow, louvered wall case over the saloon table (left page, below). If you look closely in the same photo, you'll see the high galley sea-rail corner, with a beautifully worked cleanout hole. In the photo above, note the exhaust hood over the stove; it's about time someone thought of it. Few things are worse than turning the boat into a steam bath on a cold evening or heating up a boat on a hot one. With a tiny, solar-powered fan, the boat will be infinitely more liv-able. The bottom right photo is of the *Cambria 44*, with the ideal fore-and-aft galley in the passageway of the aft cabin. In the drawing below of the *CR40*, note the excellent layout, with two large private cabins, a huge dinette, a true shower stall, and of course stowage lockers galore.

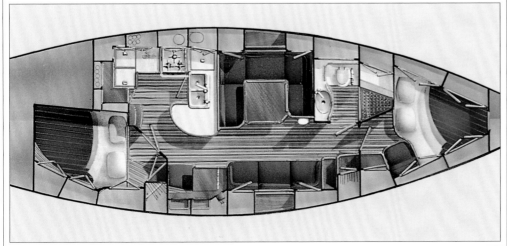

The hard-to-match details on these pages lift Cabo Rico into the very forefront of boat-building. What they do is not only the best of fine craftsmanship, as the photos attest, but also the best of fine thinking. The nicely made wooden box (above, center) contains spare screws,

that is the very best bookholder I have ever seen. The end of the removable teak bar is routed out to slip snugly over the nubby fixed to the shelf's end. The louvers (bottom opposite corner) are difficult to make but are very flat and elegant and as pretty on the inside as out. The porcelain sink (below) is per-

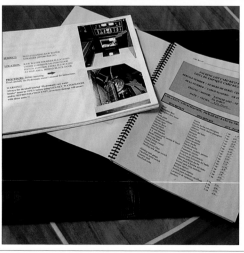

plugs, and the gelcoats and paints that match your boat. To its right, the base and trim of the air-conditioning vent is not only beautiful, but its location, in a hard-to-fit-to high corner, ensures infinitely better air circulation than the typical floor-level vents that cool your feet and little else. On this

page, the bow platform (above) features excellent stainless steel work to protect the teak from the two anchors. In the photo next to it, the companionway ladder is shaped out of a solid piece of teak, with sloping sides for safety on a heel, and has deep grooves for a forever nonskid. Below

fectly trimmed out, and left of it is a photo of the remarkable owner's manual, bound in fine leather, of course. But in it you will not find the customary incomprehensibly written instructions many builders gather up from various suppliers. Cabo Rico outdoes them all with a photo of the item they happen

to be talking about, a description of its location in your particular boat, and very clear written instructions—in English *plus* another language of your choice—in two different colors to keep everything easy to follow. *Magnifique!* Below is an illustration of their new, regal, triple-headsailed *CR56*.

'I can't help myself. We end up putting too many hours into each boat we build because I build each boat as if it were to be my own. Life is so short; if you can't feel proud of everything you do, what is it exactly that you've got?'

HALLBERG-RASSY

To say that Magnus Rassy has boatbuilding in his blood is about as true as that statement can ever be. He grew up in the boatyard his father started in 1965 with what most agree was a visionary cruising boat. Together they have built a line of one of the most successful cruising boats of all time.

The changes that have occurred since 1965 have been in one sense cataclysmic; in another, few. Few because that same center-cockpit, fixed-windshield look is still there, and so is the sturdy construction; but cataclysmic because Germán Frers began designing the line in 1989, the same year Magnus came aboard. What had been functional, workmanlike designs, Frers de-bulked, and the boats are now sleeker, elegant, and fast.

Above the water, the change is obvious: The waterlines have lengthened, yielding more slender hulls, and gone are the big flush decks that used to necessitate rather high topsides with portlights in the sheer stripes. They have been replaced by quick sheers and more rakish overhangs, topped by low trunk cabins with subtle tapers, soft curves, and artistic proportions. This is a major miracle in a center-cockpit boat. The sterns have changed drastically as well; they are all reversed, with those most practical swim platforms and steps, and are all pleasantly rounded with that unmistakably supple—and much-copied—Frers flare that blends the transom so well into the hull's sides. If it sounds like I'm overpraising Germán Frers, perhaps I am, but to me he is one of only two yacht designers in the world who are also truly gifted artists with flawless sensibilities.

Underwater, the HRs are unrecognizable with modern flatness, short bulb keels—the bulb beautifully Frers-ized—and ultra-deep foil rudders.

Magnus, who has his father's joviality, big-boned movements, and even some of his hand gestures, put the Frers' influence this way: 'Apart from the beauty of his designs, we think he's a master because he can combine those beautiful lines with very good sailing performance and good volume, which yields extremely livable, comfortable boats. Many designers excel at one of these, some at two, but very few excel at all three like Germán does. He has given us much more elegant boats. His underbodies are modern with much more speed. And the boats are stiffer with a lowered center of gravity so you can reef later and sail faster. The sterns are fuller for more power and more interior volume.

All in all, these are huge steps forward from the old long-keel, internally ballasted boats we had before. We build eight models from 31 to 62 feet, all Frers designs. We tend to keep our models quite a long time, compared to most builders. I think our average model life is one of the longest in boatbuilding, an average of twelve years.

'Our boats are still built to be solid, reliable, and fast long-distance cruisers. What we emphasize in designing a model is getting the displacement right. It has to be designed to carry equipment, big tankage, good loads for long cruises. It is of little value to design a dream displacement that you will never keep, and end up loading down the boat until it sits well below the waterline and no longer performs.

'As for our reputation for building a solid boat, we have improved on that. We have replaced the strengthening grid we had in the topsides of the hull, and we now build a stronger hull that combines woven roving with traditional chop strand and Divinycell foam core. Where structural parts are bonded to the inner skin, we use a heavier, denser foam. To stiffen the boats even more, we have added a grid floor structure with longitudinals and transverse beams, all of hand-laid-up solid glass. Apart from distributing the loads of the new short keel over the hull, it also does the same in case of grounding—distributes the impact over the whole bottom of the boat. The engine bedlogs are part of this grid. In the bow, additional bulkheads are bonded in under the berth to stiffen the whole forward section for pounding into waves. To create a truly monolithic structure that does not rely on mechanical fasteners, we bond our hulls and decks together at deck level, with fiberglass laminates. We feel it's the most solid, leakproof, and secure way. Above the laminates, the hull-to-deck joints, at the top of the coamings, are filled with a mix of resin and particles of Divinycell.

'One thing my dad always stressed was that in a serious offshore boat, everything, whether it's mechanical or structural, should be accessible and repairable. We always keep that in mind. For example, we put the deck onto the hull as soon as the bulkheads are in, so that all components—tanks, engine, everything—have to be brought into the boat through the hatches; you have to take them out the same way if there is a need to. All our wires we put into conduits so you can add or change wires, and the refrigerator cables are twisted to reduce radio interference. We stress big engine rooms on all models—very important—not only so you can work safely and securely around the engine, which we feel results in much better engine maintenance, but also to have everything in one place—pumps, filters, and all the tools you might need, always well lit and accessible,

instead of being buried in some locker or the bilge.

'Before coming here, I worked at a boatyard in Switzerland to learn German. They mostly serviced and maintained Hallberg-Rassys so I got a good idea of what was right with them and what wasn't. We think of a lot of little things, like the fine tube feeding from the lowest part of all our fuel tanks to a small manual pump in the engine room. This way, if you suspect any water in your fuel, or see some in your fuel filter settling bowl, you just pump until you get clean fuel. We have built more than 8,000 boats; we have a lot of good feedback from our owners, so we can keep improving.

'Our thinking in rigging has remained with a well-supported, stable mast, and we tend to do double spreaders—no runners—for stiffness and safety. The masts are all deck-stepped; we feel it's better to avoid leaks. A massive laminated-mahogany post transmits the compression down to the mast step. On boats over 45 feet, we have a cutter rig as standard, but it is also available, if people want it, on the smaller boats.

'In the cockpit, I guess you could say we have actually developed backward. The first boats my dad built had solid windshields with rigid tops. Then, for years, we went to collapsible canvas tops; now, on the bigger boats, we are back to rigid tops. To me, they're wonderful in both hot and cold climates. So are the collapsible dodgers, soft tops, but if you talk to people who have them, they'll tell you the tops are almost never down. So why not make them permanent physically when they're permanently in use anyway? But one thing that's vital to us is that the center window in the fixed windshield can be opened for ventilation.

'Comfort is so important on a long-distance cruiser. You can stand discomfort on a weekend boat because you'll be home soon, but when you're circumnavigating or on an extended cruise, you *are* home. In the last ten years, people have been asking us for more and more equipment—electric winches, electric windlasses, and in-mast furling. People just expect a boat to be more easily managed. I think I can safely say that over 45 feet, people expect to have push-button sailing. And it's not that people are getting older; for us, it's the opposite. Fifteen years ago, almost all our clients were over fifty-five; now many of them are in their thirties. And they love comfort; we are often asked for full-spring mattresses, just like at home, so on the 53 and bigger it's standard. With us room and comfort were always at the front of our thoughts.

'As for who our competitors are, it's hard to say; there are all kinds—other boats, the house, even the spouse. I'm not joking. Once a husband and wife came to the yard to look at the boats,

and the husband was very serious in wanting a new boat, but the wife wasn't. At the end of the day, the wife said, Now you have to choose—either a new boat or me. Two years later, he came back and picked up his new boat, with a new wife.'

There are a lot of temptations on the HR boats to make you think twice about the future. In fact, their boats are full of the kinds of thoughtful details you'd expect to find only on a boat that someone has lived aboard for a long time. On the exterior, two small steps molded into the transom also have teak on them for safety. The stem fitting that holds the anchor rollers continues down past the sheer so the plates act as chafe guards against anchor flukes. Then there are the brass strips where you step on the teak caprail, to cut down on wear. Similar strips are laid as chafe guards on the caprail under both dock and anchor lines. The windshield has two giant handles to help get you safely onto the side deck. And the bow pulpit incorporates a lowered forward portion with a step, for easy access to shore when you tie bow-to.

The interior is no less full of pleasant surprises. A manual bilge pump is intelligently located at the navigation station, so that in case of a holing, you can sit calmly on the nav seat, pumping away relaxed with one hand, while with the other you can work the microphone of your VHF yelling, 'Mamma! Mamma! Get me outta here!'

Even on boats as small as 36 feet, the whole side of the engine compartment opens up so you can get to every part of the entire engine. And the space dedicated to the engines qualifies, in many of their boats, to be called 'engine room.' In them, there is of course an automatically activated light—as soon as the door opens, a light goes on. And natural-flow air ducts bring air into and out of the engine room. For additional comfort while motoring, a sheet of rubber is laminated right into the deck in the engine-room area so that no sound is transmitted throughout the hull. To make life easier for those of us whose memory is no longer quite encyclopedic, all hoses, filters, seacocks, and pumps are labeled. And the wrench for cleaning your filters lives in a little bracket right beside the filter. It is tied there with a lanyard, so you don't have to empty every locker aboard to find it.

All locker doors are louvered for ventilation, and the ceiling is open, top and bottom, for air circulation, so no mildew can settle in. A nice European touch: strips of wood in the overhead panels to reduce the sense of plastic. The cabinet fronts all have solid faces, and they use solid mahogany even for the sides of the drawers. Inside the lockers is a careful detail—all tubing that passes through here is protected with a rigid casing to pro-

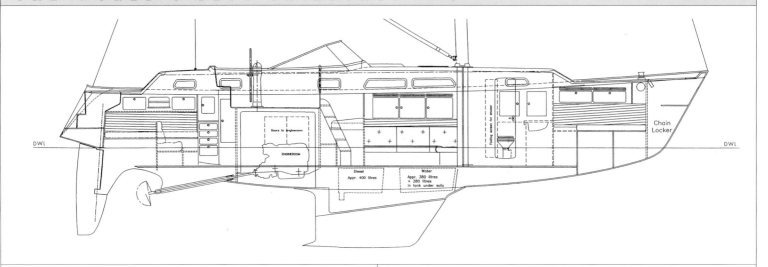

tect it from sharp or heavy objects that may, in rough seas, damage it. The companionway steps are laminated from layers of solid wood, allowing for upward curves outboard so you have safe footing on any heel. The nonskid in the ladder is eternal—eight V-shaped grooves routed an eighth of an inch deep into the steps. The dishrack in a galley locker has little movable baffles to fit whatever odd dishes you may have. The berth bottoms have myriad of 1-inch-diameter routed holes to promote air circulation and prevent condensation. They are neither painted nor varnished, because the Rassys have found that raw, untreated wood promotes condensation the least. The heads have ceramic or Corian sinks, and recessed curtain rods and curtains are standard on every boat, so you don't have to tape your place mats and T-shirts to the portlights for privacy, as we do on ours.

When I complemented Magnus on the innumerable intelligent details, and asked him how they came up with them all, he smiled shyly: 'After 8,000 boats, sooner or later, we figure things out.'

'Are there any new things left to learn?' I asked. He laughed; 'Every day.'

They have even learned to put a secondary trap filter under the drain screen in the shower to catch hair so it does not foul the dedicated shower sump pump. I asked Magnus how often you have to clean that out, and he chuckled as he stroked his fine Scandinavian hair: 'That depends on how fast you're going bald.'

The yard itself is a lesson in modern boat-production technology. A computer-controlled routing machine, the size of a truck, cuts all plywood parts to perfection. No tear-outs, no

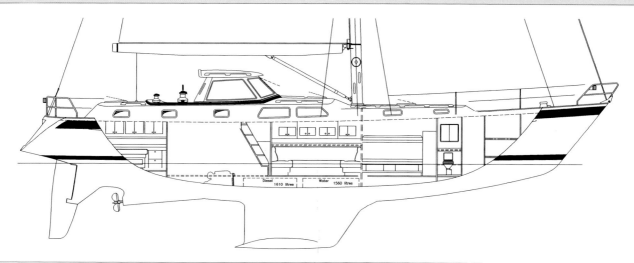

slips; a vacuum holds the sheet of plywood firmly in place. One person runs the machine. There is virtually no waste. A rotating brush cleans up the plywood and sucks up the dust. The only manual work is the numbering of parts once they are cut.

In the old days, they used to varnish the cabinetry inside the boat after all the installing was done. But in an enclosed space, some dust always lingered, so it was difficult to get the perfect finish. Now, they prevarnish even the smallest piece outside the boat with a fully automatic machine that's completely dust-free and about half a city block long. It sands, removes dust, then sprays and at the end dries. Whatever the shape of the wooden part, the machine accesses every corner. Sensors detect the pieces coming through and spray only right at the piece so there is no wasted varnish. They build up six coats. No dust, no fumes, completely people- and environment- friendly.

Anyone working near solvents wears a breathing apparatus. Vacuums are everywhere to keep the workplace dust-free. People and the environment count for a lot in Sweden. It's little wonder, then, that most workers stay for many years. More than forty people have been with them for more than twenty-five years, and one has been there for forty-seven. When you feel so protected and so appreciated, it's easy to put your heart and soul into building one of the world's best boats.

Oh, yes, one last thing. They have a large saltwater tank out back into which every boat is launched before it is shipped. The engine is started up; all fittings, gear, and are systems checked; then all sails are hoisted and it is test-sailed, often in severe conditions. The tank is called the North Sea.

These are the new-generation Hallberg-Rassys—sleeker, more powerful, and beautifully detailed. The great leaps are due to the genius of Germán Frers, who has redesigned the whole line, which now goes from 31 to 62 feet—most with all-furling sails. New are the low-profile trunk cabins—replacing the big flush decks—with resultant lower freeboard. What has remained are the ample safe decks; the big, comfortable center cockpits; and that most valuable con-

cept, the fixed windshield with opening center portion. Their slogan is 'There's no need to be soaking wet from head to toe to enjoy sailing.' Some of their boats even come with something all designers should consider nowadays, a fixed hard top over the cockpit—see page 48. The two photos on this page are of the 43, their newest design. Note the hollowed-out, fixed-stepped transom and the easily driven hull, with the beam carried well aft to form the broad, powerful stern. A close look will reveal those perfect Frers curves in the transom, on the house corners, and the cockpit coamings. On the left page is the very sweet 36 of the same excellent proportions. What are invisible on these pages are the new underbodies—all fin keel with a very deep foil rudder with a good-sized skeg for support.

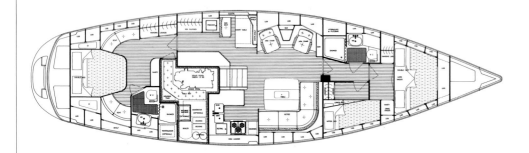

Hallberg-Rassys have remarkable interiors; with their center cockpits, the volume down below is nearly inexhaustible. The drawing is of the 53. Note its likable two-tiered berth cabin forward, ideal for kids (photo below); the great aft cabin with the huge berth (below, left);

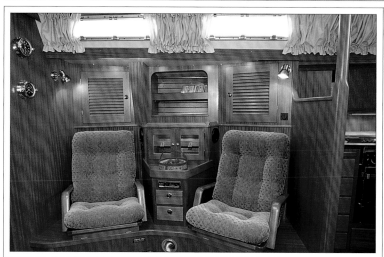

the drawing-room-like navigation area-cum-passageway with acres of bookshelves (left page, top right); the most comfortable saloon chairs, complete with a glass-fronted cabinet (above); the perfect G-shaped galley with countless handholds and safety bar (above, right). All these things make spending time below something to be looked forward to. The saloon (below) is of the 62. It shows the beautifully wood-trimmed overhead, nicely rounded molded searails and corners, and elegant recessed lights. In the same vein, note also the nicely recessed light at the foot of the bed of the 53 in bottom left photo. Hallberg-Rassy has even thought to put curtains under the skylights to keep out the heat of the sun. And some of their mattresses have real coiled springs, just like your favorite bed at home. Pleasant dreams.

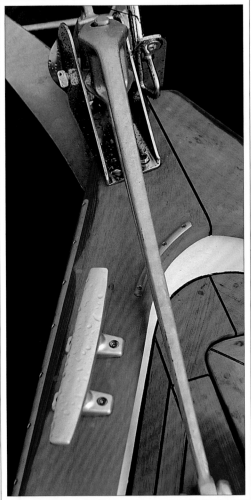

A t Hallberg-Rassy, the thoughtful details are everywhere. Top left corner—a long brass strip outboard of the mooring cleats protects the teak caprail from dockline chafe; another—nicely curved, inboard—protects against anchor nicks. In the photo above, the laminated, curved companionway steps offer secure footing when heeled, and—you have to look closely—their forward portions have five deeply routed grooves to offer excellent ridges as nonskids. In the same photo, note the omnipresent hand-loops. In the small photo at top, right page, care for the

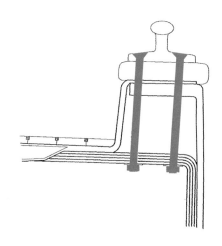

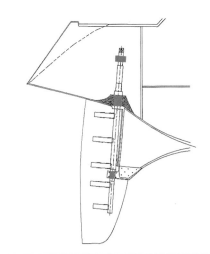

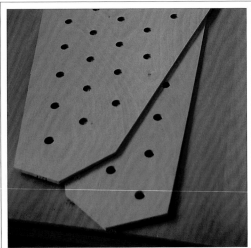

workers is extreme. In cockpit photo, note solid grabrail on outside of fixed windshield. I very much like all the untreated teak, the world's best non-skid, where it's really useful—on coach-roof edges, cockpit coamings, and cockpit seats. Below left, opposite, the best caprail joint; next to it, perforated,

'breathing' bunkboards; next to that, propane-tank locker in side deck, right over galley stove, keeping the vulnerable tubing to a minimum, Then there is the first-class landing deck with nonskid steps; and last, the beautifully sculpted foil rudder with small skeg.

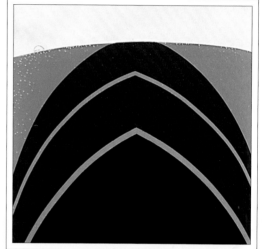

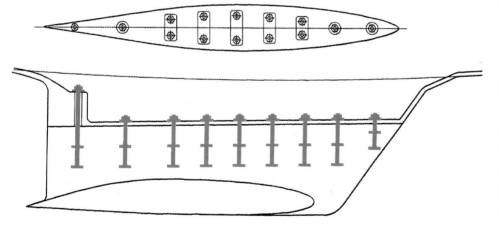

On the way back to the mainland, you drive through the fields and woods of the island of Orust. To slow down what few cars there are on the silent back roads, the Swedes don't put up speed bumps or signs. Instead, at the driveway of each house, placed right on the road, is a wooden half-barrel teeming with blazing flowers. A beautiful reminder that there are people here. It's a very human place.

HINCKLEY YACHTS

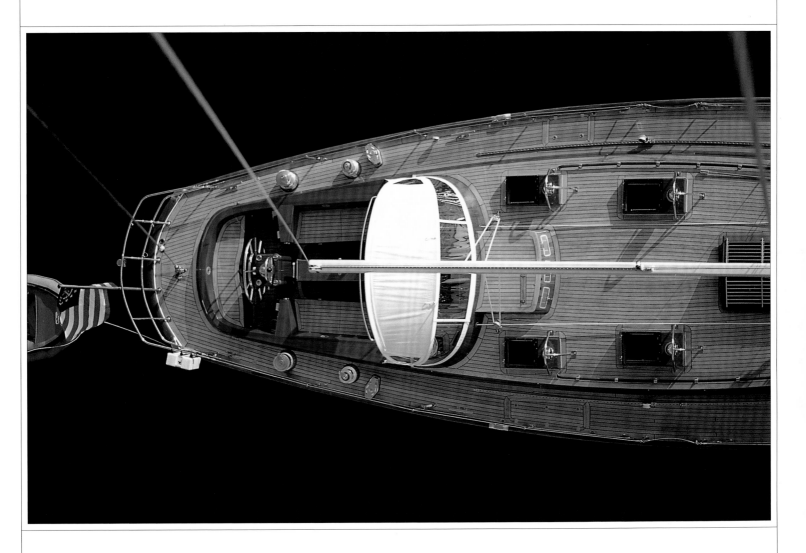

I have never been a fan of being a 'fan.' There is something disturbingly sheeplike about wearing somebody else's well-marketed insignia while uttering witless words of support. But when I see a graceful Sou'wester sailing by, I'm ready to don a beanie, wave a banner, and roar out, 'Go, Hinckley! Go!'

There is something almost inexplicably captivating about the long line of master-crafted boats from fabled Southwest Harbor, Maine. It started with the Bill Tripp-designed *Bermuda 40*, arguably one of the most aesthetically balanced sailboats ever drawn, which remained in production almost thirty years—certainly a world record in yachting history. And it is continuing with the Sou'wester line of six boats from 42 to 70 feet, five of them designed by McCurdy & Rhodes; the other, the *70*, by the highly respected—and rightfully so—Bruce King. They have all retained the same sensibility, while adding much performance and volume, and somehow, almost miraculously, maintaining the relaxed elegance of the lines, especially in their aft-cockpit, low-deckhouse versions. Their designs, coupled with super-meticulous construction, have produced some of the most revered yachts the world has ever seen.

The changes at Hinckley since my last visit have been numerous and enormous, but they are all nicely dovetailed with the remorseless continuity of quality. The biggest change is that Bob Hinckley's office door more often than not wears the 'Gone Fishing' sign. He has officially retired, sold the company to a Boston group, and once in a while comes back from soaking worms to help with the transition. While Bob's absence has left a palpable void for those of us who tend to talk about sailboats with an insatiable passion until the barman kicks us out into the night, there remains the traditional Hinckley insistence that all aspects should be considered before a decision is made, and even then the best decision is to reconsider it all again. Some corporate types might call this indecisive over-mulling, but those of us who believe the quality of sailboats to be as sacred as any saint's shinbone consider it absolutely justified thoroughness.

So, while there are no enormous visible changes to Hinckleys—except, of course, as with almost every yard in this book, the boats just keep getting longer and longer—the invisible changes are great indeed. Or, as Peter Smith, chief engineer at Hinckley, explains: 'Every boat we make, we try to make a little bit better than the last. Fifteen years ago, we were using the best materials we could but we kept looking around for better things and made the first jump from straight E-glass to Kevlar E-glass and used that for a long time. And then we used some impregnator machines: You drive the fabric through a resin bath, and you have a couple of stainless steel rollers with which you can dial in the distance you want between rollers, depending on the fabric weight. Then you wring it. That way, you can control resin quantity in the fabric.

'Then, for a while we worried about cold joints and tried to come up with a way of eliminating them. Well, along came the SCRIMP system, where you infuse the resin all at once into your entire laminates laid dry into the hull. That was seven years ago. There was a lot of resistance to it at the time, but now we find the resistance is to the old hand layup.

'The SCRIMP process begins once the gelcoat has set. The layers of material are laid in dry—the entire outer skin, the core, and even foam for some longitudinal stiffening beams. Then you lay in your tubes to feed the resin. You have to reinforce your tubes with wire so that they don't get crushed by the pressure once the vacuum is started. When you're satisfied with the level of vacuum, you begin to infuse the resin. Now, where and how densely you put your entrance tubes depends on the laminate and the material properties you're dealing with, as well as the difficulty of the mold to get resin into. Let's say you're doing a deck and you have a main-track reinforcement that may have up to thirty layers of carbon in there; well, you have to infuse almost directly into that spot, because you need to have the resin run equally among all the parts. You infuse resin in and you take it out as well. So the resin is flowing through a circular loop. We infuse a whole side of the boat at once; the whole process takes about three hours. When everything is wetted out equally, you seal it off; you turn it all off and sit and wait.

'It is said that 1 percent of air content can reduce your strength by 10 percent. The vacuum system gets out all the air possible, and it cuts down considerably the amount of resin used. But what is just as important, it creates an even resin-to-fiber ratio—every square inch of the boat with similar laminates will end up having exactly the same quantity of resin. It's not possible to do that when you are using a 3-inch-wide brass roller. We actually found that we use about 50 percent less resin than we did with hand layup. We are beginning to get close to pre-impregnated laminate results.

'The other greatest change since your first survey is that we have changed from the all-fiberglass hulls. We now do what we call a 'DualGuard' composite construction. All our hulls have Kevlar outer skin and carbon-fiber inner skin, with aircraft-grade balsa in between. The Kevlar is extremely abrasion- and penetration-resistant. So the hull is bulletproof on the outside. The carbon inner skin gives you a very stiff laminate, so our overall result is a lighter, stronger hull. We typically use two layers of Kevlar above and three below the waterline on a *42*; then comes the core, followed by a carbon laminate on the inside. Our laminates test out far stronger than what we were able to achieve with hand layup of normal fiberglass in the past.

'The vital point is to engineer each part of the boat for the local loads and stresses. So while our laminates are basically uniform throughout, some parts have unidirectional glass and carbon built up on them for added stiffness. To add extra rigidity to the hull, we use longitudinal stiffeners. In the bottoms of the boats they're typically 2 inches wide at the top, about 8 inches tall, and spaced at about 24- to 30-inch centers. In the topsides, they are typically 8 inches wide at the top, about 1 inch tall, and spaced at about 20-inch centers. There are transverse members as well—one under each bulkhead to act as a foundation, cushioning, and also to provide continuous stiffness from sheer to sheer. Others are under the chainplates to distribute the load over a greater area.

'Added reinforcement comes from the heavy floor grid. It is based on foam core, with a multitude of laminates over and around them. Overall, we have reduced our hull weight a good 10 percent in fifteen years. And we have gained added stiffness, which helps in the performance and longevity of the boat, plus of course all that abrasion and penetration resistance. I mean, you are not going to stop a container, nothing will—and we're not trying to build a floating jackhammer—but with logs and docks and grounding, Kevlar is a great help.

'As for the coring, we feel that balsa is simply the stiffest core material we can get. The beauty of the SCRIMP process is that all the scores, all the cuts, the kerfs in the balsa, get filled with resin. Traditionally, balsa was frowned upon as a core material because any time you would penetrate the skin, you'd get water into the balsa and it would migrate through the balsa and destroy the whole core. With SCRIMP vacuum-bagging, each

little square is encapsulated in resin and, as I said, the cracks are all filled with resin, so even if you did have some damage to the hull, there is no way for the water to migrate. To achieve that sort of complete resin penetration using traditional hand layup is just not possible.

'We use a lot of Nomex honeycomb board for bulkheads. It is a sort of Kevlar paper; it's fire-retardant and very light, strong, and stiff; then we put a 3 millimeter veneer on either side. The Nomex is lighter than balsa—you just can't make trees grow at 3 pounds per cubic foot. Most airplanes are built with it. Since I started here twenty years ago, let's say in a *42*, we have lost about 2,000 pounds out of the boat as a whole, as well as increasing stiffness and impact resistance. Now, for really big impacts, such as containers, we have begun to make part of the anchor locker as a full, cored bulkhead that works as a crash bulkhead. If you ran into a container, that would take the maximum of the impact load. We have some very small panel areas in there reduced by the horizontal bulkhead and a ring frame. In the bow itself, to support the anchor rollers and the forestay, we have about forty-five laminates of E-glass. It's about 3/4-inch thick—it would be twice that thickness with hand layup.

'The second-biggest structural change after the hull has been the mast. We have almost completely forsaken aluminum—very few owners request it—for carbon fiber. The few problems that people had in the early days of carbon-fiber masts came from misengineering. We have never had one fail or even a fitting tear out. As you can see, each one of the laminates—a mast has forty to fifty—each one of these lines you see is where they have done de-bulking, which is putting a vacuum on the laminates to that point and pulling all the laminates together before laying on any more. This way, you don't get any wrinkles, which in fact are weak spots. These masts are done in an autoclave, a captive container that produces a negative atmosphere to pull all the layers down. We use aerospace glue that is so strong that you pull the laminate apart long before the glue fails. NASA is a good place to copy materials from; they work in a pretty stringent environment with no room for failure or mistakes.

'The biggest advantage of carbon fiber is its lightness and stiffness. You lower your CG, and that helps reduce your pitching moment. You are reducing your tube weight by 50 percent, so in confused seas, your boat is going to sail better with the centers closer. It's exactly the same idea as keeping the ends of a boat light. The closer the weights are to the center, the less hobbyhorsing, the better the progress, and a heck of a lot better the comfort. With a lighter mast—don't forget that's a 50-foot lever up there—you cut back very noticeably on both pitching and yawing. The mistake on cruising boats is that the weight saved in a carbon-fiber mast is too often replaced by wires such as TV antenna cables and weather antennas. One should be aware of all factors when watching out for weight.

'With improved production methods, the carbon masts are only about 12 percent more expensive. Even Huisman, who was a diehard aluminum fan, has thrown in the towel. The one drawback to carbon fiber, at least in theory, is the question of lightning. Lightning tends to literally fry the epoxy that's in there. But if you're well grounded, you should be fine. We have had a couple of boats that have taken some lightning strikes without problems. I mean Freedom has been out there with their unstayed carbon masts for more than twenty-five years without problems, and so have the giant towers for windvanes that TPI builds.

'On many other things, we have made small refinements. Through-hulls and seacocks we have changed from bronze to Marelon plastic, a nylon-filled resin. The big advantage they have over bronze is that they are not subject to electrolysis. We have used them for fifteen years; if you maintain them, they should last forever.

'The exhaust fittings and some final piping, we lay up in solid glass to eliminate joints and add dependability and longevity. When we can, we use a dry exhaust, where all the water is taken out of the system. The advantage is that it is quieter, so fewer people will feel like assassinating you in silent anchorages when you have your generator running. With the engine there is less back-pressure.

'We have kept the skeg-hung rudder, but we have three bearings—your typical Hinckley overbuild. All the loads are really being taken by the bottom and middle bearings; the upper bearing is just to support the autopilot. We know it's severely overbuilt, but it's one of those things you don't want to fail.

'We use cable steering instead of hydraulic because it gives you a better feel. And hydraulic I have always thought of as too complicated, something to have only when you don't have access to running a cable; when you simply can't get there from here. We have looked at the Whitlock rack-and-pinion direct drive, primarily because you can bolt a hydraulic autopilot pump right onto the steering system rather than having a whole separate unit. There might be something there.'

And sprinkled in these last few comments by the chief engineer are the germs of the Hinckley philosophy—the secrets, perhaps, of why these boats captivate, beyond common rationale, even the most analytic and critical among us. For beyond their grand good looks, the Hinckleys are 'severely overbuilt' for 'dependability and longevity' because a serious offshore-cruising sailboat is full of myriad small things that you absolutely 'do not want to fail.' And even if you don't spend days crawling through unfinished boats, poking about, posing questions, it is simply enough to look at a Hinckley and you will immediately sense, viscerally, all the quality lurking beneath the perfect surface.

Some may object and say that while Hinckleys are indeed beautiful, so is their price. True. But when you consider that 50,000 man-hours go into building a 70-footer—that's about twenty-five working years by a miraculously versatile shipwright—then perhaps it doesn't seem such a bad deal after all. The other objection that has been voiced is that for their length, Hinckleys give you miserly accommodations. In some models, that's true, but sailing, above all, is an aesthetic and—if you will allow me—spiritual experience. It is completely impractical—you often end up where you had no intention of going; it is commonly unpleasant; you are wet and cold or boiled and exhausted, and people are snoring and scratching inescapably close by; and it is a culinary nightmare—you eat barely recognizable amalgamations out of tins, boxes, tubes, and bags. In short, it is as close to a prison experience as you care to get, except you have the added bonus of getting seasick now and then. So why do we go? For the silence and the beauty, and a chance to dream. And in a world where those three things are becoming rarer by the second, having a magnificently designed yacht both in detail and in lines, with that too rare a thing—a human-sized cockpit where you can lie back on moonless nights and court the stars—is something that makes the experience even more sublime. Cubic feet be damned. The number of bunks to hell. You only live once.

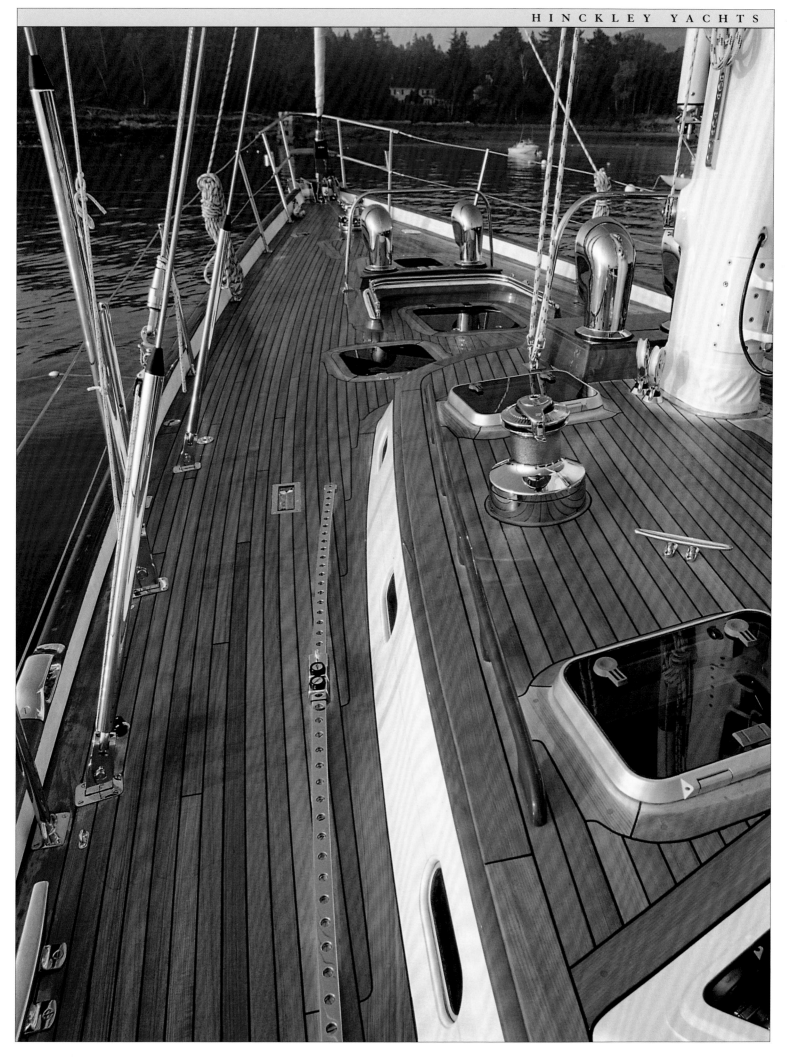

It's sigh time. The highlight of this double page is the Bruce King-designed marvel, *Avatar*—below and top right—certainly one of the most perfectly realized yachts in existence. While it's true that on a boat of her size—70 feet on deck—there is ample room for subtle curves and ele-

gant inventions, it still takes a great designer—for my taste, he is the world's best—to pull off so many brilliant touches in one boat. The profile shot shows off her spectacularly proportioned house with the ingenious raised portion forward of the dodger, which, with its three small portlights for-

ward and one on either side, allows you to have a quick look around without opening the hatch. The Dorade boxes double as skylights; the main skylight is a classic; and the five flush-fitting tinted hatches in the foredeck (see also page 68) are works of art. So is the raised portion around the mast, which is an engineering coup. It acts as a Dorade box for two cowls, allows the use of four electric winches whose motors would otherwise protrude into the cabin, and allows the flush hatch forward of the mast—an item that could have consumed 2 or 3 inches of headroom. It's a perfect lesson in how to turn an engineering problem into a design masterpiece. The center-cockpit raised-house version (below) is pulled off as nicely as these things can be, but to me, it's too much beauty given up for a modest gain in comfort. The photo top left, shows the graceful hull of the 59.

Well, what can I say? Hinckley interiors are a feast for the eyes. One of my all-time-favorite boats is the *Sou'wester 42*, below and in the small photo to the left. The starboard settee has been beautifully curved for both comfort and looks, and it's well worth the effort. The chart table has gained a grabrail/searail, and the galley now has molded Corian tops—both very practical ideas. In the small photo at left is the ideal quarterberth with good side access. I would put, at its foot, an opening portlight in the cockpit side for ventilation. Above it is the ideal seago-

ing galley of the 52, aligned fore-and-aft with perfect bracing anywhere on any heel. And, in the photo next to it, the port side has a fine little two-bunk cabin. On this page is the museum-quality craftsmanship of *Avatar*. Apart from the ventilation masterpieces of the fanned louvers, and the beautiful carved whales, are the excellent raised-panel doors, wonderfully detailed cushion rails, and to top it all, an inlaid table that one might want to hide in a cupboard so it doesn't get scratched. Look at the stainless steel mechanism below the table for a great piece of engineering and fabri-cating. All that allows the table to be raised, lowered, and also expanded, depending on whether you want a dining or a coffee table. The real genius comes into play in allowing the table in its 'dining' position to move in close over the settees for comfortable eating. Sailors have never had it so good.

Arguably the most gaze-worthy detail page for lovers of sophisticated yachts. From top left, a laudable piece of stainless fabrication for mounting controls, while the next photo, clockwise, shows the prettiest instrument mount and dodger base in captivity. The next three small photos show, in turn, a very low-profile double Dorade box forward of the mast; an excellent long loop handrail and boathook stowage; and some perfect teak deck joinery. Below, far right, note the massive stainless steel protection on the classic skylight, a longer view of the very safe and easy-

to-revarnish handrail, and the world's most elegant Dorade box combined with a low-profile open hatch aft of it. The photo below, of the bow, shows the unmatchable complexity of the stainless steel crafting at Hinckley, along with a beautiful little grate on the bow rail to make shore access easier when tied bow-to. It is also a fine lookout platform for navigating through shoals. The sailing shot—I couldn't resist—is of my favorite Hinckley, the *Sou'wester 42*, with her perfect proportions, elegant detailing, and a typically Hinckley-robust stern ladder with very safe teak steps. Now if they could only make her into a 45-footer with an aft cabin without disturbing the lines. The bottom left-hand corner photo shows off hardware. Note the careful placement of all electric winch buttons—tucked around the cockpit coaming and completely out of the way for safety, but still readily accessible.

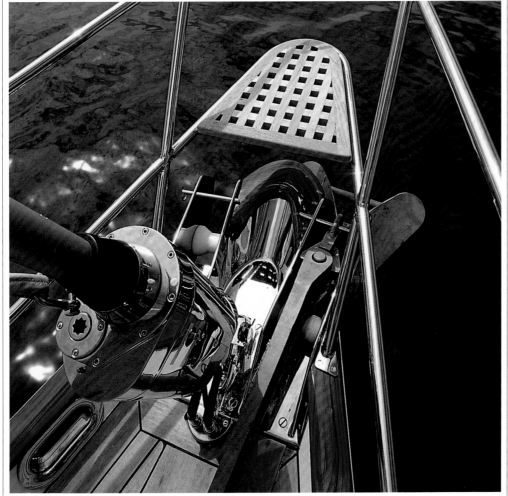

They are refurbishing some of the original *Bermuda 40*s at Hinckley. All the repairs found to be necessary have only been cosmetic. Those boats are almost forty years old. With the recent technology of resin infusion, carbon fiber and Kevlar being added to the perennial fine craftsmanship, attention and care, the Hinckley you have built today might just outlive the cosmos.

INDEPENDENCE
CHERUBINI

T he town of Portofino, at the end of a narrow winding road on the
Côte d'Azur of Italy, is perhaps the most charming port in the whole
Mediterranean. Nestled among verdant bluffs, its lean, colorful houses,
built by fishermen and sea captains, perch brazenly on the very edge of the
deep, dark-watered cove. It is the perfect setting for a world-cruising sailboat.

Portofino is packed with pretty yachts, tied stern-to under the old castle and along the quay, or anchored stern and bow, cheek-by-jowl in the bay. The harbor gleams with Swans and Oysters, sleek one-off racers, and glitzy custom yachts. The townspeople are used to them, the tourists are used to them, and the sailors from the world over don't give them a second glance. But when *Amazing Grace*, the 48-foot schooner designed by John Cherubini, slipped into the bay one day, something strange happened. The sailors stopped and the shopkeepers came out, and even a lady with babe in arms stopped along the quay and stared wistfully at the graceful *Grace*—her classic sheer, her beautiful woodwork, her long low house, her bow, ports, and skylights of long ago. And you could see in their eyes a dreamy longing for slower times, calmer days, when life still had charm, when people had time to look after the boats they loved, when boats hadn't yet begun to look like long-range missiles.

And once the schooner was tied stern-to below the chapel, people came and stared close-up. Some of them almost whispered, and almost all of them asked what kind of boat she was, and where she was built. And Rich Rinaldi, the rather shy, quiet owner, patiently replied, 'Independence Cherubini, Delran, New Jersey.'

I guess you could say John Cherubini was slightly ahead of his time. He designed his *44* and *48* almost twenty-five years ago, based on his great affection and appreciation for Herreshoff's *Ticonderoga*, which unassumingly beat the pants off everyone in nearly every race for decades. He anticipated, by many years, the new passion for beautiful classic lines and classic details of

which Bruce King has become the justifiably revered guru, for his small miracles like the 34-foot *Lancashire Rose* to 140-foot mega-wonders.

Most of the King boats are cold-molded wood, giving them a genuinely unique personality and enabling a natural, unaffected use of wood that is at once visually stunning and structurally ideal. The Cherubinis are in that sense much the same. In fact, the thing that makes them stand out from all other boats in this book is that they have a fiberglass hull for assured longevity, coupled with a wood deck with magnificent deck beams, beautiful cabin sides, and enormous compression-bearing capability.

I have had the fun and pleasure of knowing Lee Cherubini, a master boatbuilder from a family of master boatbuilders, for more than twenty years. His dad, Frit, now retired, started the company; his Uncle John designed the boats, and his Uncle Joe, a master woodworker, and cousin Rick, master carpenter and ABYC electrician, still lend a hand in the shop from time to time. Lee has the quick movements and big passion of a man in love with his craft. He loves building the boats, he loves sailing the boats and he loves talking about them—their every piece, every detail.

'I think it's important to use each material where it does the most good,' he begins with the zeal of an evangelist. 'My first choice is always fiberglass for the hull, composite laminates, Vinylester resins. Not only have they proven reliable and virtually indestructible, but they certainly give the owner the best value. So in the hull we use fiberglass to take advantage of its strength which is tension, and in the deck we exploit wood for its greatest strength, which is compression.

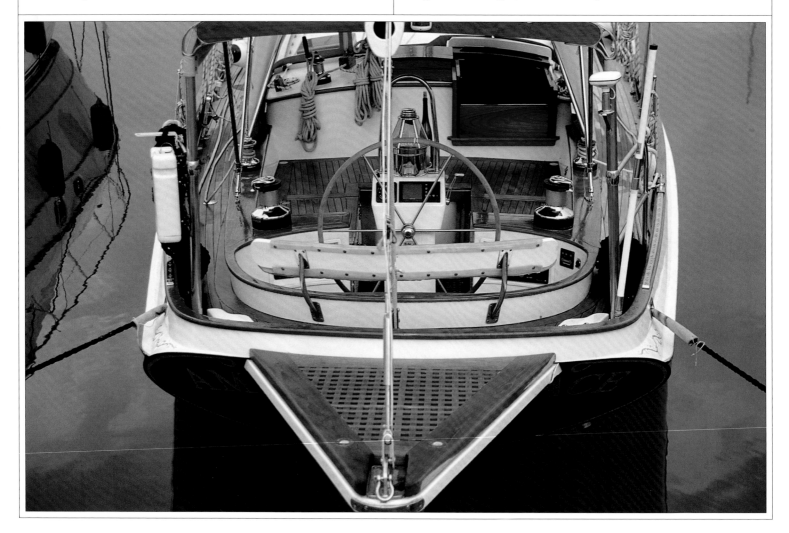

'We are thinking of going even more hybrid; my Uncle Joe is going to build his *44* that way. He wants a 1/4-inch fiberglass outer skin of four or five layers of 1708 biaxial in epoxy resin, laid-up in the mold. Then we will vacuum-bag in about four layers of wood veneer from the sheer to the waterline; below that, we'll have solid glass. The boat will be almost indestructible, plus the inner hull will be beautiful wood—a sort of bullet-proof Stradivarius.

'We use Vinylester on the outer laminations and all the tabbing of bulkheads, as well as the integral tanks. The resins have become infinitely better. We use split molds to enable us to extract the hull with its considerable tumblehome, but we lay up the hull in one piece with the molds locked.

'As for special reinforcements, I think unidirectional E-glass is ideal to tie together the chainplates with a yoke that passes right under the mast. I would, in fact, like to custom-make our own hybrid composites. The idea should be to use the best material for each application. Take our wood decks. Some people say they're too labor-intensive, but look at how perfect a material it is for that application, structurally. Remember how Tom Dreyfus used to test the IOR boats he built? He'd tighten a piece of wire from the bow fitting to the stern, make a pencil mark on the mast, and then pump up the backstay to 5,000 pounds. Your typical Airex-cored 40-footer would bend 1 1/4 inches or so. You literally pull up the ends of the boat like a banana. We tried this, slack rigging, then we cranked the rig as tight as we could; the wire beside the mast moved from one side of the pencil line to the other. No more.

'We use the compression strength of wood—its best mechanical property other than fatigue resistance—to the best advantage. And don't forget our cabin sides—1 3/8-inch solid mahogany; you'll never compress that together. All things—the bulwark, the cabin sides, the cockpit coaming—are structural, rigidifying components. Then there is the solid piece of mahogany inside the bulwark that's 7/8-inch thick, bonded to the sheer of the hull. It all adds up.

'The problem is, this kind of intense detail is mostly buried under the finishing, and it takes a very knowledgeable sailor to appreciate it all. He understands why a *44* is a 10,000-man-hour boat, and the *48* is about 12,000.

'But getting back to using the best material in a place: Take our chainplate system. We make a structural box that forms a cavity of 7 inches by 18 inches by about 5 feet long. We use unidirectional fibers, which then go all the way under the mast step and up the other side to form a girdle of four layers. Inside the box is a 3/8-inch-thick, 2-inch-by-2-inch stainless steel angle iron that runs the full length of the box underneath the flange. The stainless angle conforms to the hull and then the U-bolts of the chainplates are bolted to it. This creates a gigantic load distributor. So you have three materials all reinforcing each other, all doing what they do best.

'Our deck is the same idea. We use 2 3/8-inch molded wood deck beams that are structural. Then the first layer of 1/2-inch deck plywood goes in with the Formica already laminated onto it, so when you lie in your bunk, you see the varnished-mahogany beams and an off-white, maintenance-free, mildew-free surface. On the coach roof, we vacuum-bag three layers of 1/4 inch to allow us to form the crown. The plywood pieces for deck and house are staggered and bonded to each other with epoxy thickened with cotton fibers to create a giant, monolithic,

beam-reinforced panel. The nice thing about the wood house and deck is that it can be changed according to the owner's taste. Aside from the obvious, such as portlights and hatches, we can even change the cabin trunk—long or short, double or single house—or put a scuttle, a small doghouse, forward.

'In the cockpit—where my Uncle John drew those swooping curves of his—instead of beating our heads against the wall, we decided to use fiberglass in order to create an absolutely leak-proof structure. There are heavily loaded areas with cleats and winches and many corners—you simply do not want any joints that might open here.

'We have modified the rig. We dropped the 30-degree swept-back spreaders with no backstay because we found two downsides. One was aesthetic—they weren't things one expected to see on this kind of boat. The more I thought about it, the less I liked them. We now use a more conventional rig with a boomkin aft to make room for the backstay. This is for the second reason: just in case you have one of those oh-my-God jibes, when the boom rises 6 or 8 feet—it'll still clear the backstay.

'Below the water, we've stayed with the Scheel keel. Most people ask for interior ballast, but we have certainly done, and will be happy to do, exterior. We just dam the mold, lay up a short stub, and then have a bolt-on lead keel. If you were to ask me which is the ultimate, I would say external ballast for impact, and also to lower the center of gravity, which would be considerably lower in our case because our casting is so long. The gain in CG is noticeable because the keel is only 12 inches high, so you can see that dropping the CG 2 inches by having the laminates of the hull bottom above, instead of below, the ballast is a hell of a lot of difference.

'In case of grounding, we don't have the problem of keel bolts shearing or bending as fin-keelers do. Not just because our shallow keel is such a short lever arm, but also because, behind the ballast, the mold drops to the bottom of the keel so you have the whole hull—not just the keel bolts—absorbing the force of the impact. These are vital points in the longevity or even the survival of serious cruising boats. The length of the keel also gives us a long contact surface with the hull. This is important for sealing and fastening. We set the keel in 5200 bedding compound, then crank down on the nuts. The adhesion is so good that when we had a boat in here after thirteen years for a refit, we actually had to wedge off the keel. We had tried taking off the nuts and washers and lifting the boat, but the keel came right along with it. It's that big of a surface area—21 inches wide. There is a trade-off with a bolt-on keel; because of the keel bolts, you lose some bilge space, but then you can't have everything.

'For the internally ballasted boats, we actually create a one-piece ballast by setting in the lead pieces and then filling the voids. We fit the cast pieces so tightly, actually cut them to fit the hull, that the space is minimal. It's a slow, costly process, but it does give you a good fit. I just like things right—that last forever.

'To make the wood that goes into the boats last long, every piece under floorboards or behind ceilings, everything, is encapsulated in epoxy before we put it in. That's basic. The edges of the bulkheads are sealed with three coats of epoxy. It soaks into the end-grain of that plywood like into a sponge. We feel so confident about our construction and reinforcement that we give a lifetime warranty on the hull to the original owner.

'To give our teak decks long life, we set the planks in 5200 bedding compound, screw them down, and then when the 5200 has set, we pull the screws back out. Then we drill for a full-depth plug so you don't end up with plugs the thickness of sandpaper, which last a couple of years and then pop. Before we put in a plug, we take WEST epoxy and, with a plastic syringe, we shoot it into the hole, so it flows right down into the deck itself where the threads were, and then we put in the plug. You remember in the old days, we used to use a two-part polysulfide on the decks. It stuck to everything that came within shouting distance; we used to call it black mung. Oh, shit, it was terrible. But now we use a pure silicone specifically formulated to stick relentlessly to wood; it also has great ultraviolet resistance. It was developed for teak decks on commercial cruise ships.

'To make life below more comfortable, we have begun using a new high-tech material called Reflectix for insulation. It's made with silver mylar; it's like bubble wrap but silver. You see a couple of corrugated layers if you cut it in half. It reflects 97 percent of the energy both ways. And it's flexible. We line the hull with that. It is actually suspended off the hull 1/2 inch to 1 inch, on little battens, so you have a dead-air space; this way, you can't trap water. It's great stuff—doesn't absorb any moisture, and the nicest thing is, it's radar reflective. And it doesn't weigh anything. You can pick up a roll of the stuff as big as a car with one hand. Over this we put our typical batten ceilings.'

So while Lee thinks of every construction detail, his new partner, Geoffrey White—soft spoken, thoughtful, with many years of experience overseeing the building of cruising sailboats—handles the daily organizing and the business end. What drew Geoff to the boats was not just Lee's ability and the boats' almost enchanting looks, but the one thing that few people realize until they sail them—their speed.

'The hollow in the bow is carried back to station four,' Lee points out, 'So the boat is very easily driven through seas. The flare gives you a lot of reserve buoyancy, and a much dryer deck. All the times I have been to sea in these boats, I have seen the bowsprit go into a wave only once. The boat picks up so much buoyancy on that last foot of freeboard that she'll just squirt ahead. When you're surfing down a wave on the edge of control, and you're convinced that the bow is going to stuff for sure, it never happens. We actually Veed the bottom of the bowsprit to take out any kind of sudden resistance. Uncle John thought of everything.

'As for how fast they are, a guy called me up after having just finished Fort Lauderdale to Newport. He averaged 10 knots—bar stool to bar stool. And that was on the little boat, the 44. You can confidently count on doing 200-mile days—reaching, of course. We took the people sailing from the boatyard next door. They race in J/Boats, big races, and they looked at the wind speed, apparent wind, and wind angle, and said, Mother of God. This boat really goes. They could not believe they were on a cruising boat. We will never out-accelerate the light boats, but once we get going, look out.

'I will not talk anyone into buying one of our boats; you either fall in love with the way they look and sail or you don't. You have to like our distinctive classic style. We do fall a bit short on volume. We're a bit narrow, but then that's why we're so fast. My uncle realized, when he was designing, that adding on beam becomes a vicious circle on a cruising boat. True, you can carry more food and water, fuel and provisions, but then you *have to* carry more because your boat is slower and your trip is going to take longer. He made a boat that goes like a Great Dane, and you don't need all those provisions because you'll cross the ocean in ten days.'

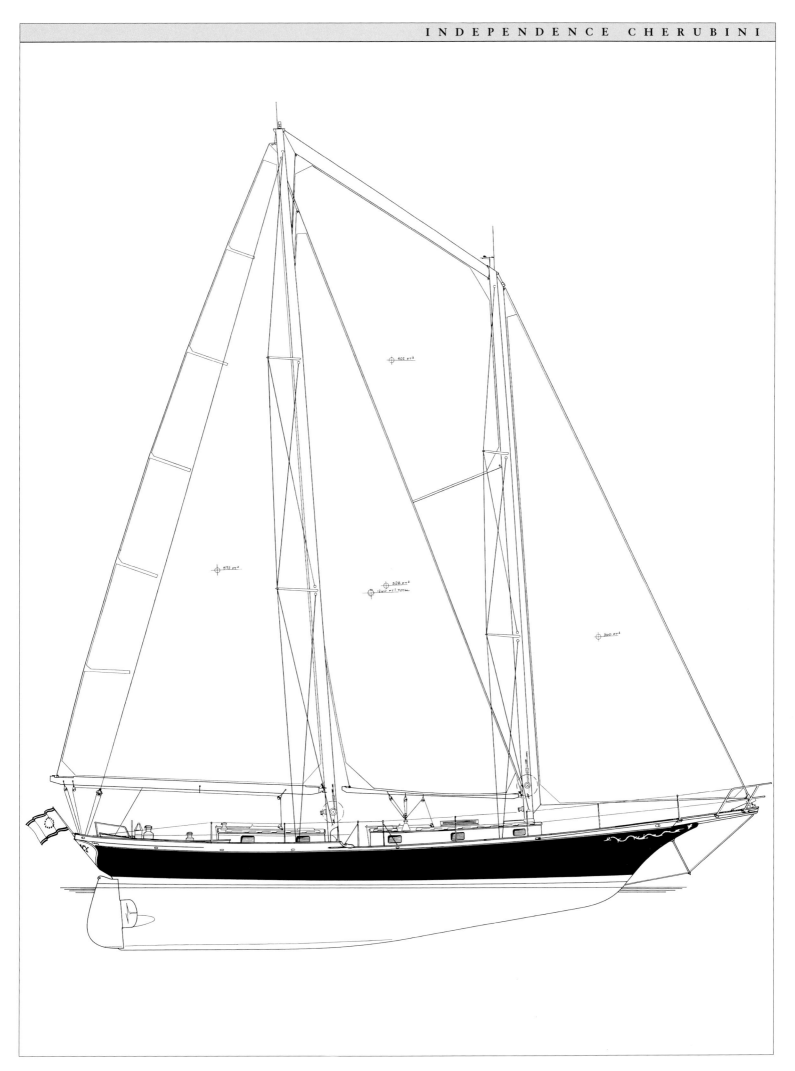

Easily the greatest crowd pleaser in any harbor, the boats designed by John Cherubini have a timeless beauty that stirs the soul. The two top photos show, apart from the amazingly graceful lines of the boats, the two different house versions available in the 48-foot schooner.

Above is a drop-dead-gorgeous split house, making her look like something right out of a Conrad novel. Above right is a more conventional trunk cabin, which can be had with or without the evocative curved house forward. The sliding hatch on that, with its compound curve, is a sight to behold.

At far left is a detail of the dazzling cockpit table, which remains narrow for drinks or, with its two leaves extended, becomes wide for dining. And as the two photos below demonstrate, she's not only a pretty face. Her big, powerful stern, moderate beam, and a fine clipper-bowed entry enable her to clock two-hundred-mile days with ease. The broad side decks, with the raised bulwarks, make movement on deck safe and enjoyable in any seas. In all, she's a perfect heir to *Ticonderoga*, to which John Cherubini pays homage with this work-of-art of a design.

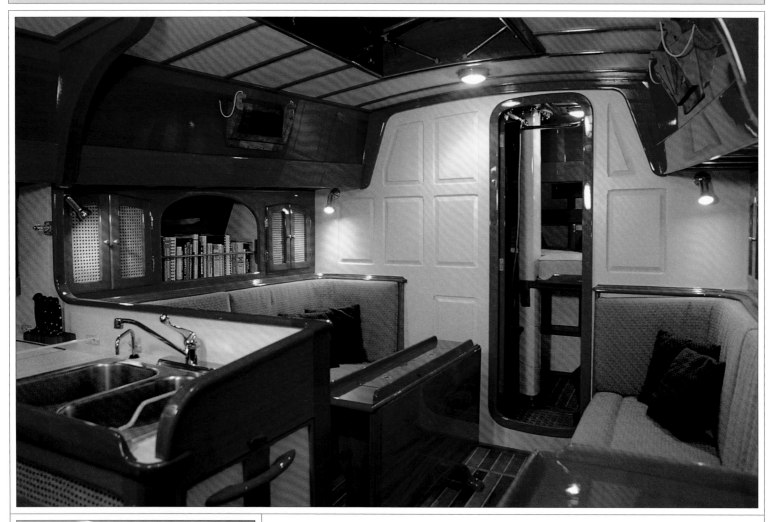

You might, at first glance, think you are looking at the interior of some masterpiece of an old classic from the early twentieth century, but these are two fairly standard *Cherubini 48s*. The photo above is a true collection of nautical art—from the beautiful raised-panel bulkheads to the trim around the bulkhead opening, the double dropleaf table, the settee trims, the arched bookshelf opening, and the classic skylight. Above right is looking aft in the same boat. Apart from the myriad beautiful small drawers, note the world's most perfect pilot berth in the passageway

leading to the aft cabin. The solid mahogany cabin sides are almost 2 inches thick and structural, as are the knees and the beams under the side deck. In the photo below, note the far-and-away-best doors for a boat—cane inlays in solid frames. There is simply no better way of ventilating lockers while adding a marvelous touch. And, for 'weight' watchers, don't forget—the cane weighs less than the new cored panels the high-tech people use. Opposite below is a door made of solid, beveled mahogany, and some very nice detailing for an armrest of the settee.

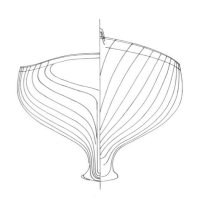

I have always believed that there are two irresistible but almost diametrically opposed attractions to sailing. First, there is the physical exuberance and adventure; second, the silence and the beauty. The Cherubini yachts are the rarity that can be all things to all sailors. From the classic and super-efficient clipper bow—top left—to the beautifully proportioned and classically detailed deckhouse, below it and right page, bottom, there is something that stirs the romantic in us all. And ingenuity is often combined with grace, as in the stunning teak dinghy chocks, to the left, that are

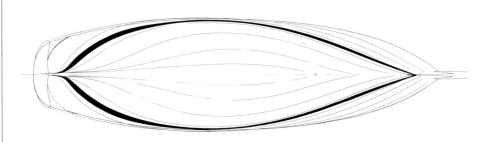

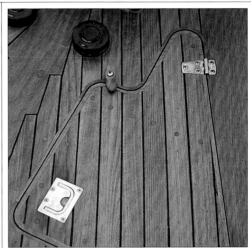

coupled with equally fine teak boom gallows. The large triangular teak grate not only reinforces the boomkin against the compression of the backstay, but it is also an ideal nonskid gangplank when tied stern-to to a sea wall. Then there is beauty for beauty's sake—the magnificent curved cockpit, with a very comfortable and secure padded backrest. The caned doors are my very favorite type, and so is the joinerwork of the door frames. The top four photos show excellent workmanship, including the one on the left page, right, which shows the lost art of splining—simply the strongest way of joining butted planks.

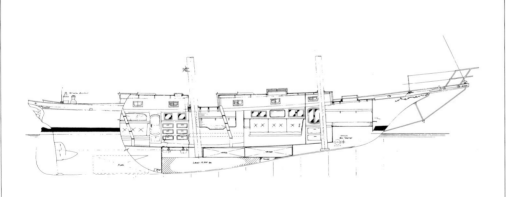

After a long day of explaining to me, with great patience and detail, all the whys and wherefores of his spectacular little ships, Lee stopped to give me a response as to how he can keep up his blazing enthusiasm after so many years. He searched for words. He was silent, remembering. 'You know, Ferenc,' he said, a little choked, 'I live these boats.'

ISLAND PACKET

Bob Johnson's passion for sailing bloomed at an early age. He was only eight when he bought his own subscription to *Yachting* magazine, and fourteen when he wrote a term paper on his future career as a naval architect. That same year, he lofted his first sailboat on the living room floor, then sailed it down Lake Worth, with his brother holding a garden umbrella for a spinnaker. He was hooked for life.

Even though he became a mechanical engineer, ending up at McDonnell Douglas designing missiles, his heart was still with sailboats. With a master's degree from MIT in naval architecture, he went to Florida and worked with Irwin Yachts and Endeavor, ending up as general manager. But he had a well-engineered dream.

He started Island Packet modestly in the mid-seventies by borrowing money to buy the molds for a 27-footer with a beam of more than 10 feet—a catboat proportion. He was everything at the company—engineer, purchasing agent, production manager and sales staff. They have since grown to near two hundred employees in an immaculate, family-owned—just Bob and his wife—facility that has its own lake, and they have developed over the decades one of the most enthusiastic and loyal followings in cruising-boat history.

But it was no happenstance. Bob Johnson had a concept in mind. As a dedicated observer, he had seen boats go from full-keel, wineglass-shaped hull forms to the *Cal 40* type with a fin-keeled, U-shaped underbody. He was struck by the fact that there had been no thoughtful, logical transition from one extreme to another. He felt that something sensible, seaworthy, and very manageable was missing.

He wanted to utilize the best of both extremes—take a modern U-shaped hull for performance and create a long keel for seaworthiness, not only by stretching the fin keel and making it shallower, but by making it an airfoil shape—he did get something out of the missile industry—creating lift. And instead of the big barn-door rudder hung on the aft end of the keel, which generated huge turning radiuses, he separated keel and rudder. Protecting the rudder—and the propeller—he still felt most important for a dependable cruiser, so he connected the bottom of the keel to the bottom of what was now a counterbalanced spade rudder. In this way, he maintained the stability and sea-keeping quality of a long keel and gained a good shallow draft. Even in case of grounding, his internally ballasted hull would suffer little damage compared to the major repairs necessary for bent keel bolts or torn-out bottoms, which some deep fin-keelers might endure.

So he set out not to compete with weekend racers but to build the best cruising boat possible. While the boats are full-out cruisers, they happen to sail darned well; the 38-footer just finished first in class in the Caribbean 1500 by twenty-five hours over the second-place boat. The *45* was first to finish twice in the same series. Apart from seaworthiness and performance, he became obsessive about keeping prices in line with the capabilities of cruising families.

At Island Packet, when they talk a lot about cruising comfort and livability, they mean a boat with a gentle, comfortable, less-fatiguing motion. This in turn improves safety, and—because of lack of fatigue—a more rested and alert crew. Their conviction is that every cruising boat should have the following key features: for a start, a comfortable, seakindly motion and an easily manageable sail plan; in plain English, a cutter rig as on most single-handed round-the-world racing boats. So, on Island Packets, furling sails—main included—are standard equipment. Next, apart from the protected propeller and rudder, they build a bullet-proof steering system, meaning rack and pinion—no cables, no pulleys, no chains. And they are adamant about the need for a recessed foredeck for safe work and immediate anchor access, because for them, an anchor is a piece of safety gear.

With these ideals and very high-quality workmanship in a line of boats based on common sense and simplicity, their boats have kept their value very well over the years.

Bill Bolin, who has been with the company a decade and a half, and looks after sales and marketing, proudly explains. 'We have been awarded five *Boat of the Year* awards from *Cruising World* magazine, but we're probably most proud of the two for *Best Value*. This means not only boat-for-initial-dollar, but also the cost of ownership over the long haul. There are a lot of boats that cost less than ours do for the same length, but in five years' time, most of their value drops 20 to 50 percent, while ours have historically maintained the same price as the day they were bought.

'*Sail* magazine told us several years ago that we have the highest percentage of repeat customers, and I believe this still to be true. There are a lot of owners on their third Island Packet and a few on their fifth. I think it's no accident that *Practical Sailor* has called us the best-run company in the business. Bob has been very meticulous in making sure that every dollar counts. And he doesn't like mistakes. Until not long ago, he used to pull every boot-stripe tape for every boat going out the door. That's dedication to perfection.

'And he has also been a firm believer in our company, giving back to the boating industry as a whole, a lot of what we have learned and gained. Several employees, including Bob and I, volunteer time as leaders on industry boards of directors with Sail America and the National Marine Manufacturers Association. And we actively participate in compliance seminars and training workshops to keep us at the forefront of changes. Bob has always felt that what was good for a builder would be good for the industry as a whole—certainly in the long run.

'To help reduce VOCs—volatile organic compounds—since many of them are classified as potential pollutants, we use hydraulic cylinders to pump catalyzed gelcoat, via a low-pressure/high-volume spray gun, onto the mold surface. This is instead of using high-pressure air systems that atomize a lot of the material. This also gives us a perfectly catalyzed gelcoat. In the more common application system, you have catalyst and gelcoat spraying out of two spigots, so you might get two drops of gelcoat and one drop of catalyst in one spot and the opposite in another. With our system, an adjustable master-and-slave cylinder mixes the precise ratio of materials for the given temperature and humidity and delivers it onto the mold with virtually no overspray. We get a glossier, less-porous gelcoat for longer life, and much less potential for osmotic blistering, enabling us to put a ten-year warranty on our hulls.

'Our gelcoat is different under the waterline and above. Below, it is terrific for blister resistance—not a blister since 1989, except for one bad batch of gelcoat, which infected three hulls that used the same barrel. Of course, we refinished all three hulls at our own expense, ground off all the gelcoat right to the laminates, re-faired and refinished, and started off with a new warranty. We like our owners to have confidence in us. But that same material chalks and oxides too much for use on topsides, so there we use one maximized for gloss retention. We have had our gelcoats lab-tested with UV bombardment and saltwater blasting and found that this new one has more than four times the reflectability after a ten-year simulation than the old one. We use different colors of gelcoat just to make it impossible for anyone to screw up, no matter how sleepy they are that morning.

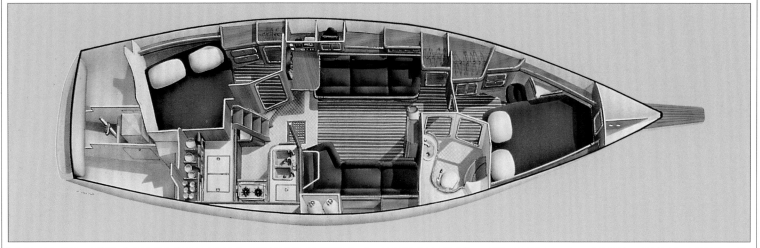

'We don't spray our resin for the laminates. It, too, comes precatalyzed, but it comes out through a roller. For our hull laminates, we use knitted unidirectional, as opposed to woven, fabrics. We start with a skin coat of mat. All the rest is triaxial glass; that is, the fibers run at 0 then 45 then another 45 degrees. In the relatively open and simple surface of the hull, triaxial is just fine, but it does not bend or conform to compound curves, so in many areas of the deck, we go to biaxial. Once we wet out, we squeegee; that forces the resin in among the glass fibers. Then we roll with brass rollers to squeeze out any extra resin. The rotating molds help the extra resin to flow out of the laminates. With this system, we're getting very close to 47 to 49 percent fiber content. It takes five workdays to laminate a hull, laying one layer on one side just past the centerline, then the hull is rotated and the same layer is laid in the other half.

'Our coring for our decks and interior liners is pretty unique. Instead of using conventional materials that are prone to rot and delamination, we actually make our own core in a liquid paste form, made up of microballoons—tiny Ping-Pong balls—and resin. The beauty of the material is that it is chemically very similar to, and bonds aggressively with, the composite structure, eliminating a major cause of delamination and allowing us to offer a ten-year warranty against deterioration, whereas many builders are reluctant even to offer five.

'So we take polyester resin, mix it with the microballoons, catalyze it, and then apply it with a low-pressure spray gun; it looks like shaving cream as it's applied. To maintain thickness minimums, we use spot gauging. When we attach the inner liner to the deck, we use a similar material mixed with mill fibers and microballoons—a little heavier, but it sticks like gangbusters. We then hand-scribe and fit our bulkheads to the deck, with all major bulkheads being mechanically fastened.

'For ballast, we use large lead castings or lead-and-iron ingots, depending on the model. With internally ballasted boats built like ours, we feel there is very little, if any, advantage of lead over iron. With the ballast completely encapsulated within the keel cavity, and with a complete hull laminate on top, we get a very strong, double-bottomed, boxlike beam down the center of the boat. For twenty-two years, 2,000 boats, and a few million miles, it's proven to be a system that works.

'Bob believes in simplicity. We build the boats one way with very few key options. The dealers are welcome to further personalize each boat to the owners' wishes; in fact, we do a lot of prewiring for various systems, but we know that the only system that is guaranteed not to break down at sea is the system that isn't there.

'And Bob also believes in very thorough engineering, to avoid changes and regrets once a new line of boats goes to the mold stage. He believes in mock-ups. We mock up the entire boat—deck and interior—to make sure everything fits. Not just obvious things, such as berths and cockpit seats, but all access to engine, steering gear, seacocks, etc. On a small model, we have even duplicated all the rigging to see if a dinghy can be swung aboard with the help of the boom, clearing the split backstay (split to accommodate access to landing platform). For example, on our new raised-saloon model, we wanted ample aft-passageway width, from main saloon to the aft cabin, to allow easy passage even with two people working in the galley. This can look

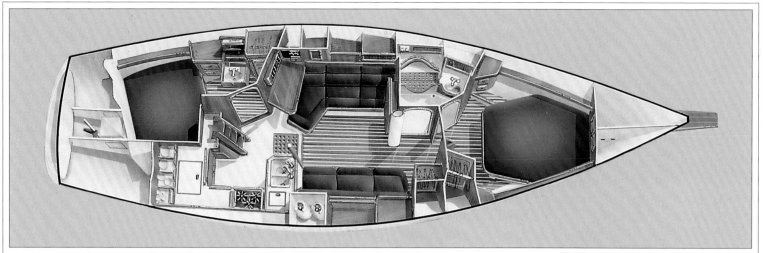

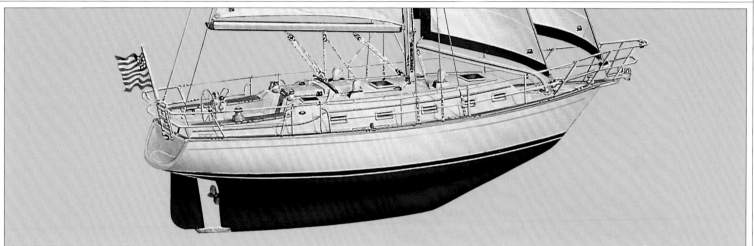

possible on paper, but it's only proven in a full-scale mock-up.'

Their quality control is just as finicky. There is a twenty-six-page quality-control book for each boat. Each item is signed off by three different people: the line foreman and the line supervisor, and then a quality-assurance supervisor checks all. This keeps warranty way down. In a trade where standard warranty costs often exceed 2 percent, Island Packet's decades-long record of less than 1/2 percent really shines. To achieve that, they do things like using a flashlight to check inside hard-to-get-at angles, and, with a wax crayon, mark off even pin-sized holes to be corrected, whether it's an inside hatch or fridge liners or even lazarette wells.

They have an impressive number of access holes to all of their floor liners, so that every piece, no matter how hidden, is bonded, on both sides, to the hull. And the finishing is thorough even in invisible spaces, so you can reach anywhere in their boats without finding a sliver or raw edge.

The chainplate system reflects both the engineering and the highest quality of workmanship. There are three chainplates on each side. A T-bar is welded to all three plates so the whole thing is one unit. Unidirectional glass comes up and wraps around the T at each chainplate and back in a V down the hull so the load is spread well over a great surface of the hull (see photo on page 91): a good, solid system with no bolts to elongate, no leaks, no mechanical attachments, like wearing a belt *and* suspenders. Even without the upside-down V-bonding, Bob says the structure is strong enough to pick up the whole weight of the boat with just the T-bar, because you have the hull flange, the deck, and the caprail on top of it.

The meticulousness of his thinking is reflected in the whole Island Packet yard. It is utterly spotless and organized in every aspect. I laughed when I saw, in the lobby, two pens on chains on a small writing table for job applicants—the chains were laid out perfectly stretched, and both they and the pens were absolutely parallel to each other. As Bill Bolin says, 'In order to work here, you have to be able to spell *anal retentive* properly.' It's little wonder that the people who come to work here stay for a long time. There are near twenty fifteen-year employees and close to fifty ten-year employees. When you think of how small the company was fifteen years ago, those are pretty amazing numbers. I cannot overstress how important the consistency of the workforce is in building continuously high quality boats.

Island Packet has been well recognized for its quality. It was the first U.S. sailboat builder (and still one of too few) to be certified under the strict new CE certification standards. The International Marine Certification Institute has awarded the entire range of Island Packet models its highest rating—Category-A, Ocean—meaning the boats qualify for 'unlimited offshore use.' It is an extremely thorough process that examines not only design and engineering but also construction and equipment details. Panels for the forward sections of the hull and deck are tested for their stiffness and oceangoing capabilities. Also examined are stability, cockpit drainage, cockpit depths, downflooding angles, wiring and lighting, port and hatch construction and installation, fuel delivery systems, and, of course, bilge pumps. The list goes on and on. In other words, they are almost as thorough as Bob Johnson.

I n the enticing photo with the palm trees is the first little Packet that started it all twenty-five years ago. The boats that followed, all from the board of naval architect Bob Johnson, who also owns the company, have much leaner but even sweeter and just as friendly lines. Their fleet—the *350* (bottom right), the *380* (two top corners), and the *420* (below) share not just good looks but also easy-to-handle sail plans. Their decks, with low bulwarks, make for safe footing on any heel. The

stern landing platforms are most practical, and the cockpits on even their smaller boats are ample, with the added creative seats worked into the stern pulpit. These, protruding beyond the stern rail, are practically 'off the boat,' opening up the cockpit for the helmsman and sheet handlers. The ventilation on the boats is extreme; the *480*, in the bottom left photo, has fourteen opening ports and seven opening hatches. Bob is one of too few builders who exhaustively engineers each boat.

I sland Packet has, over the past twenty years, developed a following whose dedication borders on zeal, mostly because of the many practical details that Bob Johnson and his team have put into these classic-looking yachts. Bob is an avowed believer of making every penny count.

Practicality, combined with efficiency, results in such features as small floor liners in a high-traffic area at the foot of the companionway, which then blends into the galley (above, and bottom right). The overhead is a rigid liner, which not only reinforces the deck but is infinitely easier to maintain,

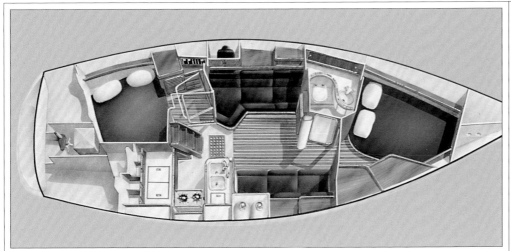

and it has a lot longer life than soft plastic ones, which can discolor or tear or, over the years, harden and break down. It also allows for molded bases for the long, easy-to-use handrails. The use of space is truly remarkable; the color illustration is a 32-footer with an aft cabin. The double berth in it is full length; the feet, ingeniously, hide under the galley countertop. The photo below is of the *350*, while at the bottom left is the *420*. My favorite small item, which one finds on all Packets, is the tempered-glass piece inserted into the middle dropboard of the companionway. This enables one to check for the safety of those in the cockpit without opening the hatch. I'm getting out my hacksaw and modifying mine.

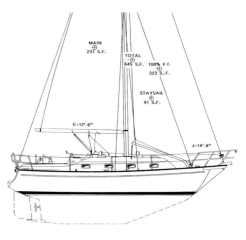

E very inch well thought out. In the cockpit photo at top left, the carefully drawn helmsman's seat allows full-length fore-and-aft seats for stretching out under starlit tropical skies. Note the perfectly placed bilge pump and the molded pocket for sheet tails. Next is a storage

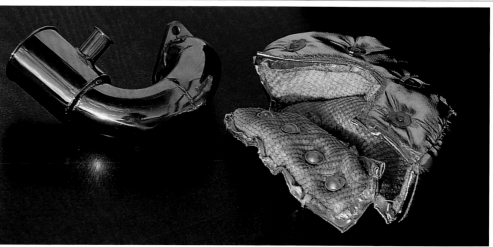

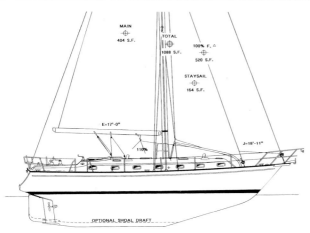

bin for dropboards. To its right are the hydraulic arm and air-less sprayer (see text). What looks like jewelry is a piece of the exhaust with a thermal insulator. Below them is the flawlessly crafted double anchor roller; below that, the immaculate mold shop, and to its left, the carbon-fiber strapping I talked about in the text. Next, the compart-mentalized refrigerator box; then a brilliant use of space under the bunk for bedding, with the lid held up by gas strut arms. Above that is my favorite—they mock up the deck with rigging to see if the inflatable can be swung cleanly aboard on the boom.

Having a naval architect own a boatyard helps greatly in avoiding the common friction between designer and boatbuilder. At Island Packet, it's most reassuring to see the knowledge, conscience, and concerns over seaworthiness, which are bred into a naval architect, win out over the judgment of the builder, whose opinions are too often compromised by the whims of the marketplace.

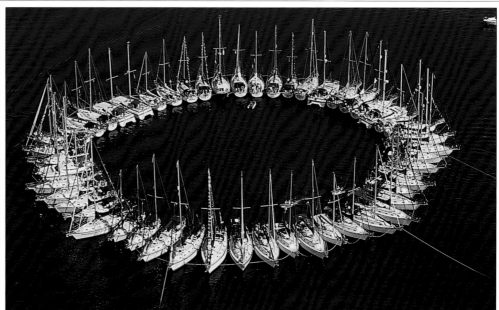

J
BOATS

'If you can tack up a shoreline into wind, waves, and current at the same speed as those plodding under *iron genoa*, then you have a performance sailboat. If you enjoy the serenity of broad reaching at nearly the same speed as boats that are motorsailing, then you have a performance sailboat. But if you have to crank up the engine even in a breeze to make a decent day's run, you're on a slow powerboat that happens to have sails.'

The Johnstone family has changed the world of sailing. And it has done more to keep sailboats as 'sail' boats than anyone else in boatbuilding. And perhaps because Rod, the designer, is 'basically a small-boat sailor' who was brought up to believe that sailing is a family affair, most of his designs have kept families in mind—in affordability, handling, and pure, outright sailing fun. Their now-legendary J/24, of which there are more than 5,200 in forty countries, is just one of their long line of what can be called, without a hint of overstatement, 'pure sailboats.'

Rod and his brother Bob, the marketer, started J/ Boats with Everett Pearson, the laminate genius, in 1977. While all three are less active in the company than they once were, their modus operandi is still intact. Rod's son Jeff, now president, looks and moves exactly like one of Rod's designs. Long, lean, full of energy, he will courteously look after you as he, along with Everett, guides you for hours through the plant, which looks like no other boatyard in the world. But all along, you get a sense of his chomping at the bit, glancing at the racing clouds, dying to go sailing.

'For us, the overall name of the game is to make sailing easier,' he begins, with absolute and sincere conviction. 'We have had a *105* in front of the house for a week, and we have gone out five evenings just because the boat is so easy to get underway and so easy to handle. Two days ago, it was blowing 20 to 25, and I took out five kids between the ages of eight and eleven, and they were up on the foredeck getting sprayed and loving it and loving the motion.

'We have stayed with generally narrow boats. We find it easier to steer the boat because it tracks through the waves better, it's not tossed around as much as a beamy, flat-bottomed boat. And since the boats have less deck area, we get a lower center of gravity, so the boat tends to have more stability. The ultimate stability—where a boat firms up—is more important to overall performance than initial form stability, where a boat might be stiff to start with, but once it heels, it keeps on heeling. The boat with better ultimate stability will be able to keep on sailing faster with fewer crew. So our hulls are generally long and skinny, with long waterline length and narrow beam waterline, which means there is not a lot of resistance.

'One of our goals in cruising boats is to reduce the number of sail changes that cruisers are often forced to do. Most cruising boats have shoal drafts and not-too-tall rigs, so they have to have a big overlapping genoa to get any kind of boat speed in 6 to 8 knots of wind. Then, when the wind picks up past 12 knots, they don't have the stability to continue with that big headsail. So by the time you hit 25 knots, they'll have gone through three or four sail handlings—reefs in the main, rolling up jibs and all. Because all that takes effort, you see many cruising boats motoring half their lives.

'Well, we thought, if we are really going to make an advance in cruising from a handling standpoint, we need to design a boat that can take the same two sails—the main and a small jib—and perform well in light air, and yet be able to depower and sail the same sails in 20 K of wind. These boats can do it. In 6 K, you can ghost at 4.5 K; at 20 K you just pull down the backstay, flatten out the main, pull down on the boom-vang, slide your jib lead aft a little bit, and keep going without reefing. One of our owners sailed around the world twice, once in each direction, and the biggest headsail he had was a number 2 genoa.

'Our mainsails tend to be the driving force in our sail plans. So if you were shorthanded and it did blow 25, instead of reefing the main, you just roll up the jib and sail mainsail only. All of our models sail beautifully with just the main. Or just the jib.

'A boat has to be easily driven. Yet we keep away from the IMS racing boats' knifelike bows. Admittedly, that helps them go upwind, but when you go downwind, you don't have any buoyancy up there, so you have to hang your whole crew off the stern rail. If your crew is just your sweety, then you don't have much in terms of willing human ballast. Rod and Al have always designed plenty of reserve buoyancy up there so the boat is relatively forgiving in its fore-and-aft trim. This is important when you have to put equipment and provisioning on a cruising boat. But the Js really distinguish themselves from IMS or raceboats, in that they have a lot more stability on a reach, which is vital for cruisers who, if they can help it, tend mostly to be reaching.

'Most people are amazed—I'm talking about those who normally get seasick—because they simply don't get sick on our boats. It's comparable to that sense of cornering in a sports car instead of a bus; it's a whole different motion. You know how on a ferryboat, people feel ill because they can't sense the axis of rotation. But in the Js, the body can easily pick out the up or down or side-to-side motion. There isn't that slow yawing. Rod has always had that knack of designing very seakindly hulls. And of course the lightness of our carbon-fiber masts cuts down on the rolling.

'A good measure is how tired the helmsmen get. We have had a lot of people comment on how they happily take extra turns at the helm because the boat is so effortless to steer. This helps a lot on saving autopilots as well. The rudders are very high aspect, so you don't have this barn door trying to jerk the wheel out of your hands. I think the narrow hull form with a large rudder and a truly balanced sail plan gives you just as much downwind stability as does the average skeg. Nice thing about a big mainsail is that it's your best downwind sail. My worst sailing experiences have been with a tall, skinny mainsail and a big masthead spinnaker. You can't drive them downwind at all, because there is no balance between the main and the spinnaker.

'Before the asymmetrical spinnakers came along in the early nineties, shorthanded cruisers had only the geniker, which was for reaching, not for downwind. With the asymmetricals, even without the bowsprit, even if the tack was right on the end of the anchor roller, you can still rotate that spinnaker out and sail 150 degrees apparent. The bowsprit would give you another 4 or 5 degrees.

'Our bowsprits for the asymmetrical are retractable into a tube incorporated into the hull. There are two bearing points: one right at the exit and one at the stern end where there is a bulkhead. So it's supported by a 4 1/2-foot section. When the pole is out, that 4 1/2-foot piece remains inside.'

All of Rod's design contributions aside, I think it is fair to assume that J/Boat history would have been drastically different were it not for Everett Pearson, the laminate guru who owned and ran TPI (see chapter on Freedom Yachts in *Volume I*). He was gracious enough to come out of retirement and spend a day with Jeff and me at the plant to talk about his favorite subject—how to turn rolls of fibers and barrels of mush into super-fast racing and cruising boats. TPI still builds the whole boat. They also engineer it, and in fact have been involved in development every step of the way. Their expertise has been enriched by

decades of experience building everything from ultralight composite trains for airports to the giant wind-generator blades, that translate readily into the fabrication of carbon-fiber masts and carbon-reinforced, structural hull components such as rudders and bulkheads. The rudders, for example, are all composite. The rudderposts are the same material as they have been using here for the windmill blades, just because those have been tested for hundreds of thousands of revolutions over many years. The cross technology here at TPI has been tremendous. Everett's knowledge of composites and laminates is not only prodigious, but he also has the most congenial and intelligent way of transmitting it to others. He walks and talks not like someone who is retiring but rather like a young man in full career stride.

'You know, on our side, the construction side, the big changes, the biggest improvement for the J/boats, has been the SCRIMP process which we started on them back in 1994. That changed everything from a very difficult quality-control aspect to something where you can predict exactly what you're going to obtain, every time. You get a very high-quality, low-weight laminate, no voids. The only way we could improve on the laminate is to go to pre-preg, oven-cured, a process very tough to handle. I think we're at about 3 percent less physical properties than you would get from an oven-cured part.

'The saving of 10 to 15 percent of weight with the SCRIMP over the traditional hand layup is not the only positive factor. Consider also the uniformity and the lack of air, and the consistently high quality. You can engineer the laminates better, fine-tune them.

'If the system is laid out well—and of course you have to understand the flow rates, the amount, the pounds, and the thicknesses of glass you have to wet out—once you work that out, the process is completely repeatable. Nothing varies. If you take the dry fibers of the laminate and compact them under a vacuum, they (being dry) compact to the greatest extent possible. Basically, all we do is fill in those consistent voids with resin. So the amount of resin that goes into that mass of consistent fibers is itself consistent. There could be variation in how you cut the glass, but since we use a computer, which cuts a perfect pattern each time, there will be no variation. Take our wind blades, which are 80 feet long. You have to cut those perfectly. If the cutting is off 1/8 inch in laminates that we put in there, it will affect the weight of the blade by more than 150 pounds. The computer takes out all that variation. Our blade weights vary under 1 percent. Windmills only turn at about 40 rpm, but the blades are so long that the tip speed is 200 miles an hour. So they have to be perfect to stay together.

'You are basically taking the spray gun and the squeegee and roller out of people's hands. Don't forget it might be a different guy laying up one side of a hull from another, or it's after lunch, or Monday. Who knows how different the hand pressure or the nozzle movement will be from day to day, from hour to hour.

'To achieve an ultimate laminate and not worry so much about the composites, you can go right against the gelcoat, but with the high glass content, the fiber pattern of the fabric tends to print more.

'Everything but that outer skin coat, to stop the read-through, is dry. Even the core goes in dry. We use end-grain balsa on horizontal surfaces, but on the vertical sides of the cabin, we go to foam. Everything is one shot, including the floor grid in the

bottom of the hull, so that the entire hull and structural grid are laid up and infused at the same time, into a monocoque unit.

'The reason you can do that is that, if you cut your glass as accurately as we do, you have a very small dimensional tolerance. So we don't have to go back and grind and fit and dry-laminate. When you run aground with a fin-keeled boat, the first thing that usually happens is the stringers at the back end of the keel pop out. They separate from the hull because the secondary bond fails. But with SCRIMP, the grid is infused with the hull; there is no secondary bond. It's all primary lamination; no joints, no weak spots. Our longitudinal hull stringers, too, are SCRIMPed in the mold to take advantage of the strength of primary bonds. And there is no practical limit to how many layers you can infuse at a time. I have a block in the office that's a foot thick that we infused at one shot.'

'The nice thing about having this technology,' Jeff Johnstone interjects, 'is that you can design boats to take advantage of it.'

In the mold shop, Everett guides us to a half-hull mold covered with arabesques of tubes and ropes and a giant sheet of see-through plastic.

'Through the plastic sheet, you can watch the resin go in. The first thing we do is put resin into the tubes of the mold of the grid. As the resin feeds down into those crossbeams, you stand here and all of a sudden you'll see it coming out and wetting out the laminate on either side of it, so you know it's being wet out. The second thing you can do to verify is to weigh everything. You know that a given weight of glass in the grid—let's say 70 pounds—will take 30 pounds of resin because we know that our fiber-to-resin ratio is 70-to-30. I think a lot of builders have to do a lot of careful lamination to get their fiber ratio even up

to 40 percent, never mind 70.

'There was one very big, well-known French company that wanted to license the process from us. We went to try to infuse the glass laminates they gave us, and, my god, we sucked the resin right out of there, so there was no stiffness left. Their whole boat had basically been built on resin strength. Just bulk. You can build up resin with a chopper gun or hand lamination to a sufficient stiffness, but the thing will weigh more than a Sherman tank; it'll be a slug in the water. But if you want a good-performing boat with a lightweight laminate, you have to get the resin out of there. But when you take out the resin, to get the stiffness, you have to put a core in. The *105* was originally a vacuum-bagged boat that was converted to SCRIMP. When we did that with the same laminate, we realized that the skins had become too thin without the resin. The strength was there in terms of tensile, but strength for impact resistance was reduced because the skin thickness went down. So, since we didn't need a lighter boat, we decided to add more glass. For the same given weight, we have an extra layer or two of glass in this hull versus the old one.

'It takes a lot of time to work out the engineering initially. You have to think everything through; you have to design it, then you have to spend the time on the tooling to make it work. Some of our main bulkheads are balsa, SCRIMPed in. Furniture, and even bunkboards in the ends of the boat, we have made with foam core with glass skins to keep the weight out of the ends. But you are paying for it; twice the price for half the weight. Don't forget we're trying to strike a balance, to create a dual-purpose boat.'

Without doubt, the fastest and most fun-to-sail line of high-quality boats in the world. Starting with the *J/80* (left), at 26 feet and 2,900 pounds, up to the queen of their fleet, the *J/160* (far right), at 53 feet and 31,000 pounds, the Johnstone family has designed and built something for every sailor. The pictures attest to the thrill of sailing J/Boats, with their retractable carbon-fiber sprits, which allow for the most efficient use of asymmetrical spinnakers. While they all plane easily, due to their flat bottoms and powerful sterns (bottom-right photo), the speeds

attained by the *J/160*—8.1 knots upwind and 9 knots reaching—have certainly made long-distance cruising an entirely different endeavor. What in the past have been Spartan sailing craft are now vindicated by the *J/145*, below left and right. While she's as sleek and light as her sisters—13-foot beam on a 48-foot boat displacing 19,000 pounds—she has a luxurious cherry or teak interior and a very safe and comfortable cockpit. This contrast is achieved by keeping the basic structure of hull and deck very strong and light, using Carbon/E-glass/SCRIMP lamination (see text).

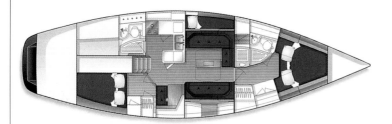

J Boats have come a long way from the ascetic interiors of the early *J/24s* to their new boats on these pages, which are as woody and cozy and as full of excellent joinery as you can ask for. But never is it forgotten that these are long-distance, serious cruisers. Notice the long overhead hand-holds in the bottom-right and top-right photos; and the side ports with quadruple dogs. And I very much like the thoughtful fore-and-aft searails in their galleys. These divide the surfaces

into small, secure areas, where things are kept from madly sliding about in rough seas or on hard heels. The photos and drawing on the left-hand page are of the new *J/46*, while the photo below is of their flagship, the 53-foot *J/160*. The drawing to the right is of the new 48-foot *J/145*. Oh, yes, the top-right photo (with all the books in the main saloon and forepeak) merits the Johnstones one of my most coveted awards—the most bookshelves per LWL. My heartiest congratulations.

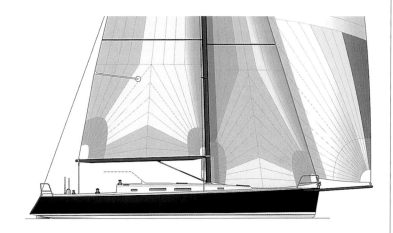

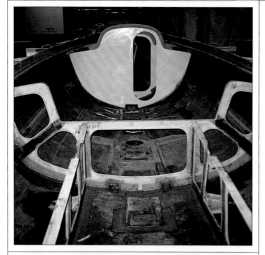

The sailing shots in the four corners capture the fun and thrills of sailing a J. The upper right-hand corner shows the extremely well-proportioned cutout in the transom of the new *J/145*. I very much like the amount of 'meat' left around the cutout, for structural as well as aesthetic reasons. The photo above, with the white interior, shows the forepeak of the racing version of the same boat—pure, lightweight, and functional. There is an optional all-wood forepeak as well. The small photo to its right is of the great carbon-fiber wind-generator blades, which TPI, the builder of

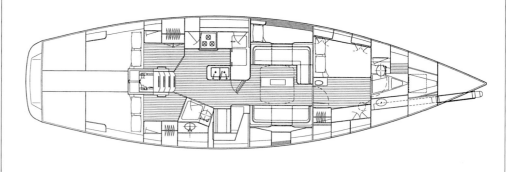

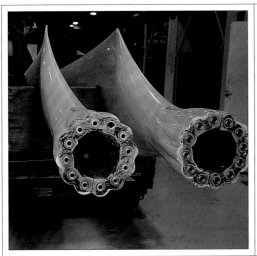

J/Boats, has been making for almost twenty years. This has given them the enormous experience necessary for making perfect carbon-fiber masts (next photo). The two small photos at far left show the weight-saving at TPI. Most structural bulkheads—all of composite—are reduced to skeletons— they provide the same strength as full bulkheads but with much less weight. The two photos below left are of the floor grid. The one with the tubes is of the grid mold, showing it being infused at the same time as the hull. This precludes secondary bonding, yielding a unified, much more fail-proof structure.

The shot of the keel testifies to the great intelligence at J/Boats—to maintain a shoal draft with excellent stability, the keel flares downward *and* the bulky, most weighty portion is stretched aft for optimum righting moment. And lastly, note in the interior drawing of the *J/160* (left page) the retractable sprit.

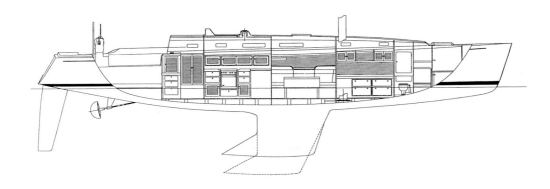

In midafternoon, in 20-plus knots of wind, Jeff and I took the *105* sailing. He had the sails up and us underway before I could lash the dinghy to the buoy. The boat flew. I tried steering with my eyes closed and could not go off our sail setting—I sensed the resistance both ways in the helm. But J/Boats are not for everyone—you need strong neck muscles. Otherwise, in a gust, when the boat takes off like a bat out of hell, you're liable to get whiplash.

MORRIS YACHTS

W hile it was common in the old days for a son to take up his father's profession, it is a rarity today. Sailors should feel proud, then—at least judging from four of the boatyards in these pages—that the building of sailboats seems to be a happy exception. There is something reassuring and human about a son following in his father's footsteps. And something exhilarating in watching him stride ahead.

Cuyler: 'We pride ourselves on being flexible and less production-oriented.'

Tom: 'On one hand, it takes more energy and creativity to work this way, but we do have a lot of history so we can price out things safely. We have had a bonus plan for more than fifteen years based on the number of hours that we under-run our projections. It works amazingly well.'

Cuyler: 'We are actually quite happy that other builders are going more toward production-type work because the craftsmen who really thrive on creativity then come to us.'

Tom: 'Here they can blend creativity with tested production techniques. And they seem to like it fine, because they never seem to leave. I'm sad to say that, in general, the old kind of marine carpenter is fast disappearing. A lot of people who today call themselves marine carpenters can only laminate curves. If they can't bend and laminate, they're lost. Real handwork—yacht joinery, dovetailing—is vanishing. All of our clients really appreciate fine joinerwork. One of them just restored his own Steinway.'

Cuyler: 'We had a European customer here with his classic S&S sloop. He knows and appreciates fine details. When he came out of the 486, he said—and I was amazed to hear this: You just don't see craftsmanship like this coming out of Europe anymore. And he had just been at A&R and Huisman, so he knows.'

Tom: 'We still try for the most elegant and thoughtful way to execute the joining of pieces of wood. But to be consistent in quality in such a variety of boats as we build, we have to have a steady crew. I never remember letting a person go except in 1982, for lack of work. I think people appreciate that kind of consistency. When one of our owners wants a new boat, nine out of ten times they come to us. And ten out of ten times they don't come alone. The female side of boat buying, I think, is one of the major changes in sailing over the last fifteen years. The design and technical features of the boat had traditionally been the domain of the male in the family. Now the women are involved in every detail from the keel up: boat behavior in seas; the ease of handling of sails; the interior layout; and they are often just as knowledgeable. Overall, they are driving fifty percent of the process—at least in our case, where we have so much personal input by each customer. We're still a family business. As we grow, the structure of the company has to change, but we don't want that structure to dominate the relationship we have with the owners of our boats.

'Or the relationship with our employees. To me, people are infinitely more important than any structure. Being in Maine helps a bit. Even here, there is a lot of influx of new people and new needs, so the pressures start to show, but fortunately we have such long winters that it keeps a lid on things.'

Cuyler: 'At least we know that whoever walks through that door on a miserable winter's day really loves our boats.'

Tom: 'One of our problems, I guess, had been that of image; everyone knew us as builders of small boats up to 36 feet. We didn't do our first 46 until 1992. All of a sudden, the magazines were knocking on the door to review them; Harken and Schaffer wanted pictures of our boats to use to project themselves. That never happened with the 28- or 30-footers. We had to literally drag the magazines up here.'

Cuyler: 'But we were always known for a kind of elegant quality. You know, Dad doesn't point out many of the little things, but aside from sailing performance and construction, he

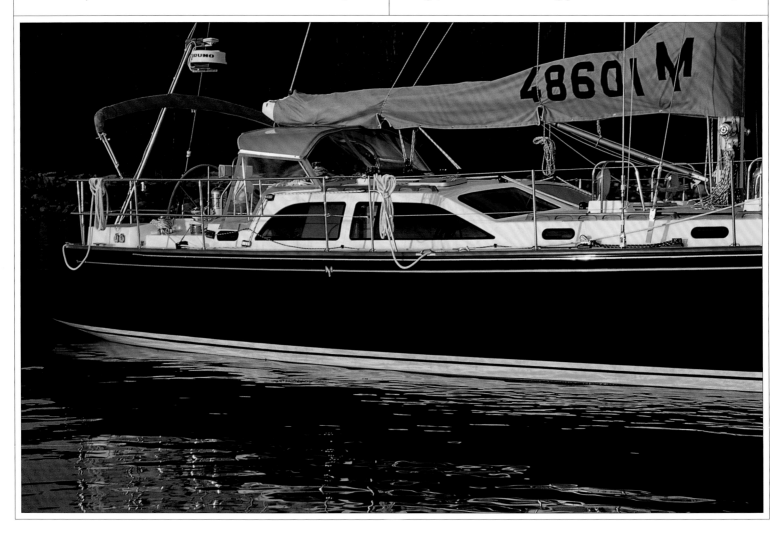

is a maniac on making every detail not just perfectly useful but perfectly beautiful.'

Tom: 'Well, why not? Look at the Italians at the forefront of all designing. Practically everything they touch is in the Museum of Modern Art. And whether it's a chair or a Ferrari or a spoon—whatever the final use of the object—when the lines are right, they are pleasing to the eye. Sailboats, whether with a traditional hull shape or a modern hull shape, as long as the lines are right, I think that we will—no matter what our taste— react by saying, *That is beautiful*. But all the lines have to work together—not just the sheer or bow, but the house, the windows, the angle of the stem, angle of the transom, the transition from foredeck to cabinhouse, all that.'

Cuyler: 'A good example is the bend in the side of the pilothouse, which also puts a bend in the side windows. Everyone comments that it has such a unique and pleasantly striking effect. It is, in fact, a line that follows through from the lower housetop to the cockpit coamings, holding together three vastly different elements. Interestingly enough, it makes the big windows infinitely stronger. And we are now looking at bent laminated glass that has almost complete reflective qualities to keep the boats cool in hot climates. We like to look into the newest and best ways of doing things.'

Tom: 'Unfortunately, we don't get to do them often enough. I'm a great believer in solar panels; we have built some into rigid tops of our boats. I just wish people would appreciate them more. You can be putting four amps into your system for twelve hours without noise or stink or pollution or expense, enough for cabin lights and instruments and, with the greater efficiency of batteries, a good panel would make enough juice to run your watermaker.'

Cuyler: 'But people are getting more adventurous. I think it helps that many of them know their boats will winter in our service yard, so we'll look after any avant-garde ideas.'

Tom: 'We're onto some pretty exciting things. We have been talking to a manufacturer about diesel-electric power for sailboats. One forgets that submarines were driven by diesel electric. This is something in development now. The advantages— particularly for boats over 40 feet, most of which have generators—would be amazing. No engine, just a generator placed wherever you want without regard to shaft, etc. Weight saving: Instead of the huge heavy diesel you have an 18-by-14-by-12-inch electric motor the size of a box of apples. No vibration; almost noise-free. Plus, as we mentioned with the watermaker, solar panels or wind generators could be helping to charge your batteries, so to some degree, depending on efficiencies, you can have your motor running on free, nonpolluting power.'

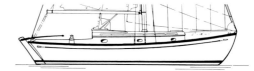

When I mention to him that he seems to be getting deeper and deeper into boatbuilding instead of retiring out of it, he laughs and points out the window toward the docks. 'That's my ticket out of here; I bought back an old Frances I built years ago. She needs some work, but then I'm going cruising. Just have to finish a major, high-tech conversion—the woodstove to diesel. But until then, I'm here. Building.'

Morris Yachts's motto appears to be, 'We can do anything best.' To the left are Tom and Cuyler Morris, Tom with one of their classic hulls, Cuyler with their latest—both designed by Chuck Paine. The photo above is of the beautifully balanced 46 with exquisite traditional lines and perfect sea manners. Below, the new 486, showing pinpoint handling at good speed around a lobster trap. She's arguably the sleekest raised-house boat ever designed, with those beautiful bent side windows (see also previous pages). She sports a spacious cockpit, hard-top dodger, and com-

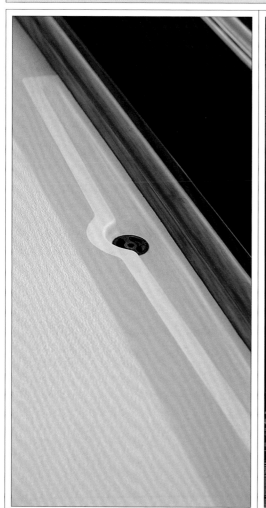

modious transom platform with even a low grabrail for lashing the inflatable and hanging a swim ladder. The boat is all waterline, and that, combined with a powerful stern and modest beam, make for a hell of a fast sailer. With its sophisticated lines and just the right amount of detail teak, she is as elegant as her classic sisters. The skinny photo above shows a commendable piece of tooling—no dirty puddles on Morris boats—the decks drain to the very last drop. Above right, the pretty stern of the 46. Note the beautiful rise to the sheer and the sleekest of rubrails. Below right is the new center-cockpit 52, which has an apartment-sized aft cabin. And last, in the small photo below is the fairlead we all dream about—the center part is hinged so you can insert or remove the rope at any point instead of having to painstakingly thread the whole thing. *Bravo!*

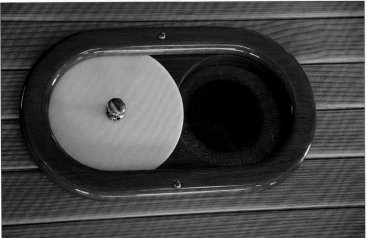

I cannot recall having seen more beautiful yacht joinery than that on Morris Yachts. They combine a quiet elegance and sophistication with perfect execution. While these pages show the more traditional 46-footer, the work in their more modern-lined boats is no less impressive. In the bottom left corner is a handhold that would easily win a Joinery Academy Award. So would the masterpiece of a Dorade-vent bottom (in the photo above it), with a barely visible brass mos-

quito screen, a sliding Teflon hatch to keep out the draft, and an immaculately crafted trim ring. The chart-table-area cabinetry (above) is so beautiful, it's almost a shame to put instruments into the very boxes designed for them. The drawers and searail details are exemplary, especially that bafflingly-shaped one in the galley counter in the photo below. If it were left to me to make that, I would be having nightmares for weeks. In the same photo, note that the edges of the stainless sink are

under the countertop for both beauty and practicality, and the hatch trims in the same photo could make you turn green with envy. In the right-hand photo above is a truly classic ship's table with leaves that hinge athwartships for better access to the settee, and again a set of those covetable drawers in its base. The nice thing about these boats is that you could save a mint by forgetting about sails and rigging and even a keel; it would be reward enough just to sit below and gaze around forever.

Morris Yachts's minor miracles are always noteworthy. Clockwise from top left: the wiring is paranormal— not only exquisitely meticulous, but on each white sleeve, on each wire, is printed the wire's function. Next is an innocent-looking, shipshape dovetailed toolbox. But that's not all at Morris Yachts; the thing fits and slides as perfectly as a drawer into the bottom of a locker. The next two shots are interiors of the 486 with room and light galore. Below the one on

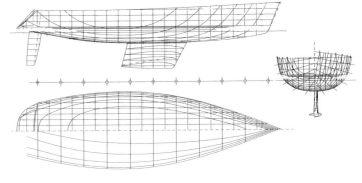

the right, is a 'blind' chainplate—no nuts, no bolts, no leaks. Below that, a little stainless steel tray that seems made by Tiffany's; note the sculpted holes for glasses/beer cans and mugs. The dropboards are not the normal wood-to-wood but instead, brass-to-brass for eternal life. Both the bow-thruster opening and the keel are sculpted to perfection; and so is the hull of the new *454*, with carbon-fiber ribs and floor grid, and the large, built-in steps of the transom. In all, about as good as yachtbuilding gets.

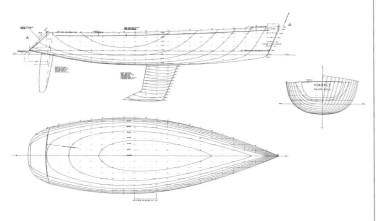

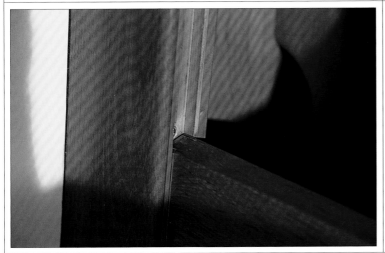

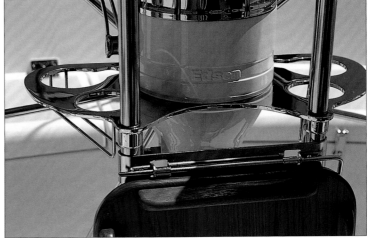

'Overall, I can honestly say that each boat is built, each phase is carried out, as thoughtfully and as precisely as we can manage. Each item, each detail, is the very best that we can do.'

And a lot of the very best at Morris Yachts is the very best in all the world.

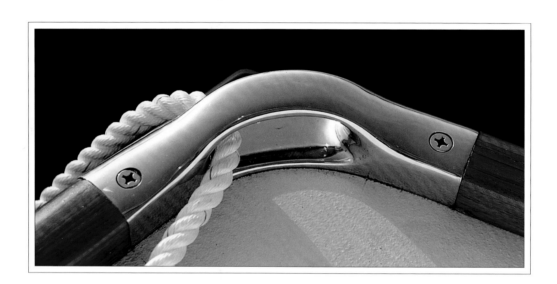

NAUTOR'S SWANS

'In the old days, we used to put in a bit extra to be on the safe side. There was so much extra, you could have given the boats icebreaker certification. Nowadays, with more research, more computer simulation, more precise engineering, we know exactly how much is needed. That's the new Nautor—leaner, lighter, faster.'

Nautor has always been one of my favorite builders. They started more than thirty-five years ago with fresh ideas, tons of self-confidence, and an all-defying new look by designers Sparkman & Stephens that was dictated by a vision of utmost utility and common sense. They coupled that with unremitting quality based on five centuries of boatbuilding tradition in this remote corner of Finland. The result was a line of distinguished yachts that sailed like a dream, cruised well, raced well, were luxurious below, and, as an added feature, were more or less indestructible.

They were absolutely unconfoundable with any other yacht; their lines were born from the brilliant Sparkman & Stephens notion that if the line of the deckhouse was carried well aft, then you could, with great aesthetic success, hide an aft cabin there. This did result in smaller cockpits and some manhole like companionways well forward, which made for rather insecure exit and entry in big seas, but then, good God, you can't have everything in a 40-foot boat. And besides, the safety of the wide, clear decks made up for that shortcoming. Anyway, the revolution was on, based on the old Louis Henry Sullivan notion of 'form follows function.' For thirty-odd years, that slightly arrogant, admittedly aggressive, but absolutely utile form remained. Swans were the perfect embodiment of the elegant cruiser/racer. Some people never took to them, and admittedly they were a bit short on 'Hinckley grace,' but when the world caught on to the astounding quality of their construction, the final word on them was almost always, 'Grace be damned.'

And so they chugged along for decades, changing models only now and then, all of them distinguished and only a single flop—the one with the rather strange uplifting plastic sides.

If you are wondering why I'm spending so much time discussing looks, it's because I fear they are about to make a mistake again, but for much less noble reasons. The design with the hinged sides was born out of an honest attempt to bring more light and ventilation and great views down below. The new design seems to have no other motivation than to change style. I'm talking about the new *Swan 45*, which, according to rumors, is the forerunner of the 'new' Swans. This would be sad, because the *45* seems a full-out racer, barely disguised in cruiser clothes—i.e., teak decks and a wood interior. It seems in too many ways to be turning the Swan philosophy on its head. In 2001, it was the talk of the London Boat Show, and while there were a lot of first-glance oohs and ahhs, too often they were followed by chuckles. I do think this is unjust to Germán Frers—one of my favorite all-round designers—who has perfect sensibilities and has, in this case, come up with a perfectly stunning design. But comments like, 'How ingenious to squeeze the interior of a 35-footer into a 45-foot boat,' one must admit, were more or less justified.

It seems that this boat was designed to look pretty and function (as far as safe and comfortable cruising is concerned) be damned. When one learns that Nautor was bought three years ago by a group headed by Leonardo Ferragamo, who leads the Italian design house of ultra-high-fashion, then one slaps oneself on the forehead and says, 'Of course.' Unfortunately, in a world whose median intellectual depth is fast reaching that of the average puddle, the all-importance of the 'pretty face' concept, perfected by the world of high fashion, has become the new anthem of us all.

The new *Swan 45* is nothing, if not pretty. With hollowed cheeks, lean lines, less freeboard to lower CG, a deck that's free of lines (buried underdeck, where they may bang when they tighten) and free of toerails (what's the big deal about trying to stay aboard?) and free of a helmsman's seat (let him stand until his knees buckle), one is tempted to ask, 'Where's the boat?'

If I sound critical, that's only because I love the old cruiser/racer Swans and loved what they stood for—the best, the most reliable, roomiest, most uncompromising, simplest, long-lasting fast boats you could build. If I had my way, Nautor would have been declared a World Heritage Site. Now, to have that compromised by the input of those whose daily concentration is on pretty but mostly throwaway clothing (who would be caught dead in last year's model?) seems somehow *un peccato*, a sin. I won't elaborate on the fashion world—I made my feelings pretty clear in my book *A Reasonable Life*—but I do fear that, while Frers is still their main designer, Mr. Ferragamo is trying to modernize the fleet with his personal sensibilities.

All the newer boats are faster, more performance-oriented, and that's all to the good. But that, of course, is at the expense of some of the traditional Swan qualities, such as handling. Just like a Chapman Lotus or a thoroughbred racehorse, they are more temperamental, requiring more attention. And they offer a lot less volume, storage, and security for cruising.

In defense of the new line, Ingmar Grenholm, Nautor's in-house naval architect, observed: 'We have to combine the new, lighter boats with more gear, more equipment, so it's a delicate balance. But we certainly were due for a change. When we were owned by the paper mill, they didn't want to get really involved and no one here had the courage to convince them to surge ahead. For them, paper will always be paper, even a hundred years from now, so to them innovation seemed foreign.' Of course, the sea has been the sea a hell of a lot longer than paper has been paper, so perhaps they had an arguable point.

'But the best part of the change,' Mr. Grenholm goes on, 'has been our very good new boss here, Luciano Scarmuccia, who was with Perini, of the big Italian luxury yachts. He's very active, aggressive, and he's put a lot of speed into the company.'

While I appreciate Mr. Grenholm's steadfast loyalty and do not undervalue either Mr. Scarmuccia's abilities or Mr. Ferragamo's unparalleled good taste in visual details, I would like to close my observations with this note. To most of us who love sailing, a sailboat is something we cherish because it can carry us far, far away from the hyperactive, often depressingly shallow, too-often-moronic activities of what we, without a hint of irony, refer to as 'life.' To try to build a boat whose main aim seems to be to impress those most enamored with this superficiality is a betrayal of one of man's last reasonable activities. Mr. Ferragamo might do well to allow the Swans to influence his philosophy of life, instead of the other way around.

All of the above is said in the hopes of trying to preserve the integrity of what, to many, have been the very best sailboats in the world. And by God, some of them still are.

The *Swan 44* was launched in 1990 yet is still the most perfect 'small' Swan around. While its hull shape deprives it of the performance of the newer, moderate-beamed, broader aft-sectioned, proportionately longer-waterlined *48* and *56*, its overall lines are the most pleasing, the interior-per-cubic-foot the most functional, its cockpit and companionway the safest.

The *48*—designed in the late nineties—might just be the best

all-round Swan ever built. Its unexaggerated, easily-driven hull, flatter bottom to get it to plane, and perfected elegance of its lines, along with two safe companionways, make it close to the prettiest and most functional of the line. The aft cabin has a very accessible island double berth, the galley is perfect, and the saloon luxurious but utile—although, as I mentioned in another chapter, beyond a 13-foot beam, saloons start to become rather bizarre with movable chairs and other oddities. A second, ensuite private cabin forward makes it an ideal family, long-distance cruiser. Farther forward still is a watertight bulkhead that not only joins up with the hull grid for extreme stiffness and strength, but also, if the bow is damaged, stops the incoming sea at that point, leaving the rest of the boat seaworthy.

Much of the energy lately at Nautor has gone into boats between 60 and 112 feet. Some aesthetically stunning (except for the *82 RS* which has a deckhouse that seems to be made out of an old car top installed backward), eminently practical, and commendably safe ideas have come out of these boats, much I would think owed to Mr. Scarmuccia's background with the megayachts. In the first category are such things as the alluring flush hatches, which not only are beautiful but also cut down on the loud *Madonnas* uttered when toes are stubbed on the traditional ones. Intriguingly shaped bulb keels that cut down on draft, and 'pop-up' fairleads and mooring cleats are others, while the *45* has introduced as standard the carbon-fiber masts. They used to have continuous rod rigging but found the bends to be weak points—perhaps vulnerable only after a long period of time, but then Swans have very long lives—so they have gone to discontinuous rigging with ball joints at the spreaders (see photo, page 127). They have also gone more to swept-back spreaders to give more fore-and-aft stiffness to the mast without the need for running backstays except when nearing survival conditions. The older boats still have running backstays.

What has not changed at Nautor is the obsessive quality of the boats. Nearly five hundred workers are as serious and disciplined as you can dream of in a boatyard. With the growth in the last ten years, they have become more industrialized, as amply illustrated by a rotating carousel in the stockroom with more than two thousand different items; all you do is punch in the code and up comes whatever you want.

Nautor's self-reliance is still inimitable. All the pieces that need precise fittings, whether in stainless or aluminum, are still fabricated *in-house*. They have one miracle machine that shapes, mills, drills, and planes so you have an infinite combination of potential maneuvers, which result in the showpieces you see on the detail pages. They still make their own aluminum masts, but, as I said, carbon is fast coming into the picture.

Their hulls—maybe my overall favorites—are still mostly single-skinned, reinforced with a massive gridwork of longitudinal and lateral stiffeners. These are all laminated in before the bulkheads, so that no panel larger than about 6 square feet goes without the massive reinforcement. For the most part, they have shied away from cored hulls because of fear of delamination, and of course the complexity of repair. And they think weight-saving for their kind of boat is most often negligible. They feel that, while you can build racing boats with a limited lifetime with all sorts of trade-offs, for boats where the owners expect uncompromised longevity of thirty or forty, or who-knows-how-many years, it's advisable to remain conservative.

They are one of very few builders who use clear gelcoat, not only to facilitate seeing and repairing tiny voids, but also because

gelcoat without pigment is tougher and less brittle than gelcoat with pigment. Some fiberglass parts are vacuum-bagged, pre-molded, and then epoxied together. They do mix combinations such as carbon-fiber pre-preg deck with a Nomex core.

The hull-deck joints are sealed and bolted onto an impeccably laminated 3-inch-wide, massive integral hull flange that's more than 1/4 inch thick. Both sides of major bulkheads are routed down and bonded, as is one side of minor or secondary ones. The two major bulkheads have huge transverse floor beams supporting them; these are in fact a continuation of the chainplates, to distribute the load over the hull.

Keeping in the vein of the impressive structurals is a huge galvanized-steel mast step that's part of a galvanized-steel floor grid onto which the keel is bolted. Thus, the weight and torque of the keel is distributed broadly over the hull. There are two 1 1/2-inch-thick bulkheads on the forward and aft ends of the steel floor grid. On the 56, the floor grid is bolted to the main bulkhead with no fewer than eighteen hulking bolts, whereas its aft plate is bolted to a lower bulkhead that ties into the longitudinal stringers with no fewer than—are you ready?—twenty-six bolts of 3/8-inch diameter. If this doesn't hold, nothing will.

The beautifully cast, sculpted keels with hollow cheeks make a spectacular aerodynamic foil that not only cuts water remarkably well but sheds it at the trailing edges with equal efficiency. The bulbs used on shoal versions are just as airfoil-shaped.

The head of the keel has a deep, bucket-shaped bilge about a foot long and 10 inches deep. This, first, creates a deep, practical sump in an otherwise flat-bottomed boat; and second, protruding as it does into the bolt-on keel, it creates a 'key', which, in case of grounding, takes some of the shear load off the keel bolts, transmitting the impact into an integral part of the hull instead of only onto mechanical fasteners.

The chainplates are mostly single-unit stainless steel, bolted to bulkheads, backed up on both sides by 3/16-inch laminates of glass that continue onto the hull, forming heavy knees. The bulkheads also have two long, 3/16-inch-thick vertical straps of fiberglass laminated onto them to carry the enormous loading of the turning blocks (which lead all the halyards aft) right down to the keel. That's about as brilliant as boatbuilding gets.

To eliminate unwanted weight, there are large holes, a foot in diameter, cut out of the bulkheads where no loads are present. This in no way weakens a bulkhead, for—as on most racing boats—only the outer ring of the bulkhead is utilized for stiffness, the center being left behind as it is mainly deadweight filler.

Where smaller areas are reinforced with carbon, postcuring is done 'locally'—that is, a small bag is placed over the area to be cured instead of the whole hull going into an oven. The stringers on the big boats are laid up in carbon but bonded into the hull with Vinylester.

The boats are full of wonderfully engineered details, such as deck drains that lead to the through-hulls with one-piece solid fiberglass tubing and bonding, thus eliminating possible leaks at mechanical joints. There is a clever locker-ventilation device in the form of a recess at the bases of cabinets—such as the kick-space under kitchen cabinetry—where the outwardly invisible horizontal surface this creates is of perforated aluminum. Coupled with a louver above the door of the cabinet, it creates perfect air circulation. And they have gathered as many drains as humanly possible onto each seacock, in the relentless belief that the best through-hull is no through-hull. At Nautor, excellent engineering still reigns.

The most graceful Swan of them all, the *45*, above, with its pure, clean lines, is just arriving at U.S. boat shows but has already taken the world by storm with twenty-seven boats on order while hull #5 is still in the mold. It is as luxurious a racer as you can get, with teak decks and teak interior. The stern is wide open to save weight in the end in order to cut down on hobbyhorsing, but this does necessitate a cattle-fence-height stern rail. The side decks are broad, the house beautiful, the new dove-gray stripes very tasteful, but toerails exist only from the shrouds forward. Note

the small headsail with a very short track, and big main. I salute the under-deck lines as shown close up in the small photo left. It leaves the side decks uncluttered, hence very safe. On the negative side, they can bang as they tighten when the headsail slats in little wind and leftover waves, and

I'm not sure about how jamproof they will be. If time proves them practical, then they are a great step forward. Below is the striking 54, much more of a cruiser/racer, showing off her power. The double cockpit and double com-panionway make it very safe in any sea condition. Above is the dramatic

70-footer, while below left is my favorite Swan, the 48. Like the 54, it has double access but only a single cockpit. The aft companionway is only a steep ladder but most welcome and safe in a storm. The stern opens down, and, together with a fold-down swim ladder, makes boarding easy.

Zen and the Art of Sailboat Interiors. When one combines the unmatchable sophistication of Italian design with the flawless joinery of Finnish craftsmanship, the result is what you see on these two pages. Since Mr. Ferragamo began to guide Nautor, the purity of the details in Swans has become remarkable. The two top photos on this page are of the new *Swan 45*. The galley seems hewn from a solid piece, with almost invisible joints, and contains nice touches, such as the anodized aluminum doors as splashboards behind the galley stove. Note the ventilation in the cabinets—a

grille above the doors, while the intakes are invisible in the 'kick-space' at floor level. In the saloon photo, there is the amazing detailing around the carbon-fiber mast. The rest of the photos, from the larger Swans, show a galley that highlights the vents I mentioned, with some beautifully minimal-

ist detailing and amply radiused corners, which are mandatory on any serious ocean-going boat where bodies in motion don't always end up quite where, or how, their owners had intended. The nav station is almost a nav lounge; and below is the sculpted saloon, with meticulously detailed flush

doors and roll-up shutters—just like on old roll-top desks. In all, the Swan interiors demonstrate design and workmanship that many boatbuilders would be wise to emulate for years to come.

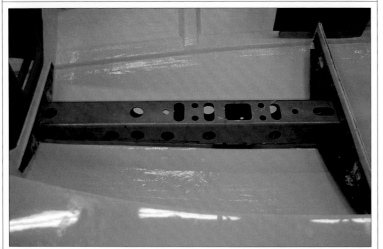

Nobody does it better. I have always considered Nautor in the forefront of hull construction. The single-skinned hulls (above) are reinforced with the most imaginative and robust grid of fore-and-aft and transverse beams. No unsupported panels remain larger than about 6 square feet. This results in a hull of relatively light skin but enormous rigidity and strength. The photo at left is of a Kevlar-reinforced hull. Below that, the steel floor supports the mast and stiffens the hull

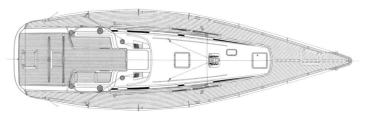

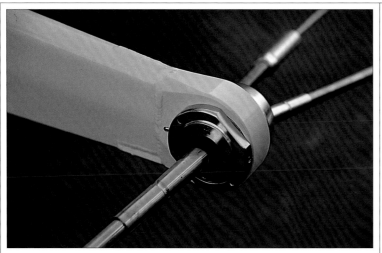

against the torque of the keel. Below that, in-house welders and metal fabricators turn out masts, spreaders, pulpits, and the miraculous goodies in the upper right-hand corner. The palatial cockpit is in a mega-Swan; below it, the cockpit of the new *45*, a masterpiece of Frers's design, as pure as a Japanese tea ceremony. Note the sheets vanishing in the deck about a foot forward of the winches. The mostly black photo is of the world's most beautiful stainless steel, composite, and teak gangway.

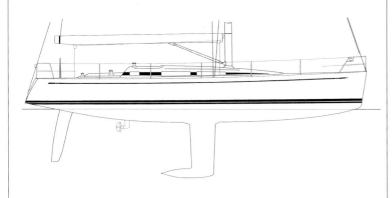

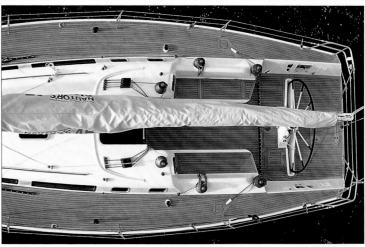

The remarkable thing about Swans, when you see them with the deck off, is that the quality of finishing inside all lockers, underdecks, even the most hidden corner, is not only excellent but extremely so. They seem never to lose sight of the fact that a perfect boat needs all perfect parts.

OYSTER
MARINE

At the risk of disappointing all purists, like myself, who have firmly felt that sailboats must have aft cockpits, I will go out on a limb and say that, as far as long-range oceangoing cruisers are concerned, when you look at an Oyster, you're looking at the future.

If you're utterly surprised to hear that from me, believe me, so am I; remember, I cruise in a wooden ketch that doesn't even have pulpits—in sharp contrast to Oysters that have everything.

I visited their docks in March at Fox's Marina in Ipswich, on the east coast of England. It had snowed the night before, but the sun was out and the harbor was full of Oysters undergoing their long, meticulous commissioning process. What they all had in common, from the smallest *42* to their largest *66* (they also have an 82-footer under construction and plans for a 100) was their acres of deck space, lounge-sized cockpits with perfect visibility forward, and extremely well-thought-out reverse transoms as comfortable and functional as a back porch. They also had Rob Humphreys—designer of *Kingfisher*, in which Ellen MacArthur won the 2000 single-handed transatlantic race—designing their fast and well-balanced, low-medium-displacement hulls. And they had an in-house group of designers who have come up with the most elegant house and deck detailing that leaves you shaking your head, wondering, 'Why can't other people do this?'

Then there is the clincher—the 'deck saloon.' Oyster is often credited with its creation. Whether or not it's so is completely irrelevant; what *is* relevant is that Oyster, in the last few years, not only has made this structure visually acceptable, but has indeed sculpted it into a sophisticated showpiece.

Now for belowdecks. If you're determined to keep your aft-cockpit boat, you must never go down below in an Oyster. You will come out like me—clinically depressed. These bloody boats have more useful interior volume than my house—and I live in an old Tuscan friary. And light? Wear sunglasses.

For those of us used to spending drizzly days below feeling like Lord Byron's *Prisoner of Chillon*, a rainy day on an Oyster would be a welcome reprieve. You could stay snug below and gaze through giant windows at the scenery. Or, as Robin Campbell, a true gentleman and a director at Oyster who was my most patient guide for two days through their plants and yard, quietly said, 'I mean, if you take a long, tiring, risky ocean voyage, once you arrive, it's kind of nice to tell from inside the boat whether you're in Fiji or in Finland.' *Touché!*

As I have always held, it takes a truly obsessed sailor-builder to come up with truly remarkable boats. Richard Matthews, who started Oyster in the mid-seventies and still owns and directs the company, certainly qualifies. What makes him unique is his broad experience in both long distance-cruising and serious racing. He always owns an Oyster and has cruised widely, including the Galápagos and the Arctic, and has always

raced. In fact, that's how Oyster started—building raceboats. He has been in fifteen Fastnets, was six times East Coast Offshore champion, and has won the Britannia Cup, SORC, and on and on. Even now, he has a 12 meter in which he does the Fastnet-type races. It's no wonder that he insists that his Oysters be designed and built to sail so well. He loves cruising but insists on fast cruising. In the ARC of last year, an *Oyster 62* was the first cruising boat over the line, beating a bunch of boats that should have been faster.

Robin is quick to add: 'But as much as we are interested in speed, we are very much, just as much, interested in comfort, quality, and safety. We do single-skin hulls and we have put Kevlar into boats on request, but we have concluded overall that our hull is enormously strong. As an example, one of our *45*s was watching a whale playing, when suddenly the boat stopped dead from 6 or 7 knots. They felt a hit on the rudder, yet there was no damage. I think there are very few boats that could withstand that.'

Their consistently solid and meticulous construction I witnessed at two of the plants that build the Oysters. Richard, by a brilliant stroke, assured himself of guaranteed high quality right off the bat when he started building. He didn't. He went to one of the oldest and best boatyards in England and asked them to build the boats for him.

An hour's drive from Ipswich, on a silent little bay, a neat, white, hand-painted sign marks the entrance to the great complex of tidy, but still romantic, great boatbuilding sheds. 'Landamores,' the sign says, '77th Anniversary.' Those of you who know the masterpieces of yachtbuilding the British produced through the middle of the last century will instantly realize what a coup Richard Matthews pulled off. Since then they have expanded greatly. Windboats (another yard in the same village) has been building for them for nearly twenty years; they own Southampton Yacht Services, where most of the larger Oysters are built; and they now also build *49*s and *53*s at McDell Marine in Auckland, New Zealand.

At Landamores and Windboats we scour the half-finished boats, and I marvel at the remarkable, classic-yacht-finish woodworking, some of whose pieces resemble Chinese jigsaw puzzles. But what is just as impressive is gazing at the fundamental strength of the overall construction—the massive floor grid, the enormous longitudinal stiffening beams, the solid-glass chainplate bases that are more than an inch thick, and the Brobdingnagian-sized keel bolts. I suddenly felt sorry for the poor whale that rammed the *45*.

'We are not weight-obsessed,' Robin remarks. 'We still do hand layup, which is time-consuming, taking up to a month to lay up and cure a hull and deck. We have a series of longitudinal and transverse stringers, which also are very time-consuming to place and lay up. It takes around nine months to produce a 50-foot Oyster, from beginning to laying up the hull until the yacht is ready for handover to the owner. This can result in fairly protracted lead times, but in the end, everybody is happy with the results.' Everybody except the whale.

That's because the hull and deck not only are bolted together like they are on the average top-class yacht, but after the bolting, Oysters are bonded together with wide laminates because, as Robin says, when you're in the middle of an ocean, you really begin to be an avid believer in building in redundancies.

The bulkheads sit on transverse foam-cored beams that act as spacers and angle softeners. They are massively bonded with

10-inch bonds onto the hull, and with even wider bonds to the deck. The bulkheads are double-bonded on both sides, and so is most of the cabinetry. The bonds are so enormously heavy that you could practically pull out the bulkheads and the bond laminates would be stiff enough to hold on their own. Those giant longitudinal beams are cored, 8 inches wide by 3 inches deep.

The chainplate base, a solid-glass knee, holds the chainplate with twelve bolts, some of them 7/8 inch in diameter, with an equally massive backup plate. To get a perfect fit on the covering plate of the chainplate, the chainplate is dry-fitted and bolted with a couple of bolts; the cover is slipped on and tack-welded. Then the whole thing is removed, welded, and polished before it is finally bedded in place. That's yachtbuilding.

There are fourteen keel bolts on the 56, all of them around an inch in diameter with two well over that. But the ultra-thoughtful thing about the keels is that around the bolts are 1/4-inch-deep recesses in the lead casting to give room for the bedding compound to form a sizable, very secure, and leakproof gasket. The outside rim of the casting has an identical recess all the way around, for the same reason. Similarly, all outside bolt holes get drilled, then countersunk to create a space for the caulking to set up and form an O-ring.

The tanks are integral with baffles and huge inspection hatches for potential cleanout, so you can really get an arm in to get out the sludge.

'We pay extreme attention to limber holes in the boat,' Robin says and when I look at him as if his deck was short a few cards—I mean, what can be such a big deal about a simple hole?—he elaborates with remarkable patience: 'Where a stringer forms a V-dam at the centerline with a potential puddle behind it, the easiest way to have the puddle drain is to drill a hole and call it quits. But this has two disadvantages—one, the hole will in time get plugged up creating a swamp; and two, you would be weakening the stringer you just spent all that effort making. So our solution is to fill the space behind the dam with a foam-and-resin mix and a bond over it, with a bias aft to allow perfect drainage over the dam.'

Then Robin adds, in such an understated manner that I had to laugh: 'I think you can see that we are most serious about quality. But what you can't see is that we are just as serious about quality control. We like to have redundancy in that, too. And personalization of quality checking. The guy who puts in the seacock signs it off, then the quality-control guy goes and checks it and puts a dab of paint on it to show he's checked it, then he signs it off. Then our project manager spends more than a day on each boat checking it, and he goes around with a mirror on a stick. Then the boat comes down to the marina and the commissioning process takes four weeks. Seriously. A team of two goes through it and does verification.

'We have a quality-control meeting on a monthly basis, with input from builders, project managers, sales team, and, very importantly, from owners. Many of our owners are on their third Oyster, and by now we are on a very relaxed, friendly basis, so they feel quite free to critique, and they often suggest very creative, honestly welcome ideas. It's by far the best market research or research-and-development one can find. And of course Richard, sailing the boats continuously, makes an ideal test pilot.

'And we pride ourselves on our customer care. We now have a chap who is almost constantly traveling the world. When a boat is about three months old, he will visit it and go through it

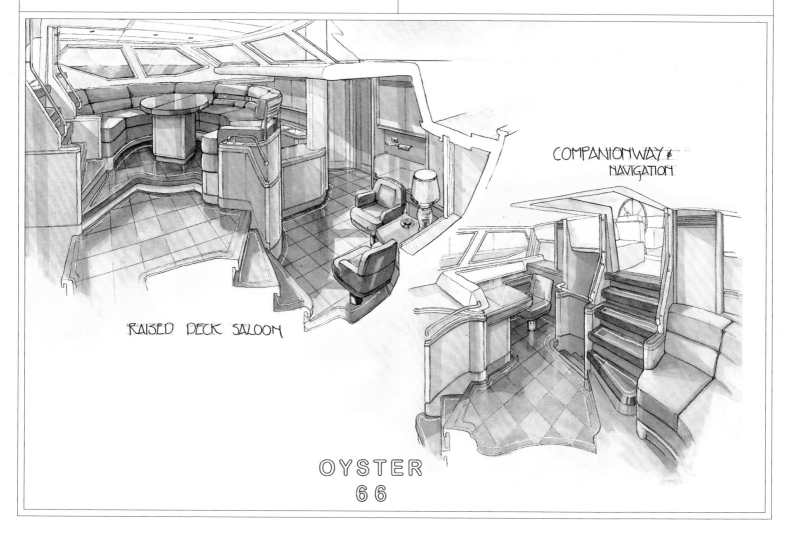

RAISED DECK SALOON

COMPANIONWAY & NAVIGATION

OYSTER
66

stem to stern. He has good Oyster experience, having circumnavigated in an *Oyster 55* and having done commissioning for a time. He goes through the boat with a very dispassionate eye, looking at not only existing problems, but any hint of a problem that might come up in the future.

'After those three months, the owner knows the boat and has also found out what he doesn't know, so it's a good time to review. This is a free service in the Northern Hemisphere, with a travel fee in the Southern. If he has any problems, we have an after-sales team of six people looking after him. Sometimes we get phone calls from people with twenty-year-old Oysters saying, *I need a spares kit for my whatever, could you courier it to Bora Bora?* And we do.

'We have a lot of our boats in the ARC. Two years ago, there

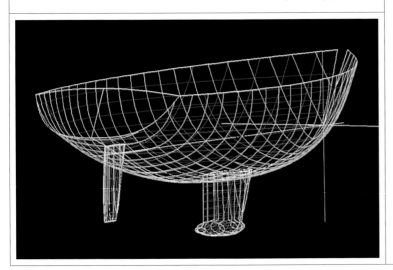

were twenty-two, last year thirteen. We send a service team of six guys down to the start—a rigger to check things out and an electronics guy to teach last-minute computer use, whatever. This keeps our owners happy, and it doesn't hurt our PR to have a huge fleet of boats noticing our guys, in bright-red Oyster shirts, scurrying around taking care of our owners, while the other owners are wringing their hands, biting their nails, trying to round up help.

'To try to prevent breakdowns, we tend to discourage a too-complex or overequipped boat. I think we spend more time unselling such things as mechanical systems, trying to convince owners to forget it because in truth they will hardly ever use it. Or when they finally do, the thing—after being idle for many months—won't work. On boats under 50 feet, we do our darnedest to discourage generators, unless you live in Hong Kong with 100 percent humidity. Generally, people listen to us because they know that all of our staff—design, maintenance, sales—are all broadly experienced, very serious sailors. Sometimes people do come up with strange ideas—they want to have their boat built backward or whatever—but then we sit down and explain to them that we have built nearly a thousand cruising boats, and we detail to them why the things that have worked, worked, and eventually they appreciate the engineering and the thought behind it all.

'Most people, justifiably, ask about our large windows. Well, we have never had a break or cave-in, and the quality and strength of windows today are infinitely superior to those of twenty years ago. On the 50-footers, for example, we have 1/2-inch tempered glass. On the plus side, apart from the view,

two front windows do open past 90 degrees, giving you about the world's best-ventilated sailboats. We are sticklers for ventilation; we have an airspace between the finishing panels in lockers to circulate air to avoid condensation. It also helps as sound and temperature insulation.

'And, as I said, we very much like systems with backups. The water pressure system has two pumps, depending how much water is required. Then, if one packs in, you have another left.

'We do use cable steering but our autopilots have a direct arm onto the rudderstock, so even if your whole cable system dematerializes, you still have the autopilot left, plus of course the emergency tiller.

'Speaking of steering, people sometimes ask why we don't make the raised saloon into a pilothouse, meaning create an inside steering station. The answer is that we think it's too dangerous. When you steer from inside, you can see well only when motoring. When sailing, all you can see is a bit ahead under the headsail and the sea on the leeward side. You could have a supertanker come from the other 200-plus degrees and you wouldn't know it until it cuts you in half.'

When Robin sees me trying different parts of the cockpit seating, trying to find an uncomfortable spot, he smiles: 'There isn't one,' he says, almost apologetically. 'The cockpit design was done by the Department of Ergonomics at Loughborough University. And they considered every square inch, not just for sitting but also for getting in and out, and not just at the dock, but on different angles of heel. So you can see that the coamings are slightly rounded everywhere—not just for looks, but also to give you a solid, flat footing on any heel. With an

extreme horizontal/vertical coaming, you would be forced to perch on an insecure edge at all times other than when the boat is sailing flat or you're knocked down.'

I'm ready to get off the boat, but Robin stops me: 'I almost forgot. Come.' He shepherds me down a private companionway into a most luxurious aft cabin—with settee, writing desk, the works. 'Try the bed,' he says, like some proud hotelier. I do. It's more comfortable than Il Splendido's in Portofino. 'Sprung wooden battens,' Robin smiles. 'With a crown to them, just like orthopedic beds, to provide more spring and the most comfortable condensation-free sleep you can find on any boat.'

I scramble up the companionway past him. 'I need a drink,' I mumble. What I really need is an Oyster, but I can only afford the drink.

The Oysters on these two pages are shaping the future of sailboat design. Each year as the demand increases for more long term cruisability, complex mechanical systems, and more creature comforts, so obviously does the need increase for more interior volume. The best solution appears to be the raised house—deck-saloon—with center cockpit arrangement. Oyster provides the most consistently elegant and ingeniously engineered of this genre. Their newest, the 49, above, exemplifies the enormous refinements Oyster has achieved. From the almost-flat raised

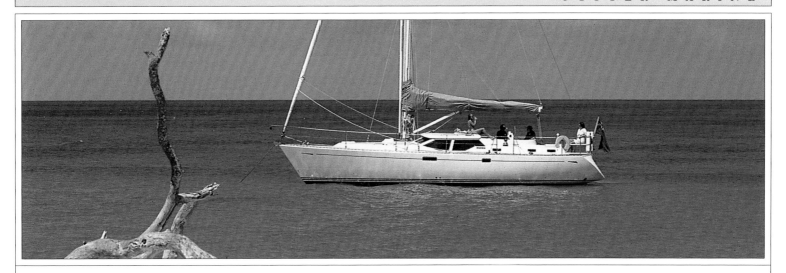

portion, to the beautifully feathered forward and aft house with teak deck inserts, to the university-ergonomics-department-designed cockpit, no detail has been overlooked. The 66, bottom left, has additional refinements such as the curved, recessed staysail track, which makes the staysail self-tending while guaranteeing perfect sail settings without resorting to the despicable staysail boom. Plus, you can have a furling staysail. Note too the in-mold nook for the life raft—under the blue cover just forward of the track. The large cockpit table, with a mechanically refrigerated compart-ment in its base, helps create a self-contained lounge from which to enjoy tropical paradises. The 56, below, shows the effortless power of the hulls designed by Rob Humphreys, who also designed the winner of the 2000 single-handed Transatlantic Race.

Welcome to modern floating palaces. With their raised deck-houses and center cockpits, these boats offer amazing interior volume, where ingenuity is combined with impeccable British craftsmanship. The very best of fore-and-aft galleys (above, and opposite page, below) is the norm. The level changes create a remarkable sense of space and allow use of every corner, yet the details are so invisible and visually clean that one never senses clutter. Note, at far bottom right, the unprecedented quantity and quality of natural light belowdecks. The saloon settees are masterpieces of comfort. But these boats are, above all, serious ocean sailers. In the

photos above, note the omnipresent grabrails—besides the companionways, a pair overhead, one along a table, and all beneath the side windows. And the searails, even on the smallest cabinets (small photo, right) have a hollowed interior for perfect grip. Note in the small photo, far left, the beautiful wood-and-Plexiglas cabinet, which yields ready visual and physical access to the watermaker's essential components that need frequent verification. These are the most commodious serious offshore cruising boats of all time. It's little wonder so many of them are circumnavigating; indeed, it might be hard for Oyster owners to want to set foot on land again.

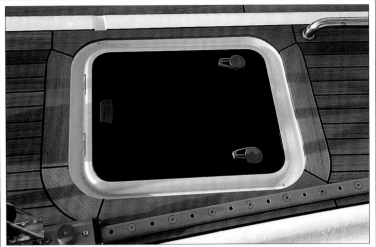

This is a feast for detail-lovers' eyes. Clockwise from top left—a beautiful, toe-saving hatch, inset flush with the teak deck. This takes exquisite engineering not just to finish out down below but also on the exterior for drainage; hence note, on top, a trough in the tooling but with the teak passing over it. Next photo is of the world's most beautiful deck hatch, which should be in every woodworking textbook. Next is a Dorade vent showing off the *absolutely* best designed and

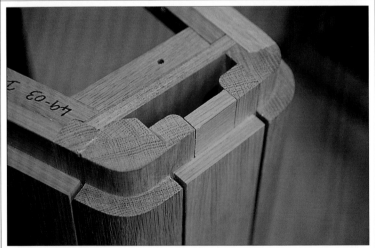

me a hernia carrying it outside for some natural light. In the bottom right-hand corner is a serious offshore detail—the floorboards are held in place by stainless steel screws set into brass housing. To its left is a grabrail worked into a table surface. Next a jewel of a computer base of solid oak and stainless steel to give you just the right angle for comfortable working. Next, an amazing searail corner that I could throw together, no problem—given a year or two and a couple of acres of oak forest

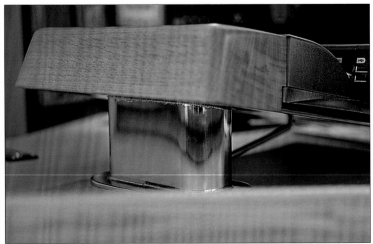

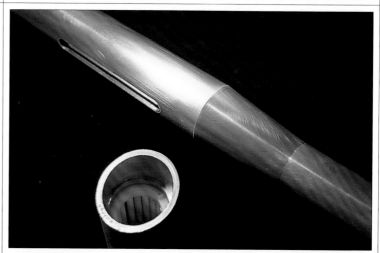

tooled in-mold Dorade box ever invented. I apologize for all the superlatives, but they are certainly merited. Not only is the Dorade box reduced in mass, but by being three-tiered, it becomes visually, nearly nonexistent. *Bravo*. Next to it is a very sturdily supported, beautifully finished, and comfortable seat worked into the stern pulpit's corner. Below it are two examples of serious metalwork: the first the meticulously turned shaft and bearing, the other a rudder gudgeon so massive it almost gave

to practice on. Above it are the intriguing 'guts' of the cabinetry. And last, the landing platform, teak-lined, of course, with a hinge-down ladder; liferaft in a most accessible bracket; and behind the little white door to the right, a shower hose with, of course, hot and cold running water. Thank you, Richard, for showing us the good life afloat.

He stops me in the cockpit and lifts the lid of the gleaming varnished table. The structural box below has a generously insulated liner, ice, and what looks like a year's supply of Guinness. The table has a stainless steel tube under it to brace your foot on any degree of heel, after any number of pints. No wonder hundreds of people are sailing these boats right around the world. Or at least until the Guinness runs out.

PACIFIC SEACRAFT

'Acanoe stern offers that vital factor of reserve buoyancy without presenting too much of a rump to the seas; it does, however, take a lot of care in the designing. If you would judge a stern, realize first that it will have more effect on the motion of your boat than will the bow. Second, when the going gets really rough, your stern will probably have to serve as your bow.'

I first met Naval Architect Bill Crealock, thirty years ago. He was quiet-spoken and thoughtful before giving an unfailingly articulate response. And he was prodigiously knowledgeable about what aspects make a serious offshore sailboat not only seaworthy and manageable but also provide her owner with 'cruising pleasure and peace of mind.' His depth of knowledge, his years of offshore sailing experience, his integrity, and his gleaming, honest eyes were so confidence-inducing that if Bill had told me, then and there, that it would be quite safe to go to sea in a paper cup, I would have happily hoisted my napkin on my swizzle stick and sailed straight west.

The years have proven me, if nothing else, a fine judge of men. The very elegantly drawn, moderately beamed, and perfectly behaved cruisers Bill has designed for Pacific Seacraft of California in the past twenty years convey the same unshakable confidence. They must have conveyed it to a lot of serious sailors over the years, because of these boats, between 31 and 44 feet, an even ten have sailed clear around the world. How many dozens are gunkholing beyond God-knows-where, no one has bothered to keep track. And even now, looking at their latest combined creation, the beautiful Crealock 44, makes you want to say, 'All aboard that's coming aboard, and so long to the rest.'

Pacific Seacraft has been building boats since 1975. The original partners, Mike Howarth and Henry Morschaldt, built their well-earned fame on the Bruce Bingham-designed, 20-foot-long Flicka, which in the seventies and eighties captured many a sailor's imagination and, suiting their pocketbooks, became the pocket-sized world cruiser—stable, all-waterline, tough as a rock. They have sailed all over the world and given enormous service to those who were quite content to go to sea while still poor and young.

Mike and Henry and the Flicka have moved on, and Bill's boats have grown longer every year, as more and more of us feel the need to wait until we're older and can afford more size, more space, more gadgets, and more comfort.

Now, two brothers, Don and Gene Kohlmann, are looking after the line of some of the most consistently reliable and solidly performing boats blue-water cruising has ever seen. Don, as affable and honest as befitting Bill's designs, has done stints as America's Cup crew with Dennis Conner at the helm; has cruised broadly; and brings to the boats a thorough knowledge of what dues a boat will be asked to pay at sea.

He talks with a calm gentleness that was common in Newport Beach when we built our boat there in the early seventies—when it seemed the whole world was building sailboats, and the whole world was full of dreams, wild plans, and cheap Mexican beer.

Don's gentleness hardens when he talks about his boats' underwater lines: 'You just can't create a hugely wide, flat-bottomed boat that has good ultimate stability. Apart from our skeg and bustle, it's our very moderate beam that helps to give our boats a lot of directional stability. With a moderate beam, as a boat rolls or heels, it doesn't become as asymmetric as a big wide boat, particularly one that has the lines tortured through the aft section for the sake of the interior volume. With those, you actually get a kind of tricycle effect. If you have a beamy boat that has a disproportionately buoyant after section, sure, you get a very showy stateroom in there, but as you heel, that increasing beam and full sections make the boat unmanageably asymmetrical. Plus you begin to lift the rudder and it begins to ventilate, and the boat gets hard-mouthed; it wants to round up. The ultimate steering boats are the 12 meters; they can have very small rudders and still be easy to steer because the hull is so extremely fine, not pumped out—no matter how much you heel, the hull shape that's in the water remains much the same at all times. With our more even distribution and very moderate beam, the boat just doesn't get as cranky as fuller hard sections would. Fortunately, there are a lot of very experienced sailors out there who are well aware of the advantages of moderate hull shapes and canoe sterns.

'What people still find troublesome, is understanding the hidden quality built into these boats that you just can't see at boat shows. People still look at the boat and then they look at the price and say, *Very nice, but gee, there is the same length such-and-such with much more room and lots of nice-looking engineering, so how come yours cost so much more?* Well, I'll give them an example—one of the truly life-and-death pieces on a boat, the rudder. A few months ago, I was going through a boatyard, which I love to do—you learn so much by asking boat-repair guys what failed on whose boat and why. So I was looking at this boat hanging in the slings and I noticed the rudder was a bit damaged on the bottom. Then I went to look at the other side and the skin was completely gone. Inside was nothing but low-density, maybe 4-pound, foam. It had a laminated polyester resin rudderstock—which is okay, I guess, if you do it carefully—but all that was really holding the skins and supporting the rudder blade was just a pressure bond, with wet mat apparently, of the skins to this rudderstock. There was no web inside, and the bottom of the rudderstock ended about a third of the way down. And the skins were at most two layers of mat and cloth. Now I could build a boat even cheaper than those guys if *that* was the way I built ours.

'In contrast, our rudders have an internal structure—a 1/2-inch-thick steel plate—a web you could call it, because it has a series of holes to lighten it. This is welded to a 2 3/8-inch stainless steel rudder shaft. Even our smallest boat, the 24-foot Dana, has a 1 5/8-inch stainless shaft. This alone is strong enough that it could act as a freestanding spade rudder, but, as extra insurance, a heavy manganese bronze gudgeon, bolted to the skeg, supports the bottom of the rudder.

'And our skeg is not just decoration. It, too, has internal reinforcement—a molded-in steel channel. It is skinned separately. Then two sections of the skeg mold, which have flanges on them, are bolted onto the hull mold. So we first skin it with Vinylester, chopped mat, and one or two laminates; then we bolt the skeg mold to the hull mold and continue laying up the skeg and the hull as a single unit. Other than the nominal laminate, it all becomes monolithic. Then, just to be sure, we fill the whole skeg with silica-reinforced resin. Then there is that 1/2-inch-thick steel spine, about 4 inches wide, cast into the skeg right down to the bottom. Remember that the skeg exists, apart from the stability factor, to protect the rudder. Well, it's not going to do much protecting unless you give it some *cojones.*

'We are going with all external ballast except for the Dana. Our keels being fairly shallow—our Scheel keel on the *44* is only 5 feet 3 inches—I think it's hard to dispute that there is a substantial gain in righting moment by going external. Our lead itself is only about 20 inches high. Well, if you gain 2 inches, that's a hefty percentage. We like to have an ample root chord—top of keel length to width—for it gives us plenty of room for the bolt pattern, lots of contact for good sealing.

'Most of our boats go out with a Scheel keel. With them, we gain almost a foot of draft. And that is a lot in most of the Bahamas or the Chesapeake. The theory behind the flattened Scheel bulb is that the bulb offers not only a concentration of ballast down low on the appendage, giving you more stiffness, but, since it is cupped, it also separates the flow between the windward and leeward sides, so you get some differential pressure there, and you develop lift. I don't dispute that going upwind, you do give up a couple of degrees, but the righting moment is the same as on our normal keel. We use epoxy with a filler to set and seal the keel. If you pulled the nuts off the keel bolts, you'd still have a hell of a time taking off the keel.

'We lay up our hulls in one piece. There is no doubt in my mind that you get more uniform hull strength this way. We switched to biaxial stitched material in 1993. On the old 24-ounce rovings, you have the fiber-crimp, plus the heavy texture that requires thicker mat between layers, and of course mats have the lowest fiber-to-resin ratios. We knocked out about 500 pounds of resin on the *37* by using stitched biaxial instead of woven roving.

'The two new big boats, the *40* and the *44*, we core with balsa to the ABS (American Bureau of Shipping) rules. The first, down to the boot stripe, the second to within 2 feet of the centerline for stiffness and reduction of weight. Bill calculated that we save around 600 pounds. So you can put in a generator at no extra weight cost. Plus we add thermal and sound insulation.'

The hand layup has always been first class with Pacific Seacraft, and so it has remained. And so is all the bonding of the furniture to the hull—all pieces are flawlessly bonded in, including under the cabin sole. The liner in the smaller boats is cored; in fact, it is a stiff member that reinforces the small area it covers. It takes about a man-week to bond in the liner piece, and you can see why if you stand on your head and look at its underside—it is bonded in even underneath, everywhere. Even the inside of the smallest cabinet piece is bonded top and bottom, including the dividers in the back of the settee, which exist only to keep all your clothes from inbreeding.

'The hull-to-deck joints are through-bolted as before,' Don goes on, 'although some of our toerails are changing because of customer requests. People just don't want to look after much teak anymore. So we buy an anodized extrusion that we dry-fit, drilling the bolt holes and doing the cutouts for chainplates and chocks. Then we remove the rail and send it out to be reanodized, to be sure, to ensure that no raw aluminum is left exposed. Not economical, but infinitely more long-lasting.'

They have made other very important changes, such as increasing the size of the bow platforms to make for a safer work area when launching anchors and installing a fore-and-aft bulkhead in the chain locker to truly separate rope and chain. And they have installed true stern anchor lockers on all their boats, even the 27-foot Dana. These come accompanied by an anchor roller and anchor deck pipe. This is a real must on a true long-distance cruiser, not just for storms, but also for the ever-tighter and more-crowded anchorages. How much more calming it is to launch a stern-anchor the Bill Crealock way instead of searching in some giant locker under long-forgotten objects, then wearing away your caprail for lack of a roller.

One most civilized and safe idea is the isolated locker aft, with an overboard drain, for holding the loathed jerry can of gas for the outboard. This, too, is a must on any cruising boat unless you're crazy like us and insist on rowing a wooden dinghy. I find few things less reassuring than gas cans lashed here and there on deck, where a spill can turn it into an ice rink.

The water tanks have transparent inspection ports—*bravo*! The double opening hatches are Bowmar *cast* aluminum instead of the too-often-seen extruded aluminum. The *40* and *44* have dodger bases in the deck molds, and just as well, for few and far between are the cruisers that go dodgerless. The bilge pump is workable while staying at the helm, an excellent idea just in case there is but one able body left in an emergency. I very much like the fuel-tank vents in the cockpit so you can monitor them while you're filling, and, equally important, there is no chance of saltwater forcing its way into the tanks in heavy seas, as can happen with vents stuck on the hull just below the sheer.

Speaking of water forcing its way in, all builders should look at the turtle hatch, or sea hood—or whatever you want to call the fixed house over the companionway hatch that keeps the ocean from coming for dinner. It is massively built, with internal baffles and scuppers molded right in. This is a costly, demanding bit of tooling, but worth every penny. As I always say, it's the small, intelligent details that make a great cruising boat—like the nifty storage place above the quarterberth for hatchboards, and they are of course lockable in place. To help keep your sanity as you're rocking and rolling downwind, their doors have anti-rattle, lockable hasps. And one of those tiny, hidden luxuries that few people discover until they own the boat is the unseen little teak pencil-holder inside the chart table. This kind of thoughtfulness is much too rare in boatbuilding. Which brings me to the cockpit sole. In their boats, where the engine is located under the cockpit, the cockpit sole is removable so the whole great outdoors becomes your engine room. I had a similar design once, and it was one of the best parts of the boat. A British yachting magazine called the removed sole 'unwieldy.' Well, good God, man, the thing wasn't meant to be a Frisbee. It has to support people jumping onto it. In any case, there is sufficient engine access from below; the sole comes out only for comfort, or emergencies.

The rig has remained cutter, and for offshore work there is no parallel, except perhaps for the small-Yankee, big-staysail arrangement on the singlehanded round-the-world racers. Since Don comes from a racing background, and also is an incurable hardware-freak, the blocks and travelers on the boats are the most efficient, easiest to work, quickest to respond. He has, however, shied away from stemball fittings. 'Our research shows that they can fatigue over the years. The big advantage of the old marine eye system is that every piece is visible, inspectable. When you're building boats that will be sailing around the world, that is a priority. Plus, with this system, you have compression tubes and fasteners going all the way through the spar; with the stemballs, you don't. To me, it's just a stronger system.'

One strong new system is their steering. It's rack and pinion, just like sports cars. No spliced cables, no jamming sheaves. It's all solid rod and gears. Nearly failproof.

There also has been a huge leap ahead in the interior woodwork. It's infinitely more elegant with inset arched doors instead of the old overlapping ones, with many more louvers, more bookshelves, and beautiful detailing throughout.

Overall, the excellent quality at Pacific Seacraft is just getting better and better. These are perfectly thought-out and thoughtfully built blue-water cruisers. We can only pray that Bill Crealock will stay around another seventy years.

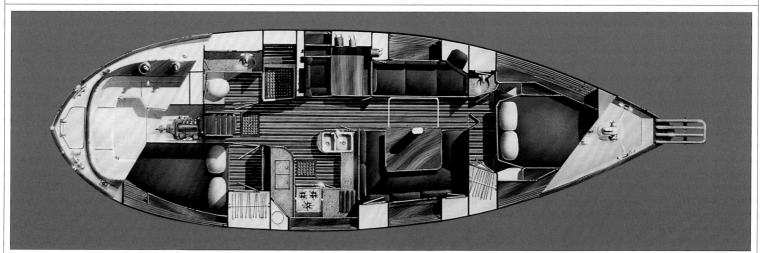

The Pacific Seacraft-built, *Crealock 37*, designed by the naval architect, W. I. B. Crealock, has just been voted into the Sailing Hall of Fame. What took them so long? All the Crealock creations—the *44* on this page, the *40* on the right, with the *37* in the small center insert—are aesthetically sophisticated, ideally proportioned, and, based on his eight years of blue-water cruising experience—some of the best-handling, most seakindly boats in the world. They all have moderate beams—hence are easily driven and steered—and perfectly balanced hulls, which make them very manageable on all angles of heel. All—including the *31* and the *34*, not shown—have lively sheers, just the right overhang and curve to the bow, a very well-proportioned deckhouse, very safe cockpits, and certainly the prettiest sterns anywhere. And those sterns

are not just for looks, but also to rise to and part big following seas, particularly in that worst-case scenario when, with sea anchor or rodes dragging, you're literally running for your life. Note the intelligently wide and teaked (for nonskid) cockpit coamings, the molded-in dodger base, and the completely waterproof turtle hatch. The 4-inch-high bulwarks provide excellent footing even on the worst heel. The amount of teak is just right for a world-cruising gentleman's or gentle-woman's yacht.

It's never an easy task on blue-water sailboats to strike a balance between a homey and a practical interior. They get much more than their share of hard knocks, drenched foul-weather gear, slippery wet boots, and lurching bodies. These photos show that Pacific Seacraft has worked out a delicate balance. On the practical side are the myriad grabrails—both the traditional wood and the stainless steel posts—the nonslip steps, and the easy-to-clean, non-water-staining laminated white surfaces. For beauty and comfort, they have teak-and-holly cabin soles, teak upper cabinetry, and the very comfortable rolled and pleated upholstery—not the great flat slabs of saggy foam found on many boats. The G-shaped galley of the *40*—at left, and bottom left of opposite page—is by far the best solution for a boat of her size and layout. Lateral support can be had on any heel without the

use of cumbersome and restricting safety belts. The cabinetry in all the boats maximizes nooks and crannies—note upper cabinets in most photos and the underdeck cabinet with sliding doors on top of the stainless pole, opposite page, bottom right. The interior of the *37*, bottom right, is scrupulously conceived, with penetration aft of the bulkhead to afford more counter space and drawers, and a good-sized quarterberth to port. The photo to the right is of the dinette of the *Crealock 40*. The table with the square hole is not some strange invention; it is simply awaiting the arrival of the mast.

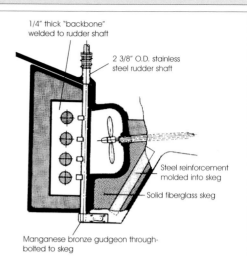

1/4" thick "backbone" welded to rudder shaft

2 3/8" O.D. stainless steel rudder shaft

Steel reinforcement molded into skeg

Solid fiberglass skeg

Manganese bronze gudgeon through-bolted to skeg

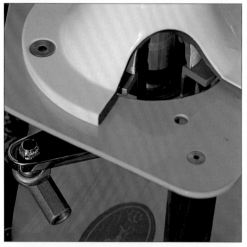

The engineering staff at Pacific Seacraft makes things robust. Top left corner, two cutaways of the Whitlock rack-and-pinion steering system with no pulleys to bind or cables to stretch; everything is solid rod and gear. The bronze ball joint allows for mounting on any angle.

Continuing with steering, the rudder structure—diagram above—shows the reinforcing steel plate (the holes are to reduce weight) that is made even more rigid by the two horizontal end pieces welded to the 'backbone'—photo, left. The skeg, too, is reinforced with steel and is solid glass—no foam

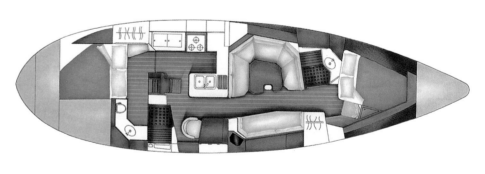

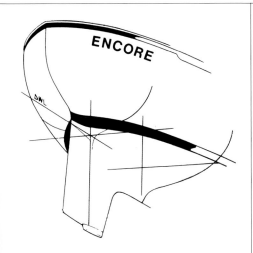

core. The photo below it shows reinforced brace-rails. Apart from giving safety and security while handling sails and halyards, they are ideal for shackling or tying off. Next to it is the Scheel keel, and to its right, the nearly bomb-proof hull-to-deck joint. The all-stainless bow pulpit (right) increases the foretri-angle and makes anchor handling and storage easier. The light you see behind the engine (above), is from the sun; the cockpit sole is removable—simply the best way to work on an engine. The rubber nonskid on the steps, above left, is routed in, not just glued on. Very fine work indeed.

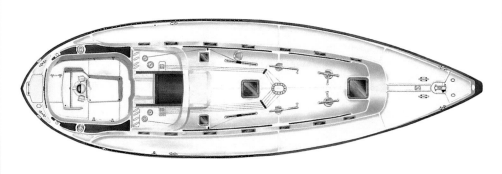

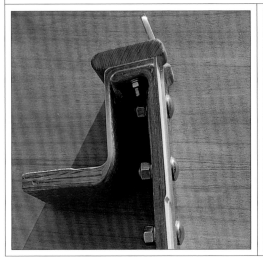

Why are these great cruising boats? How's this—the bulwarks are an excellent aid for freshwater catchment in a tropical downpour. Once it has rained enough to clean your decks, you can close the shut-off valve on the deck drain, installed for just this moment, plug the scupper, open your deck fill to your water tank, and simply fill 'er up. *Bon Voyage*.

PDQ
YACHTS

'Our catamarans, with their stable platforms, small sails, and effortless handling, simply keep people sailing longer. One of our owners was eighty-two years old when he bought one of our boats—just stepped off his *Sparkman & Stephens 53* and sailed from New York to Maine.'

The first long cruise I ever took was on a multihull. It was on the west coast of Canada in a sea of islands, with fair winds, small waves, and the monohulls heeled here and there with their crews braced and wedged. I just stood at the helm with both sheets in my hands—like driving a team of horses—and the boat resisted so little that I didn't even have to cleat them. We flew. And on the deck, my friend and his wife lay in the sun as relaxed as if they were lying on a beach.

And below, the boat had space everywhere. It was only 36 feet long, but there were three good cabins and, with the hulls so far removed, good room and a sense of airiness abounded. The cockpit was a lounge, the deck like a tennis court. You could drop sails anywhere, fish from anywhere, sprawl to your heart's content. And a breath of air was enough to make her scurry right along. The best part was in the evenings. While the monohulls all anchored together in deep water, we with our 3-foot draft found bays and nooks where no one dared to follow. Solitude. Paradise.

I'm sure few things are as alien to most monohull sailors as the idea of a gawky multihull; but just try sailing one and see if you can resist. Their irrepressible popularity struck me not only at every recent boat show, but also when more and more of the images that our team of photographers took for our *Seven Seas Calendar* had multihulls in them. When I asked myself why, the answer was obvious—they are able to go to the more interesting places that deep-keeled monohulls have to avoid like the plague. And apart from their shoal draft, apart from the comfort and volume, there is the thing most sailors love—speed. Now don't for a second think of all catamarans as lightning-fast Hobie Cats shooting roostertails and passing powerboats. But the PDQ 42-foot Antares only a week after launch, and manned by a man and wife with minimal sailing experience of any kind, effortlessly hit 15 knots in 25 knots of wind. I don't know about your boat, but the only way I could hit 15 knots with our 41-foot pretty-fast monohull would be to push it over a cliff.

To windward, the smaller PDQ, the 36-foot Capella, will go neck-and-neck with a similar-sized cruiser/racer, but she will jump with a bit of sheet easing, and in VMG—velocity made good—will outperform the monohull by about one-third. So, if the monohull can do 6 K, she'll do 8; and you can expect to motor faster by nearly the same ratio. This performance is due to their long, fine hulls of a 12-to-1 ratio. Imagine having a 48-foot monohull with a 4-foot beam. So these boats can be driven by relatively small, easily manageable sails, which you will be handling on a very stable boat.

Simon Slater and Harvey Griggs started PDQ Yachts in Whitby, Ontario, fifteen years ago. Harvey has a PhD in structural engineering from MIT, which is exactly the kind of partner you want when you want to build a structurally perfect multihull. Simon has an affable intensity and a traditional Canadian overhonesty, which frustrates marketers but endears him to the likes of me, wanting facts and truth.

'I built my first catamaran when I was fourteen,' he said, so matter of factly that I felt guilty for not having done the same. 'I even made the sails. I had been on catamarans since I was seven; that's how this all started. My dad had home-built cruising catamarans that the family spent the summers on. We were three kids, so the comfort counted. He was a mechanical engineer, one of those guys who could design and build.

'When my brother was twenty-two, he took a 30-footer my dad had built, and went down to the Caribbean, alone. It was just so easy to handle. It had furling everything. It had a double A-frame rig—very unusual, especially for its time—gear, sails, and all for seven thousand dollars. So I was always exposed to a lot of innovation, with great attention to keeping costs reasonable.

'Anyway, by the time I was twelve, I was racing catamarans full time. We'd have more than a dozen boats out there for weekend racing, all designed and built by eccentric geniuses who were convinced they could design and build better than anybody.

'I did give monohulls a chance. While I worked at Doyle Sails, I raced on monohulls but found that pretty dull—sitting on the rail until your legs bled, the helmsman so obsessed he stood at the helm without letting go of the wheel for twenty-four hours; never ate, peed down his leg. I said to myself, does fun have to be this horrible? I went straight back to catamarans.

'Our company started when a friend, Harvey, wanted to have a monohull built, but my dad convinced him to give up on those

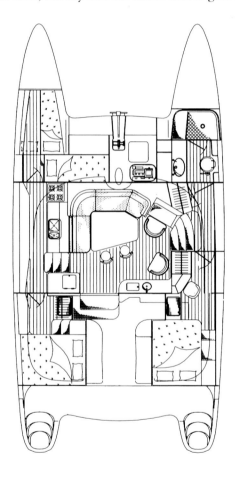

slow *dugout canoes* and have some fun. So we built a 36-footer, which we thought a couple of other people might like as well. We are now closing in on hull number 100. And they all had fun. We suggest cruising speeds of 9 to 12 knots for that boat.

'When we started, there were no real cruising catamarans that had a good turn of speed. The ones that were being built in Europe were all for charter—giant things with four cabins, four heads, that sort of thing. Our boats are for a couple. The owners expect to have guests, but most of them, most of the time, will be sailing alone. It is interesting that of the first six *42*s, only two had an extra head.

'As for who buys catamarans? Mostly people who want to sail pretty fast but in absolute comfort, and with moderate effort on

a very stable platform. Some of our owners are people who had been very active in sports all their lives and have developed some knee or back problems. For them, the stability of a flat platform is not just very appealing but absolutely mandatory.

'Of course, some people just love all the room inside. Honestly, you would have to be looking at a monohull 30 or 40 percent longer to get this kind of accommodation. And you know the weights and sizes of sails and winches that a boat that size would require. Never mind the expense. Most love the big, safe decks, and the large cockpits with the hard top where people spend most of their time. And many just can't go back to the closed-in interior of a monohull once they have seen the raised saloon on the *42*, where you can sit and, through the windows

all around you, have the best view in the harbor or at sea. We don't have an inside steering station, but you can easily set your autopilot and come and sit in the saloon and keep watch. Then some people simply want to sail in the Bahamas, and with our 3-foot draft, they have the place to themselves. And it is nice to be able to stand in the water and clean the bottom of your boat or check your propeller. Or walk to shore.'

I ask Simon about people's concerns about catamarans. He lists them almost with relish. There are few things Canadians love more than criticizing themselves.

'The greatest anxiety is *Where can I moor it?* Fortunately, it always turns out to be easier than one thinks. While most places don't have room for fifty cats, almost all have room for a few.

'Next, people worry about handling the boat in harbors and tight places. But the first time they go out with the twin screws—there is a separate sail-drive diesel in each hull—and turn the boat in circles on its own axis, they all come back smiling.

'Then there is flipping. We have all seen the aerial images of round-the-world racers being rescued from their overturned cats. Well, when you consider some of those guys do 35 knots without blinking, come hell or 20-foot water, then it's not surprising. However, Lloyds of London, who keep very tight statistics for obvious reasons, assures us that the proportion of cruising cats flipped is no higher than that of cruising monohulls flipped. The big difference is that our boats—with no ballast, and four watertight compartments—would be very comfortable, full-of-supplies, gigantic life rafts when upside down. There is even a hatch between the hulls where you can get in and out. In contrast, most monohulls upside down are rarely heard from again.

'No one has flipped one of our boats, so we can't tell from experience, but we've calculated that you need to do something very strange to do it—you have to be reaching in a gale with all your sails up and sheeted completely wrong, totally amidships as if you were on the tightest beat. I have never known a sailor whose instincts would allow him to do that.

'One minor adjustment is with anchoring. While you set your anchor like any monohull, to keep the boat from sailing or angling to the wind once the anchor is set, it's best to bridle off both bows. And people think that with the light displacement they can use teeny anchors. But because of the windage, we have to calculate the cross-sectional area, not the displacement, when we design the anchor weight. So, on a *42*, which is 16,000 pounds, you end up with a 45-pound anchor.

'Now, I must say that there is one big adjustment for monohull sailors—the motion. It's lighter. It tends to be stiffer but with more hobbyhorsing when going to weather in a stiff chop. If you come from heavy-displacement boats that tend to plow through the waves, the quick motion will be a surprise. But then you'll be getting there much faster.

'Going to windward, you don't get that sense or feeling of being in the groove, and you can't hear the water rushing by, simply because you're well inboard to steer. So if you are used to a monohull, you have to change your sensory cues and rely more on visuals or instruments. Once the wind picks up and you can feel the hull begin to lift, then it's different. When beating, the leeward hull is carrying the load, and it goes down 3 or 4 inches. The thing that is beautiful about our long, skinny hulls is that the faster they go, the more stable they get. Downwind, when you start surfing at 20 knots, the stability is almost shocking. To build the boat for those speeds, we have to design the systems to take great loads, virtually what you would have if you were ocean racing.

'There is the assumed reputation for being lightning-fast. But the reality is that, without surfing, the 20-knot speeds that people talk about is a stunt. We might do it when we first launch the boat with nothing on it, and we go out with the boys to try to see what we can break, but you are not going to do that day in and day out while cruising—not if you want your family to go out with you again. But you can do 10 knots very, very comfortably on the *36* with no effort, with your eyes closed.

'The one thing we do caution people about is this dichotomy—that you have all this volume, hence an enormous temptation to turn the boat into a mini-storage; and as soon as you do, you lose performance. So don't even contemplate dirt bikes or snowmobiles on board.

'This might seem funny, but since our boats have such shoal drafts—the 36 draws only 3 feet—people worry about grounding because they love to go into places where they can wade ashore. Well, we build our hulls with that in mind. The keels—even though they are very fine NACA foil shapes—are structurally distinct from the hull. In other words, if you do happen to run aground so hard that you hole a keel, you are not holing the hull. It is isolated and watertight. And they are built very strongly; you can easily have the boat rest on them for a few days.

'To achieve rigidity in the empty keel—we don't want to fill them with foam because they would take too long to fix and would take forever to dry before they can be relaminated—we build small composite bulkheads. The keel is laid up in one piece in the hull mold, then we lay in the bulkheads, then we seal it all off with the hull laminates—in effect, creating the second bottom.

'We don't just guess at our structural requirements. Harvey, with his MIT degree, is very good at working out panel stiffness, panel strength, any kind of loads. We pay attention to the most minute construction detail, so we have managed to avoid the hull flexing that some multihull sailors have found on more lightly built boats. And we tend to design way on the safe side. With the high speeds and rudder loads, we use the Whitlock rack-and-pinion steering—the direct-drive rod with no cables—with a transmission box that gives a nine-to-one reduction so you can have a small wheel. The nice added gain is that the autopilot motor is built right into the transmission, so it is mechanically less prone to failure. It's as simple as you can get.

'We did have an advantage over older builders in that we started fairly recently, so we had no prejudice in building methods or materials. We just started building with the newest technology and best methods available. We went with stitched instead of woven rovings right away, because the unbent fibers give you instant strength. We vacuum-bagged right away, because it is the most secure way of attaching a core to the laminates. We laminate the structure by hand after the gelcoat, using mat, then biaxials, triaxials—all stitched. Then we place the Core-Cell, a high-density PVC foam, and then the inner skin. We very much tailor the laminates to the needs of each area so we can save weight. And, also to save weight, we make all our bulkheads composite—that is, we use a foam core with fiberglass laminates on either side. For the same reason, we make most of our furniture out of a honeycomb board, which is just as strong as plywood but about a tenth of the weight.

'Since we use no liners for interiors, we have great flexibility for customized layouts. We don't have to limit the boat to either galley up with the saloon or down in the hull. With the galley up, you get great views while you're cooking; with the galley down, the whole raised area becomes a huge entertainment space.'

There is another small thing—totally personal—that I have to mention in favor of catamarans—the large, rigid top. With the sun becoming more fierce with the depleted ozone, a top on any sailboat has become a must. Frankly, I have never seen a Hinckley without the dodger up. So, since the homely canvas ones are always up anyway, why not make them permanent and part of the original design? PDQ's hard tops are first class. So, designers of monohulls, take some lessons here—hard tops are the next sure thing in sailing evolution.

And so might be Simon's and Harvey's catamarans.

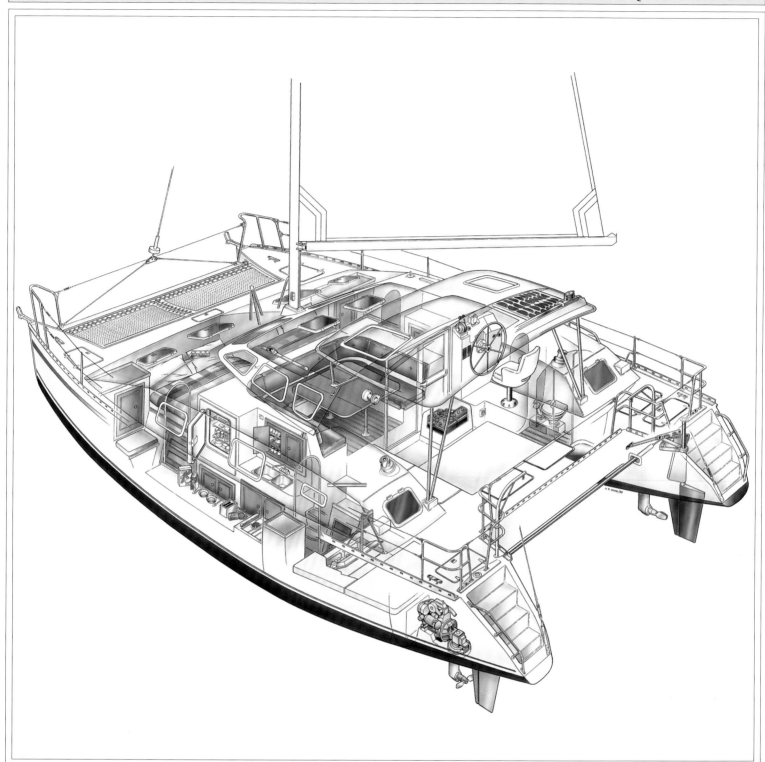

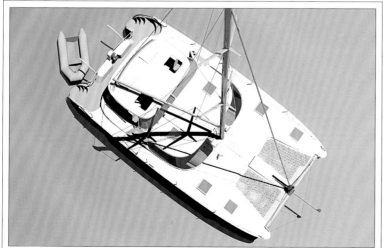

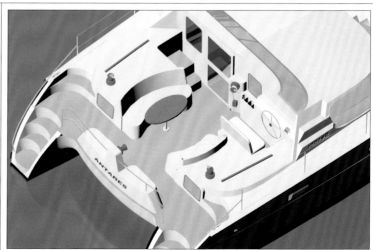

The popularity of multihulls has grown exponentially in the past decade. Not only are they dominating around-the-world racing and conquering chartering, but they are now appealing to family cruising with their easy-to-handle, go-into-any-shoal-water, stable-platform sail-

ing. The leading builder in the last category, for me, is PDQ Yachts, with their well-engineered, robustly built, fast catamarans. The illustration top right shows the just-launched 42-foot *Antares*, which, on her maiden cruise, comfortably clocked 15 knots. Her vast cockpit is protected by a rigid top. Her

enormous foredeck is densely webbed to allow for passage of wind and water as well as create a comfortable walking and lounging surface. Together, they add up to enough surface area to constitute a small European country. Her raised saloon is a seascape-gazer's dream. The photos are of the 36-foot *Capella* (I applaud the designed-in solar panels), which, with her 2-foot 10-inch draft, could sail in a bathtub. She sails at 9 to 10 knots. Both boats are 'beachable' (top of opposite page), with heavily reinforced keels. These shallow keels are 'sacrificial,' being isolated compartments so that if damaged, no water will penetrate the hulls proper, and the boat can keep sailing nicely on. Both boats have twin engines, allowing them to spin in their own length for easy harbor handling. I can't wait to cruise on one in the Bahamas.

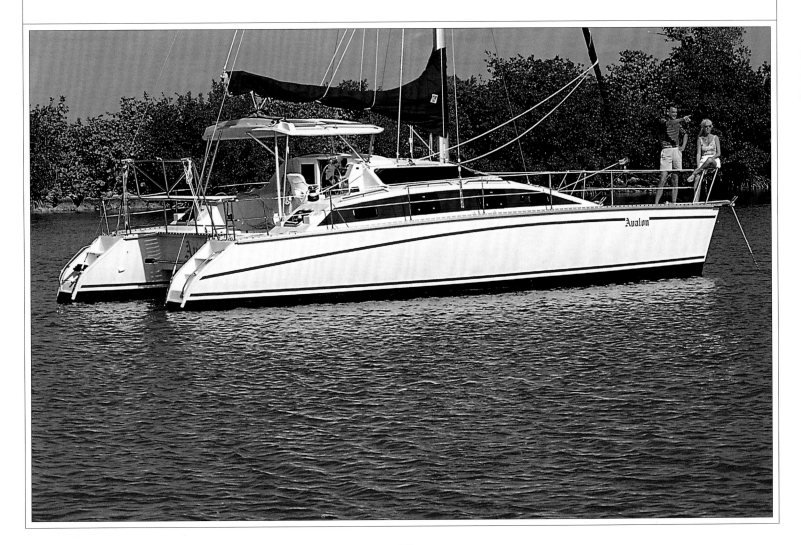

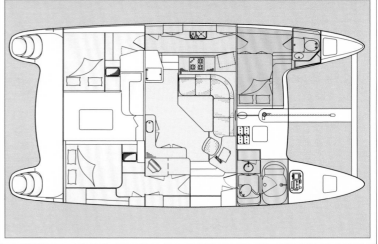

You have to rethink everything you know about sailboat interiors when you consider catamarans. The central feature is the enormous raised saloon, from which you can see the whole world while sitting at the table. The beam of the boats allows for a second saloon in the cockpit, which, with the rigid top, is the most used part of the boat in warm climates. On these pages are photos and drawings of the 42-foot *Antares*. On the opposite page, note the perfect fore-and-aft galley—long and narrow, located three steps down from the saloon. The home-length counters allow any number to work together without crowding. In each hull is an engine located below the sole in the center of the boat. Thus the ends remain light to avoid hobbyhorsing. Lifting the sole turns the whole area into an airy engine room. Note the tricabin, two-head layout in the accom-

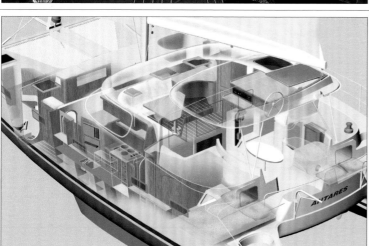

modations plan; you'd have to have a 15-foot-longer monohull to achieve room of this kind. Both of the aft cabins have large, home-sized double beds, and both cabins come with intriguing emergency in-hull hatches next to the beds—dark Plexiglas with the bar handle. These are not only reassuring in that most-unlikely event of a flipped boat—with four watertight compartments, you'd have an enormous, most comfortable liferaft—but are also extremely useful for creating first-class ventilation by drawing in the cool, shaded air from between the hulls. The photos show the very fine joinerwork; what you cannot see is that all the cabinetry is built of honeycomb board to keep the boats very light and sailing fast.

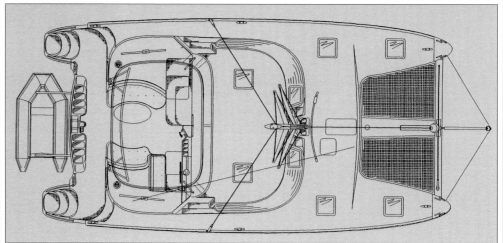

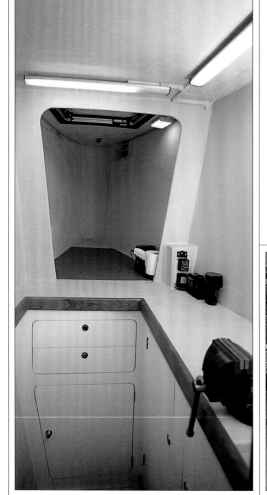

The interior photos of the 36, left, show a simple galley (top) and a small workshop in one of the bows (bottom). The far-right photos show the 'bathroom' of the 42 with a closable shower stall made in a single mold. This is leakproof and easy to keep clean. Above right is the core being vacuum-bagged into a half-hull; the miles of rope allow the air a way out. Below right is the complexly and very-well-tooled deck of the 42. Beside it is one of the 42's nicely rounded sterns, with very comfortable boarding steps and a hefty grabrail. Note, below the hull, the dark foil rud-

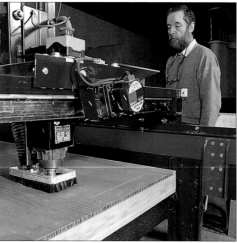

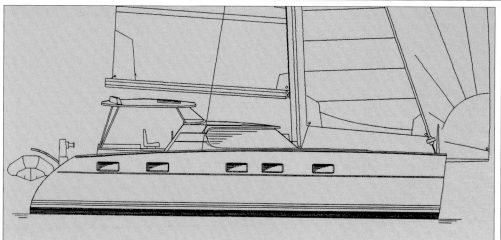

der. The steering is rack-and-pinion—all solid rods and gears. The engine access in the *42* is almost unlimited, both forward and aft. The blue machine, in the photo beside it, is a computerized router, which cuts all bulkheads and cabinetry with great precision, saving on costly trimming, detailing, and waste. In the deck drawing of the *42*, note the low-profile dinghy chocks, the swept-back spreaders and single shrouds, and the small forward-curving track in front of the mast for the self-tacking jib. Pretty Darned Qood.

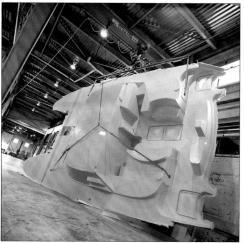

Before leaving, I just had to ask Simon what the PDQ stood for. He laughed: 'Performance, Dependability, and Quality. Or, Pretty Damned Quick, depending on whose version you believe.'

SABRE YACHTS

Back in 1969, Roger Hewson, an aspiring Olympic sailor from Montreal, came down to the Maine woods and laid the foundations for Sabre Yachts—literally. With his own hands, he hammered the forms and poured the cement for the big shed. His first boat was the *Sabre 28*, of which they built an amazing 588. Since then, their line of boats has become a reference for sensible but elegant, modern yet enduring sailing yachts.

The Sabres are one of the most welcome additions to this volume—not just because I'm a firm believer in consistency in quality as one of the best guarantees of good boatbuilding, but also because the design of the Sabres maintains a classical good sense that unflinchingly incorporates everything truly worthwhile that modern yacht design and technology have to offer. From the broader, more powerful stern quarters, and the reverse transom with its accompanying landing platform, boarding steps, and swim ladder, to the single shrouded triple-spreader rig that adds stability through less weight aloft, they have managed to keep creating the best of the new but always dressed as elegantly as a yacht of old. My good friend Warren Tiley is on his third Sabre, and he'd rather surrender a vital organ than change builders.

The sensibly distributed range of four boats, from 36 to 45 feet, should comfortably fulfill the desires of most sailors from singlehanders to couples to a large family. And here I might as well air a personal conviction that should shock many and perhaps please a few—a sailboat much beyond 45 feet is mostly a waste of money, materials, and time. This stems from the fact that to sail well, a boat must remain relatively narrow of beam—so you cannot have 20-foot beams on 50-foot boats to accommodate double cabins amidships. This midship area, where one spends most of one's down-below time, is truly useful only to a maximum of 14 feet. At that beam, a U-shaped dinette to one side with a settee on the other—with a pilot berth, some storage or bookshelves behind both—makes maximum use of the guts of the boat. Once you go beyond that beam, the settee no longer interacts with the dinette, and one thus witnesses the most absurd inventions, from a third row of seats to ballroom-dancing-sized open spaces. The ends also tend to go well beyond the utilitarian into the too-large and too-open-to-be-safe spaces.

Now back to the sensible Sabres.

One of the great luxuries of a boatbuilder is an in-house naval architect. Sabre has one in Ken Rusinek, who heads their design team that finishes off what hull designer Jim Taylor starts. He, along with Chris Evans, the chief operating officer with a degree in forestry, were ideal guides through the plant.

'We tend to be dependably consistent,' Ken began. 'All our hulls are very similar. Very well mannered, U-shaped, with a small, vestigial skeg, which more than anything helps the flow into the top of the rudder. We stick with it because it helps a lot when you're going upwind, since it acts as a longitudinal fence to stop the cross-flow on the back of the hull. The cross-sectional area is so small relative to the lateral plane of the boat that you're not getting a lot of directional help. I mean, it does have some nominal effect, but that's not why we put it there.

'But we do offer a decent range of keels—the most classic is the centerboard, then comes a short-wing keel, and then a deep fin for those who never expect to be in skinny water. While I was brought up a firm believer in centerboards, I must admit that, on the other hand, I've never heard a wing keel clang, or a pennant break, or a bushing needing replacement, and it never suffers the fate of a bent or jammed board. As for those who can't decide between a deep fin and a shallow wing, we have made the bolt patterns of the wing keel and the fin keel identical, so they are interchangeable if you do change your mind, or go from cruising to racing or vice versa. I should add, though, that it is a big, costly undertaking that needs to be done by a knowledgeable yard.

'I mention the keels to point out our flexibility. We have always positioned ourselves as a builder who would make appropriate modifications for the client's use. We do have standard boats—say, a *Sabre 40*; it's just that we have never built one. Everyone has his own ideas of what works best, and we really want each owner to feel that his Sabre is special to him. This is very different from the more value-oriented builders, who will modify very little to nothing. With us, you can even choose your own stern—traditional or reverse transom.

'It's a fine line, because we don't build custom boats, but rather very personalized and individual production boats. We have a list of standard options, which are known about and promoted. Then we have custom options, which are those unique ones that the client really wants, to create the boat of his dreams. Those we always listen to; then sometimes we tear our hair, but I would say that engineering approves and we quote on probably 90 to 95 percent of the requests that we get, and of these quotes, we build about 90 percent.

'The one thing we do not alter is our hull laminates; we don't add Kevlar or carbon fiber, even on request. We did build the boat that won the Around Alone Race; which was an epoxy SCRIMP carbon-fiber vessel, so we are capable and experienced enough to apply the newest technology; it's just that we've had great success with the structures as they are.

'I do think a lot of people react too reflexively to something they read, forgetting that there is a vast divergence between real gain and perceived gain. For example—too often we see Corian countertops, washers and dryers, double air-conditioning systems and megagenerators coupled with a tapered mast. Now it's true that it's a long lever arm, and perhaps it makes sense on

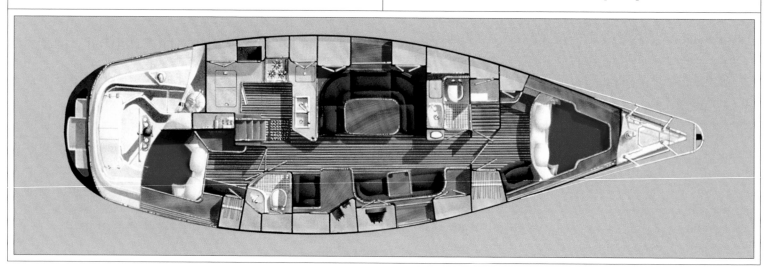

paper to try to save 15 pounds for a bit more stability, but by the time you cut and weld, fill and fair, you're not far from where you started. And with these miserable few pounds, do you think you begin to balance the thousands you have added below? Sure, a carbon-fiber mast with 50 percent weight-saving is different, but you get my point. It has a lot to do with the media. Every time a magazine article comes out expounding the merits of this idea or that widget, we usually steel ourselves for the next onslaught of requests. I wrote for *Soundings* as technical editor, and I swear I had more influence on yacht design as a magazine writer for two years than I had in being a naval architect for thirty.

'At any rate, as I said, we are consistent with our hull laminates. We have gelcoat, mats, biaxial knitted, then the core, then more biaxial knitted on the inside. We also add a whole plethora of local reinforcements—in keel floors, on the centerline, around shafts. All biaxial glass. We were one of the very first to use biaxial knitted back in the early eighties, because the people who first made it were right here in Maine. And it just so happened that Roger Hewson is a family member of the maker. We had an in.

'We core our hulls. The two smaller boats are cored in the bottoms but not the topsides. This is different from most builders, but in fact it is the bottom where the loads are higher. Your slamming loads are higher, the keel torque is higher, the rudder torque as well. So it makes much more sense to put the core in the bottom in a smaller boat, where, with lower freeboard, the spans in the topside panels aren't great enough to warrant stiffening. On the *45* instead, with its larger unsupported panels, we vacuum-bag core into both bottom and topsides. And all our bulkheads, and all plywood elements that are bonded to the hull, get a foam fillet between the two to avoid print-through and to stop shock loading. If the hull gets loaded, we don't want to point-load that spot. We build strong but we are weight-conscious, especially in the ends to avoid hobbyhorsing. So we have carbon-fiber rudderposts.'

Coming to the mold room, Chris adds: 'One thing we are intransigent about is the consistent quality of our hulls. It seems utter folly to spend even a dime on some fancy finishing detail unless you have built the very best hull you possibly can. So, in our lab, we check every batch of resin and gelcoat as it comes in; we do viscosity tests, gel-time tests, peak exotherm—to be sure the new batch of resin and gelcoat is consistent with the previous batch, so we can use the same catalyzation rates, etc. If a batch is out of spec, you can have, say, a viscosity problem, and the resin runs down the mold as it sets instead of staying and curing in place. It might look fine as you roll it out, but then you walk away and the resin drains and you could have a resin-starved area in the laminate. Suppliers do the same tests before they ship us the resins, but they can make mistakes. And who knows, if we didn't do the tests, they might just drift. So we keep them alert.

'We're always concerned that our suppliers take the same care in producing our parts that we do. For instance, with our aluminum tanks, we want to be sure they use the right welding equipment and the right alloy of welding rod to match appropriately with the aluminum we specified for the tank; otherwise, there can be a galvanic reaction between what, in fact, are dissimilar metals. The classic justification was known decades ago, in the days of wooden boats—a foundry would cast all of the underwater bronze fittings out of the same batch of alloy to avoid dissimilar metals. Perhaps we overengineer, and overworry, but we like to sleep well.

'Take our fuel tanks. On the *45*, we designed them very narrow athwartships; very tall, modestly long. So when heeling or lurching, you'll still be able to pick up fuel when you have only a little of it left. The wider fuel tanks are fine for coastal stuff, but if you're going offshore, you really need a tall, narrow fuel tank. People ask me if that is important, and I say if you're going down Casco Bay, then not at all, but if your plans range far away, that's a different story. Offshore, in some distant place, the ability to use that last 10 or 15 percent of fuel may just make the difference between good news and bad news in your next letter home. You do learn a few tricks after building 1,800 boats.' Then he laughs: 'We're a company where, when we learn something we immediately apply it to the next boat. Or I could be more candid and say that, when we find we've made a mistake, we try our damnedest not to do it again.'

Whether it's hindsight or pre-engineering, they sure have some very fine ideas. Most of the cockpit locker lids have gas struts to hold them open while you're digging below. These eliminate the instant-guillotine effect. Near the companionway there is the by now fairly common dustpan in the cabin sole, but what is unusual is that by lifting out the dustpan, you get access to all of your seacocks—head intake, engine-cooling water, saltwater pump. And to tell you which is which, they are permanently labeled.

For boats that are left unattended any length of time, an independent hour-meter is wired into the automatic bilge pump so that if the pump runs, it records on the hour-meter. When you come back and see that the pump has run an unusual length of time, you know there's a problem.

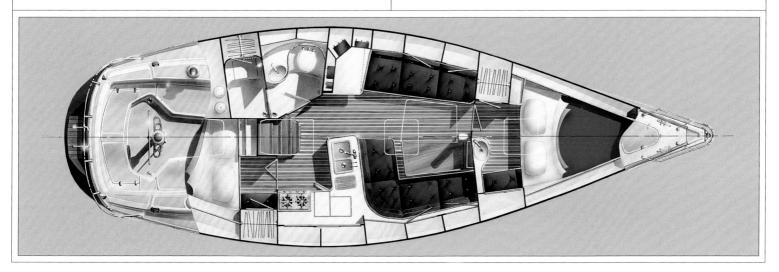

My hat goes off to Sabre Yachts. Over the decades, they have maintained an almost-uncanny consistency in their elegant designs, so that while their newest models look unmistakably modern and 'new,' the ones they're replacing, inexplicably, never look 'old.' One reason is that they have always been one of the leaders in good sense, coupled with a sophisticated northeastern sensibility, resulting in ageless boats that maintain both appeal and value. Their four boats—the 362, 402, 426 and 452—are all of moderate beam, powerful stern, fine

entry, and very good looks, with just the right amount of teak—toerail, eyebrow, handrails—to set them apart. The *362*, below left, and on page 174, has perfect proportions. The *402* on page 175 is even sleeker, and the *452*, in the other four photos on these two pages, has a truly leggy look, with the house extended slightly onto the foredeck. The transom of the *452*, in the small photo at left, is as beautifully rounded, hollowed, and practical as I have found. Note the ideal T-shaped cockpit above—sculpted to accommodate the large wheel but narrowed forward to provide secure foot bracing on a heel. Below, note the remarkable tooling that hides the turtle hatch and creates a flush setting for the largest of ten—yes, you read it right—opening hatch/skylights. With the additional ten opening portlights, plus the main hatch, belowdecks can be made into a veritable wind tunnel.

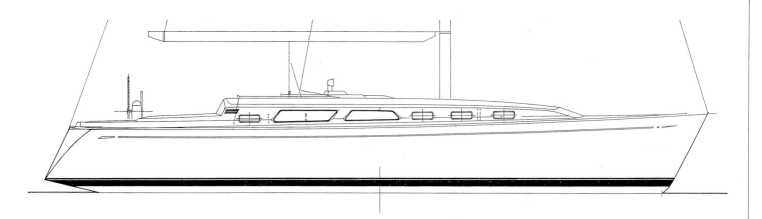

The engines come with two alternators as standard—a high-capacity one for charging the ship's service batteries and another for the engine-starting battery. There are also two separate, complete circuits so that even by mistake, you cannot drain your engine-starting battery, even if your house batteries are run all the way down. And for ultimate security, the batteries are in a fiberglass case with heavy tie-downs to keep you from playing dodgeball with 100-pound items when the going gets giddy.

The stainless steel mast step, about 3 feet long, spans three heavy glass lateral beams of the keel-floor structure. These are twice as wide and twice as heavy as the standard floors forward and aft of it. The engine bedlog is massive—4 inches wide, of laminated wood entombed in glass. Here the glass is heavy enough to take the structural loads, with inserted metal plates to take the engine loads. The wood is for sound deadening because the change in density helps eliminate the transmission of noise down through the stringers.

The top bearing in the rudder is a constantly adjusting ball, to accommodate the tension through changing rigging loads. The emergency tiller has a separate opening. Its handle is T-shaped so it can remain effective while manageably short. And to allow for ease of steerage, it is made so lines can be run from it to the winches.

I cannot say too much about the attention to ventilation. With Sabre, it's an obsession. On the *45*, there are eleven ventilation hatches plus opening ports in every cabin. If that isn't enough to keep the air moving, I don't know what is.

The propane locker is intelligently located in what would otherwise have been a little-utilized space in the side deck.

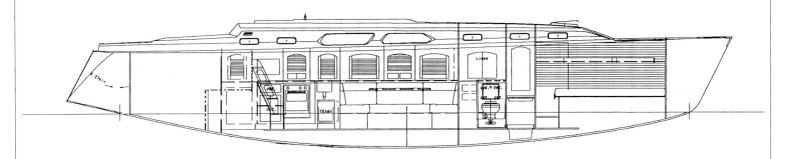

Since this happens to be right over the galley stove, you are spared many feet of propane tubing—and the less of it, the better. Then there is the world's largest sail locker, with a step in it for easy and safe access and a pocket for the hatchboards. And, very thoughtfully, a place to hang loops of line. The instruments are integrated into the sea hood, and there is a most useful little locker in the cockpit for small items that otherwise end up irretrievably at the bottom of huge bins.

One very elegant finishing touch is that the hatches—even that for the anchor well—are all squash-molded. This is a press molding where you have molds on both sides of whatever you're laminating, so that both sides end up with a finished surface—a long step from the hard-to-maintain painted rough surface you get with the single-mold layup.

If you are gazing at the interior layouts and wandering how they have managed to get a decent aft cabin even into the *36*, look hard at the exterior photos and you might get a clue. The companionway is set slightly forward of the aft face of the deckhouse. Or perhaps you could say that the house runs past the companionway. While this shortens the cockpit a bit, it does yield good headroom below, and, as an extra bonus, creates the coziest seat on any boat—right on the bridge deck, protected on both sides, under the dodger. Let it blow, let it blow.

Chris, the forester, adds: 'We are as environmentally responsible as we can be. We use a hand-picked cherry interior because we prefer wood that comes from a managed forest where the trees are planted, cut, then replanted. Teak, on the other hand, comes from the rain forest and is seldom planted again.'

Start out by flipping back to page 165; now that's about as cozy and romantic as a sailboat can be. That's part of the saloon of the *452* (the layout plan is on page 166). The saloon is seen in its entirety on page 170. Note the exceedingly comfortable corners of the settees, topped off by great lengths of molded searails. Under the portlights—you have to look closely—you can make out the looped grabrails that run the full length of the saloon. These offer the most secure of grips in a seaway. On page 171 is the galley of the *452*; note the nicely detailed and hardwared, front-loading refrigerator door and the full-length stainless steel safety rod at counter height. Here, too, there are grabrails under the portlights. On these pages: above left corner is looking aft in the *452*, while below is the beautifully appointed aft cabin with rigid laminate overhead, a plethora of most useful solid-fronted drawers and cabinets, solid wood stripped ceiling, and, most important, a good-

sized opening aluminum hatch. The cabinetry, in the right of that photo, has large, removable panels—with flush-fitting handles—to give near-total access to the engine. The other four photos are of the *402*. I compliment them on installing an elegantly cabineted washbasin in the forward cabin, above. Below is their striking, solid-wood center table, with massive wood knees. Oh, yes; I applaud their beautifully arched louvered doors.

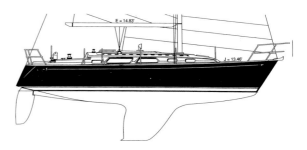

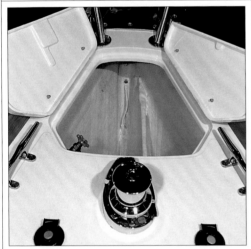

A great boat comes from meticulous attention to tiny details. In the upper-left photo, a fine chisel is used to find and fill minuscule pittings in the rudder. Below that is the quadruple support for the stanchion bases, while below that is the compartmentalized foredeck well, making anchor hauling and rode stowage an easy and enjoyable one-man job. Above, center, is the rotating, one-piece hull mold. It allows laying up to be done on a near-horizontal surface most of the time, thus avoiding resin drain-out. The next photo shows the lab where Sabre analyzes every

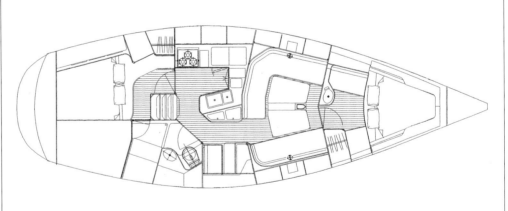

batch of gelcoat and resin to guarantee consistency. This page: above are the ingeniously made companionway steps—slightly raised, ash nonskid strips set into routed grooves in the teak treads. Next is the 'shippiest' and most solid solution for a fold-down table; below that is the laminated shower stall. Below left is the *362* under sail. The photo below and the line drawings are of the *402*. In the profile below, note the deep bilge sump keyed into the keel, and the two keel options. In her layout, aft to starboard—rub your eyes—a real sail locker! When was the last time you saw that on a boat?

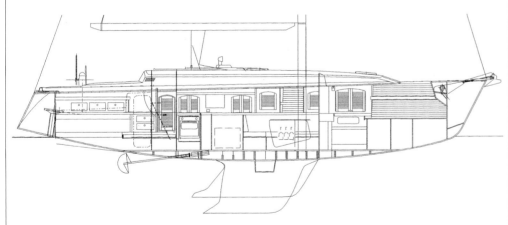

'And we try hard to create a good working environment. All our hand tools, even the scissors, are of a form to keep your wrists straight, in line, so you don't run the risk of having carpal tunnel problems. And what goes around comes around. When you do your best for people, they do their best for you. I honestly think it's the only way you can build a first-class yacht.'

SAM L. MORSE COMPANY

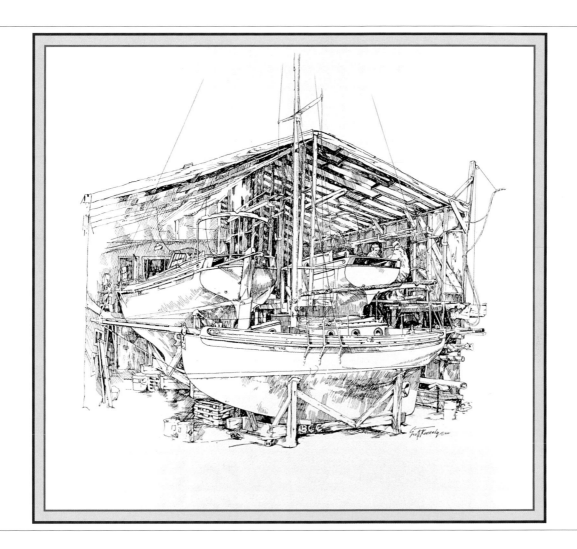

V oyaging belongs to seamen and wanderers of the world who cannot or will not fit in. To be truly challenging, a voyage, like a life, must rest on a firm foundation of financial unrest. Only then will you know what the sea is all about. But in the worship of security we fling our lives beneath the wheel of routine. The years thunder by. The dreams of youth grow dim where they lie, on the shelves of patience. *Sterling Hayden*

It's strange how sometimes an insight comes to you out of the blue, often about something you've known well before. And when it does, no one is more surprised than you.

I had spent a couple of days at the Annapolis Boat Show, screening boats for this volume, poking into whatever was accessible on the gorgeous Hinckleys, the perfect Aldens, the indestructible, powerful Swans, and the palace-like Oysters. And I was awed by their ever-growing size, the brilliance of their technology, the complexity of their systems. I had a great debate going on within me as to which was The Perfect Yacht—the ones above or the bulletlike Baltics or the daringly innovative Turner or the J/Boats that fly as much as they sail.

It was late the final day, with the rain drizzling down, when I walked along a part of the docks I hadn't bothered with before. There were some daysailers there, and wooden skiffs; then there was the Pardeys' little Bristol Channel Cutter-type boat that Lyle Hess had designed. It was one of the smaller oceangoing cruisers at the show. Its house was square, its decks wide, its bowsprit pesky, its gear modest, its lines and honest simplicity redolent of the sea. And without thinking, without analyzing, in the midst of the billions of dollars' worth of yachting glitter, for the first time in two days I felt something stir inside me. I gulped hard, and the words leapt like a breaking wave until I mumbled them aloud: 'Now there's a real boat.'

There is something about these boats—the Bristol Channel Cutter and the smaller, even more feisty Falmouth Cutter—that seems to attract some of the most likable people around. First there was Sam Morse, with his honest eyes and kind manners, who started the company almost thirty years ago. When he was ready to retire, along came George Hylkema, and soon thereafter, Roger Olson who, after sailing 50,000 miles in his Bristol Channel Cutter, became a partner and eventually took over the company until the land began to burn under his feet again and, in his new Bristol Channel Cutter, he returned to the sea. And now there's Sumio Oya, who is exactly like you always wanted your favorite uncle to be—warm, thoughtful, disarmingly honest, with a quick, uncontrollable laughter that, no matter how old you are, makes you laugh like a kid again.

He was born in Japan, and the cadence of his words, and the care with which he utters them, makes you listen with as much attentiveness as you listen to a good friend. By the time you've spent a day with him, you feel as if you've known him for years.

'Ten years ago,' he begins with a deep breath, and you look forward to the story, 'I was the general manager of a high-tech manufacturing company. We made broadcast test equipment, high definition, that sort of thing. The four big networks were our major customers. I did that for sixteen years. When the stress was kind of maximizing, a friend invited me to go sailing one day. Before I was a sailor, I used to get seasick on a ferry that crossed a river. But I went; I dreaded going, but I went anyway. We set sail. After less than a mile, he stopped the engines. There was just the sound of the wind and the waves. Instead of being seasick, I felt—for the first time in I-don't-know-how-many years—relaxed. All my stress gone. At peace.

'That night, I went to a bookstore and bought your *World's Best Sailboats*. I'd minored in art and love good design. I read through the book, loved the photographs, and within a month I was sitting in this office in front of Roger. I was fascinated with the shape of his boats. He spent the morning with me telling me about them—each part, how it's built, why it is built

the way it is. Since that day I have been hooked on the boat. I wanted so much to be a part of the Bristol Channel Cutter that finally, three years ago, I bought into the company. Roger stayed on for two years to teach me all about boatbuilding.

When I planned to buy the company, everyone said not to. The boat may be very tough, but maybe not the company. But I couldn't resist. I didn't want Roger to retire and have the boats disappear. And when I saw the quality and saw the shipwright working, so proud of his work—and he had every right to be—I thought, if the company was managed well, it could survive.

'We have only three workers. The foreman who was here for twenty-five years retired, but the shipwright, who was his partner here all those years, is now the foreman. I'm sure we could make more money by building bigger boats—say a 45-footer. It would certainly be more profitable, but my goal is not maximum profit. I had been there with the high-tech company, doubled and quadrupled in sales every year, but I could not find any satisfaction. Chasing money, you never get enough; you only get killed. And chasing money is such a limited goal for a human being. People need something more. I sure did. Money you can always find, but time, your life—once it's lost, it's lost.

'Here I do what I love every minute. I'm happy here. I love to see the faces of people who are thrilled to get their boats.

'What is wonderful about these boats, is that there is something timeless about them. When I was in high tech, we used to change designs every week, prices changed every fifteen days. Here it's: *We have built it this way for twenty-five years. Why change when you have something so good?* So we change only minor things, to perfect things.

'I just can't say enough about Lyle Hess; he designed such a perfectly thought-out boat. But then in came Roger, with all his sailing experience in it, and made some very good changes. He had taught engineering and design before he sailed off to the South Seas and Singapore and on to New Guinea. He improved the sail plan to give her more drive to weather.

'We made some minor interior improvements as well. A recent owner wanted a dinette, so we reconfigured that to port. With that, we increased the size of the pull-out double berth. Small, ongoing improvements to a timeless boat. And we changed from Volvo to Yanmar and improved the engine access. We improved the tanks, the head system. Then we switched the water tanks to under the floor. Little things, they can mean a lot.

'We are building a boat now for a very knowledgeable owner—he had owned a Hinckley and a Swan—who wants to visit the Arctic Circle. This boat will incorporate Kevlar to reinforce an already substantial hull for travel in icy regions. The strength is about ten times that required by the Coast Guard.'

There were three boats under construction the day I visited the yard, and seeing one just out of the mold, my first impression was, 'My God, but it's a beautifully shaped hull.' And far past the beauty, the boat is perfectly thought-out. The cockpit well is small, so you can brace on a heel, with good, high coamings to support your back. The decks are very wide and safe with the high bulwarks; the ventilation below is perfect—with the huge forward hatch open, and the skylight open and the main hatch open, the damned thing is practically a top-down convertible.

As they have been from the start, the hulls are laminated by Chrystaliner, the fiberglass experts in the area. They have been at it for almost forty years, laying up, among others, Westsails

and Alajuelas. Their work is impeccable. It is all hand-laid by a multigenerational cadre of craftsmen.

The engineering is as meticulous as the layup itself. The aperture for the propeller is beautifully faired. The tooling in general is very fine. The bottom of the skeg is filled in solid with resin and fibers. The hull flange on which the deck sits consists of all the hull laminates turned back; hence, it is integral and massive. The hull-to-deck attachment bolts are staggered every 4 inches—one inboard, one outboard—ensuring a perfect seal and a more reliable torque distribution all the way around. The deck is dry-fit, drilled, lifted, cleaned, then set in 5200 polysulfide—guaranteed by the manufacturer until a minute past doomsday—then bolted.

The coring for the deck is marine plywood, and that is about

hull and deck. Where the bond is to be laid, the bulkhead is drilled every foot with a 2-inch-diameter hole. As the bonds are laid in both forward and aft, they are pressed onto each other through the holes, so the bond forward of the bulkhead actually bonds to the bond aft of the bulkhead. In other words, the bulkhead is 'locked in' at every foot. In contrast to this, most builders lay bonds forward and aft with the bulkhead in between. The Sam Morse system protects against any conceivable delamination between layers of the plywood itself, or the delamination of the bond from the plywood. Admittedly, both are rare events in sailing, but then why not be prepared—just in case? It's time-consuming but indestructible.

As for the cabinetry, the boats are still stick-built—no liners—and every cabinet, every piece of wood is bonded into the

as compression-proof as you can get. And its insertion is no slapdash affair. The plywood sheets are grooved on both sides—first to facilitate bending, and second to ensure perfect adhesion to the resin and fiber bonding agent.

The ballast is internal, made up of four nicely cast lead ingots. The mast is keel-stepped, and a very thoughtful aspect of it is the Delrin plate that separates the ballast bond from the aluminum mast base, keeping it out of the way of any water that may be trickling aft from the chain locker.

The bulkheads are set back from the hull onto tapered foam fillets to avoid hard spots against the hull, and to create smooth, gentle curves for the bonding. Here I have to remind you of a Sam Morse specialty—the bonding of the main bulkhead to the

hull, one at a time, to perfection. And the bonding is enormous. Even inside the cabinets, it is so immaculate and so perfectly parallel that they must use either a ruler or voodoo. The cabin-top, underdecks, and the hull above the waterline are insulated with rigid foam.

I know there is much debate about which steering system is the most reliable for an offshore boat—rack and pinion, hydraulic, or cable. The Bristol Channel Cutter settles that once and for all—the tiller. It doesn't bend, doesn't fray, doesn't leak, doesn't squeak and most important of all, never breaks. And not only is it breakproof, but it is utterly simple to connect to a wind vane, which in turn is about ten times more reliable and foolproof than an autopilot; and lo and behold, it doesn't require generators or engines to provide electricity. The system gives you calm and freedom. Were those not the things that attracted you to going to sea in the first place? Just asking.

I don't want to repeat what I wrote in *Volume I* about these boats, for as Sumio said, they have changed little. And perhaps that is the point—that they were well thought-out from the beginning. Now it is true that the accommodations are not palatial compared to others in this book, but then so what? As long as you have good settees and a good table, and a good pilot berth, what is the advantage of a wider saloon? So you can get thrown around more in a seaway? Or to let you sit farther from your loved one? And why a huge galley? Are you going to make Thanksgiving dinners twice every day? Sure, you might have to think and organize a bit more as you cook, but hasn't

wooden 30-footer recounted dozens of stories. But they almost always involved people from large and flashy boats. Bristol Channel Cutters are so charming and friendly looking that people will probably give you things instead of taking from you.

And one last thing—your life. How many more years will you have to toil in the salt mine so you can buy a bigger, more fancy, more gear-laden boat? If I may quote Conrad:

'I remember my youth and the feeling that will never come back any more—the feeling that I could last forever, outlast the sea, the earth, and all men; . . . the triumphant conviction of strength, the heat of life in the handful of dust, the glow in the heart that with every year grows dim, grows cold, grows small, and expires, too soon, too soon—before life itself.'

'At the high-tech company,' Sumio says softly, looking at the

thinking been shown to stave off Alzheimer's?

And if you say a bigger boat gives you more storage, forget it. Go sailing; leave your junk at home or give it to the poor. This boat is so simple and unbreakable you won't need many spare parts. And if you say that you would like to have all the comforts of home, then maybe, just maybe, that is where you should stay. For if you don't go to sea to experience something different, to feel something different, to have new thoughts and emotions stir you, then why bother going to sea at all? Why go cluttering up pristine, distant harbors with all that gear and junk?

And if you think bigger boats are safer, think again. The most frequent danger long-distance cruisers seem to encounter is robbery and piracy. A friend who circumnavigated in a humble,

dusk, 'I had great status and all the money I could want. Yet I wasn't happy. Then five years ago, my father, who was a doctor, was dying. I had always thought he had an ideal life, accomplished a lot—he owned a hospital, helped people. A week before he died—I had been looking after him for six months—he became like a child and said, *Oh, I wish I had done this, had done that, retired earlier. I knew life was short, but this.* And he looked at me and said, *Never worry about what others may think. Do whatever your heart says.*'

A boat for real sailors. The Bristol Channel Cutter, a miracle of a design by Lyle Hess, owes much to the classic pilot cutters that can take any seas without wearing down her crew. Lin and Larry Pardy sailed an almost-identical boat around the world with no engine—that's how lively and manageable this piece of art is under sail. With her waterline length equal to that of many 34-footers, fine entry, and a plumb bow (now emulated by Grand Prix boats and the new

Swan 45), she is a demon to windward. On a reach, with her well-powered aft sections, she has been known to log 180-mile days, and she can average 150 miles a day on an ocean crossing. Her hefty tiller steering is the most reliable in the world. Her cutter sail plan of just under 600 feet makes sail handling a dream. With a furling genny, there is no need ever to venture onto the bowsprit, except to have a little fun. Her decks are broad for sure footing, and made even safer by the extraordi-nary high and beautiful bulwarks, which, being raised off the deck, can easily shed any quantity of boarding ocean. Her cockpit well is ideally small for bracing and holding little water, while the cockpit itself is comfortable, with nicely contoured coamings. Her boom gallows make movement aft as secure as in a playpen. I honestly don't know what more you could ask for.

The interior offers two impeccably thought-out versions—a classic, symmetrical center table, below (without the table), and the new dinette, above. Both have the snug and very useful pilot berth, which ingeniously opens into a very bright and airy double berth, left. On the opposite page, the galley is a good size, made more utile by penetrating aft under the bridge deck and by having a fold-down counter that locks between the galley sink and the chart

table. Aft of the chart table, the quarterberth offers the second excellent sea berth. It is one of the very best I have seen any-where—easily accessible and, what's most rare, airy. Note the ideal storage for its bedding, outboard, behind the solid-teak board. The photo at right shows the enclosed forepeak, where live the head, much storage, and, if requested, even a work-bench. The white surfaces on the overhead, bulkheads, etc., is of forever-perfect, gelcoated laminates.

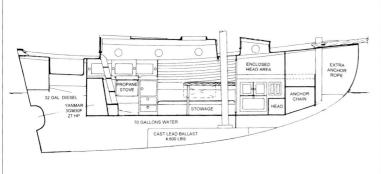

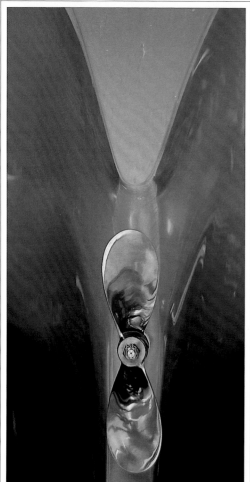

Bottom left-hand corner—the boat that flies. Top left-hand corner—the world's most affable boatbuilder, Sumio Oya. Below him, the exquisite tooling of the BCC hull, which, in the small photo beside it, is being reinforced with Kevlar—the yellowish laminates—to add extra

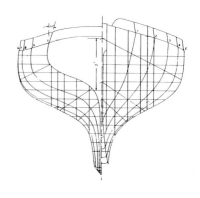

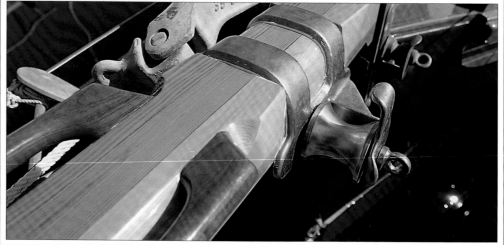

impact resistance for a customer who plans to sail in the far north's icy regions. The stainless steel bow fitting, in the photo above it, enables the retraction of the bowsprit, to save on moorage fees. The photos on this page show off not only fine craftsmanship, but—if you look at them together—the boat's airiness and ventilation. With the hinged forward hatch (below) open, the huge skylight open, and the large companionway hatch slid open—not to mention the eight bronze ports—the boat is practically a convertible. She might just be the most tropics-suited boat in the world.

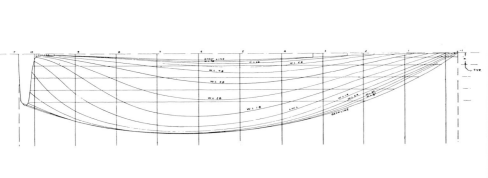

'I will never get rich here, but all I want is just to keep these boats going. To give people a chance, like I had, to have their dream. I feel it my duty to keep this company as is, until I'm too old to run it. My hope is that it will outlive me, that I can hand it down to someone who loves these boats just as much as I.'

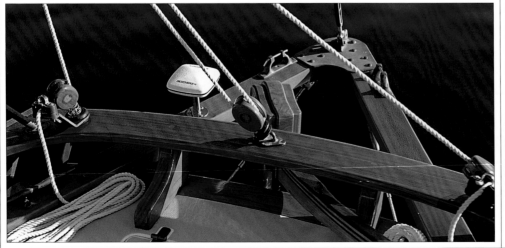

SHANNON YACHTS

W alter Schulz is one of the last of a wonderful breed—the complete boatbuilder. He designs boats, invents rigs, invents hull shapes, and then, unlike most others who work only on paper or computer, he takes saw and rasp and builds a half-model. And then he builds the real boat—always interesting and invariably one of the world's best yachts.

Walter could not look any more like the salty mariner even if Hollywood were to reinvent him. His great gray beard, his saucer-size intense eyes, big seagoing hands, and a voice that sounds like it's coming at you through a layer of shifting gravel, along with the ever-present, seldom-lit pipe, give you the indelible impression that God invented the seas and boats just for him. He *is* sailboats. He builds them, loses sleep at night worrying over them, and when he talks about them, he does so with enough passion to make any gale crawl away humbled. But at heart he's as gentle as a lamb.

Walter's Scutter Rig

'I don't care what a sailmaker tells you,' he growls, 'you can't reef a sail by furling it more than 33 percent and still have a sail form. This myth that has been generated, that you can have a 150 percent genoa on furling gear and it can become whatever sail you want it to be by reefing down is, pardon the expression, bullshit. When you furl up more than 33 percent of a sail, it's not a sail anymore; it's a bedsheet. You ever try going to windward with a bedsheet?'

Rising from this immutable observation, Walter went and invented a new rig; neither sloop nor cutter, it's aptly called the 'Scutter.'

'I can't take credit for that,' he declines. 'Boats in the last century used the same idea. And all the singlehanded around-the-world race people use versions of it too. So what is it? Well let me tell you first *why* it is. The single biggest reason we went to it was to keep people in the cockpit without having to go and do sail changes in bad weather, in dire conditions, and still have a good variety of sail combinations at their disposal. With this rig, the genoa is two sails and the Yankee jib is two sails, so you have four sails forward of the mast to keep you going safely. The average Shannon owner is fifty-six years old, while some are in their seventies, so I want to give them whatever I possibly can to keep them from getting overfatigued—to keep sailing, and keep sailing safely. I have middle-aged people going all over the world in my boats, so I can't be jerking around, putting them on a single-headstay sloop.

'Then there's the cutter. On a conventional cutter, the genoa is just too much of a pain to use when you're tacking back and forth in a real blow. It wraps on the staysail stay, plus you have all that sheet to haul. And then if you furl it too much, forget trying to sail to weather. If you get rid of the genny, what have you got left? A bitty staysail where the top of the stay is halfway down to the spreaders and the tack is too far back, hence a luff that is just too short to make the boat go. You just can't claw off a lee shore once you're over 30 knots—not with a staysail on any cutter. Our inner forestay is almost 40 percent longer than a traditional staysail stay. That's a hell of a lot more luff to drive you.

'What you need way out on the headstay, the outer stay, is a good-size, sturdy Yankee jib with a long luff, one that'll pull and pull until the world blows away. Now most people say, *When the wind picks up, get that headsail far back into the boat.* That's nonsense. A traditional staysail well inboard toward the center, when you're hard on the wind in 50 knots, will give weather helm, which in that much wind is the last thing you

need, either for the helmsman or the autopilot. That's when they both are likely to break down. The autopilot simply gets overwhelmed. And then what do you do? You steer by hand. If you're a middle-aged couple in weather like that, how long are you going to be able to sit out there and have your arms cranking? I mean, I have been out there for eighteen to twenty hours in serious grief; you get so tired you can't recall your name, never mind navigate and handle the boat well.

'So on our Scutter rig, we put a Yankee on the headstay at the tip of the bowsprit, and then about four feet back, at the stemhead, we put a nice big, fat genny. Both of them on roller furlers, of course. We have a third removable inner stay by Spectra that attaches to a ring in the deck right where the old staysail used to be. This is for a hank-on storm jib. A survival sail. That's for 80 knots of wind.

'I get as much sailing time on my boats as I can, to see if all this stuff really works. Everything seems like a great idea standing on a concrete floor inside a nice warm building, but at sea? Some years back, I was sailing off Ireland with Monk Farnham—he's seventy-five, and I'm cold and wet. We're beating past Fastnet Rock, wind right on the nose, seas like I've never seen—craziest, wildest, weirdest seas. One sea comes over the bow and hits me in the face, bam. The next one comes and hits me in the back of the head; there was no pattern that you could steer to. Having a powerful Yankee up there pulling for us saved the day. A sloop or a cutter with a rolled-up genny and a bitty staysail would not have done it. It simply cannot go within 50 degrees of the wind; no way. You're just not going to get off a lee shore.

'Another time, I was out on one of our 47s in 65 knots. Here's

how that went. We left Newport in 15 knots, with the main and genoa out, for the 400-mile jaunt to Annapolis. Just me and a couple of kids from the shop with not much sailing experience. In a few hours, the weather deteriorated. I first reefed the main, then reefed the genoa. Then, as it got worse, I got rid of the genoa, pulled out the working jib, the Yankee on the foremost stay, and carried that and a double-reefed main well into the 40s all that night. Wind kept up, even at dawn as we were beating off Montauk. Then it kept climbing. Here I am, one of the kids flat on his back sick, the other glassy-eyed staring, so here's me, basically alone. Well, I'll be damned if I hove to. I just doused the main completely and reef-furled that Yankee jib. Handled all those sail changes, the whole thing, from the cockpit. And we were tacking back and forth, too; not just hanging on. So we kept on going, sometimes at 3 knots with the damn seas so big. One old man in the cockpit steering and pulling on lines.

'We had one guy with a Scutter rig on a 39, never owned a sailboat before, almost no experience. He picks up the boat, spends two weeks shaking it down, then takes off for Bermuda. I mean, my heart was in my throat when he left. Well, he got there in three days, twenty hours. Averaged 7.4 knots on a boat with a 32-foot waterline. The rig is just so easy to get used to.

'Morgan Freeman, best damned actor in America and the world's nicest guy, owned a *Shannon 38* for ten or eleven years, sailed a lot by himself in that ketch. He flew in one night from making a movie, and I start explaining to him how simple this new rig is to work and what a great new invention it is, and he looks at me and he says, *What the hell took you so long?* We ended up building a *43* with the Sketch rig variation for him

and his wife, Myrna. On the Sketch rig, we get eighteen different, perfectly functioning sail combinations. All from the cockpit. No wear and tear on body or nerves. The real issue to me is fatigue; you have to be attentive to every aspect of sailing when you design and build a boat. I don't mean just the sails and rig; I mean how easy the galley is to use, how easy it is to move around the boat, hell, even to go to the head. In bad conditions, just getting into your foul-weather gear, is a major undertaking. Fatigue. The Coast Guard keeps records of all the major accidents and fatalities that happen on boats. Ninety-five percent of them are related to fatigue.

'I think that one of the big reasons why so many of our boats are doing long voyages is that they simply don't beat up their owners. When they get into a bad storm, they know they can trust the boat. There is no fatigue from anxiety. If you get a boat that's fast but tires the crew so much that they haven't the strength left to get the maximum out of the boat, then where is your gain? Where is the advantage?

'We often have average doctors and accountants in offshore races beat a crew of sailmakers just because they don't get tired out, can make better judgments, remain inventive, remain alert to change, and have the strength left to react to it optimally.'

The Shoalsailer

While Walt has earned his reputation designing and building boats for the extreme rigors of ocean sailing, he has always been enamored with cruising in shallow coastal waters. 'I love gunkholing. Getting away from crowded anchorages when I am on a boat with Janet, my wife of thirty-one years. While the keel/centerboard hulls of my Shannons draw a lot less than the fixed-draft fin keels of most premium offshore yachts, I still found myself looking for a boat that I could actually sail in only a couple of feet of water. That led to my Shoalsailer, which I envisioned as the ultimate coastal cruiser. I am embarrassed to admit it, but it took me seven years to work out the design problems. But I felt a little better when the Shoalsailer's hull turned out to be so innovative that the U.S. Patent Office gave me a patent. That's almost unheard-of for a hull shape. The benchmark for shoal-draft boats was set by Ralph Munroe in 1885. He was the man who opened up Florida tourism at the turn of the 20th century. He developed the Presto Ketch. Someone gave me one of these old centerboard ketches, 37 feet, berthed in Greenport, New York. Half a wreck; I sailed it up here. We tried to get up to this narrow cut—Plumb Gut—trying to beat toward it with this huge shoal beside us. We took four or five runs at it and kept getting pushed onto the shoal. So

one of the guys says, *Why don't we just cut over the shoal; with the board up, we only draw 28 inches.* Well, I said, we can't put the board up because then we'll get blown sideways.

'We're in a bar that night and one of the guys says to me, *What the hell good is a shallow boat when it's only shallow downwind?* That night I didn't sleep; I started my seven-year saga that became the Shoalsailer.'

The Shoalsailer's massive 12-foot-9-inch beam keeps the boat almost completely upright when beating; its VMG is close to a *J/35*'s; and it can sail in just over 30 inches of water with daggerboards up or down—and that's the depth of an old-fashioned bathtub.

'The amazing thing is that the hull shape alone gives you lift going to weather. The boat will sail 35 degrees relative to the apparent wind, with no leeway with the boards up. The boat is so wide that it doesn't heel much—5 to 10 degrees of heel is all. I designed the sections for each heel increment.

'It has a living-room-sized cockpit, with dual steering wheels. We have Kevlar for abrasion in the hull laminates, plus a crash sole that has watertight integrity if the hull is holed. So you can calmly beach this boat. We even designed a double roof with airflow between the skins to keep the belowdecks cool while you're sitting at the shore where there's less wind.'

Besides the big items, like rigs and hulls, Walt and his crew also stay on top of the small details, such as the interior woodwork fit and finish. 'A few years ago, I got bored with people judging boats based solely on how glossy the varnish was, so we put in a state-of-the-art, pressurized, air-conditioned varnish room, and now we are doing varnish work as well as anybody in the world. Building most of the interior out of solid hardwoods means that these boats will keep looking good even after my grandkids are gone. And my finish carpenters know that they'll have to fix any sloppy joints, as I am a real pain in the ass if I ever find anything crooked.

'I feel especially good about our boats' popularity with boatyard workers around the world. I love it when a boatyard guy with grease under his fingernails comes up to me and says that Shannons are his favorite boats. I worked my way through college as a boatyard mechanic, so I know how aggravating it can be when you can't get to something essential like a filter or a starter motor without ripping the boat apart. Our systems installations are clean, simple, and accessible. And if an owner or somebody in a boatyard is working on one of our boats and has a question, all he has to do is call and he can talk to the person who actually did the installation, sometimes even on a twenty-five-year-old Shannon. Holding onto my key people over the years gives a continuity to the company.

'Our customers seem ever more knowledgeable *and* demanding, so we have to engineer special systems for their needs. They really force me to stay on the leading edge of everything, from desalinators to fuel polishing systems. The hot area lately has been in interfaced systems—you know, the daylight-viewable laptops with raster chart nav systems overlaid on the radar image. On the first Shannon that I took to Bermuda in 1976, we found the island with a sextant and an RDF. I wonder how many sailors today even know how to hold a sextant. Now, with WAAS GPS hooked to the laptop, you can watch your boat on the computer screen pull out of its slip in the marina.

'And we've utilized the latest technology in interior design. The first generation of CAD software was useless for doing yacht interiors because of the compound curves of a hull. Once

SHOALSAILER 32 | MID-SECTION

they came out with programs for hull shapes, I knew this was the tool for designing the one-off interior that goes into every Shannon. I can move bulkheads now and not have to worry if a bunk is going to want to stick out of the hull by 6 inches when we build it. That used to happen more than any yacht designer is willing to tell you. It's been great, except for the headaches of teaching myself another software program.'

The bulletin board at Shannon is filled with postcards and photos sent in by Shannon owners from exotic locales such as Madagascar, Glacier Bay, and the Rio Dulce. Walt says, 'Everyone here in the shop lives vicariously through our boats that go to places most of us will never get to see.'

I almost forgot—all their boats, including the *39*, *43*, and *47/52*, are 20 percent lighter and 40 percent stronger than just a few years ago, due to the use of biaxial stitched instead of woven rovings, linear foam PVC cores, Vinylester resin, and the use of S-glass, which is a little stronger than E-glass.

On weekends, Walter relaxes: He rebuilds old wooden boats. The latest is a 1930 William Hand motorsailer. But one day he will stop building, designing, and inventing boats that kind of remake the world. Thankfully, he has taught his builders and designers well, passing down a lifetime of knowledge as carefully as he does everything else.

ere are Shannon's classically pretty, nearly indestructible blue-water cruisers, and at the bottom right (and on previous page), Walter Schulz's ingenious creation, the beachable Shoalsailer, for coastal cruising even in waist-deep water. In the photo below is the 39-foot Scutter—no spelling mistake—with the Yankee furled forward, while the genny (also rigged to the masthead) flies slightly aft. See the text for the reasoning behind this brilliant solution for a serious, ocean-sailing rig. Above is her sleek, larger sister, the Shannon 43 Sketch—flying the same headsail

arrangement. With the addition of the mizzenmast, you get the most versatile sail combinations imaginable, and, most crucially, they all perform exceptionally well over an immense range of sea and wind conditions. Above, showing off her power, is the queen of the fleet, the *47*, again with the Scutter rig. All of the Shannon's offshore cruisers feature a choice of keel/centerboard or fixed draft, classic cutter or ketch or Scutter/Sketch rigs. They also have very fine detailing, enormously strong construction, and an almost-endless series of creative improvements, most of them due to the inexhaustible dedication of their designer and builder, Walter Schulz, in photo left, pointing out his weekend passion—restoring classic wooden boats.

These interiors are about as 'shippy' as you can get. Apart from their evidently excellent joinery, Shannon's fortes include their inventive layouts and sophisticated custom details. Above, in the three photos of the *43*, I very much like details such as the drawers under the settee (left) and under the double berth (center), instead of the customary drop lids that you have to deal with while wrestling with cushions. The double hatches over the saloon give excellent light, the laminated overhead is elegantly trimmed and maintenance-free. On the opposite page are photos of the *47*, with the luxurious forward cabin (top, center), the intriguing classic cabinetry (left), and the beautiful burl-inlaid coffee table (right), which, when needed, rises and opens for dinner (see photo below it). In that same photo, note the grabbable searails and the V-grooved solid wood on

the bulkheads. The line drawing is also of the *47*, with that romantic forward berth, and my favorite, the small aft cabin to port with a bunk and a desk that doubles as the navigation area and a writer's hideaway.

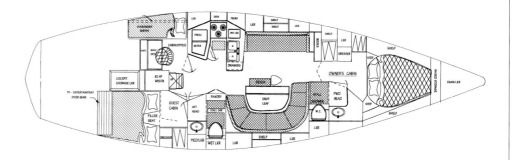

The hulls, above right, are of the Shoalsailer. Note the unusual hollowed sections bow-on, and—in the hull in profile—the slot for one of the daggerboards, which, even in the down position, does not increase the boat's draft. The other photos on this page show the offshore Shannons. The galley, below, has a well-located, accessible plate rack, and the best knife storage for a boat, set into the countertop. In the photo beside it is a perfect shallow pantry. In the upper left-hand corner is a bit of timeless cabinetry. The opposite page shows cockpits that blend classic teak details with the modern curved helmsman's seat, nonskid seat surfaces, sheet-tail stowage below the winches, and even a predesigned space for stereo speakers. The bowsprit platform is of massive chunks of solid teak, with heavy-gauge stainless chafe preventers everywhere. In the top right corner

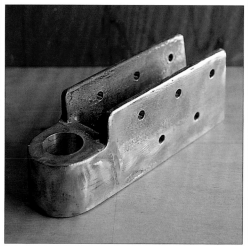

is the hefty bronze gudgeon that foots the rudder. One of the best things you can't see here: the reverse transom opens to release the life raft right into the water. No need to cart around the weighty thing on deck—a brutal task in a presumably brutal situation. First-class offshore thinking.

'When I started the company in 1975, with just a dream of building the best blue-water cruising sailboats in the world, I never imagined my life's work would turn out to be so gratifying. For our twenty-fifth anniversary here in Bristol Harbor, we had a couple of hundred people and a slew of the more than three hundred Shannons we've built so far. It brought tears to my eyes.'

SWEDEN YACHTS

'We don't like to invent new things just to get attention, because too often what looks at first original and striking will very soon look silly. Instead of changing things, we like to perfect them.'

It is always a joy to take a trip to Sweden. Not only am I drawn by the stark beauty of its western shores—the magnificent boulders, the silent woods, the long evenings—but there is a gentle humanism to the whole country, a reasonable pace, a reassuring calm. The towns are modest, of exquisite quality but of very human proportions; the houses are family-sized; and bicycle paths and sidewalks are as common as roads. It's one of those rare countries where people are still considered more important than cars. And you get a sense that they seem to consider all aspects of change before making it—the merits, the demerits—and even then, they seem to feel, it's best to think it all through again. There also seems to be an unspoken consensus that if a thing is worth doing, it's worth doing very, very well, or not at

'The biggest change we have undergone is size,' he begins, laughingly patting his midsection, which has, over the years, gained a little girth. We have made three 70-footers and two 80s. When you were last here, most of our boats were 36 and 38 feet; now they are 40 feet and up. In 1976, when we started, our *34* was considered a very nice boat; you could really live very decently with a good aft cabin and all. So we built that for seven years before we changed it completely.

'We evolve slowly. Like a Mercedes. Over the years, it keeps the grille, the insignia, but behind them, hundreds of small details make it a totally different car. We are still very conscious of speed, as you know, and like to stay near the top in that.

'But the big change that has pushed us is the attitude of sailors. Comfort on board is a very high priority today. It used

all. It shows in everything they make—from their triple-glazed windows, each of which is worthy of a master craftsman, to their baffling Saabs, of which I have owned three, and found, to my amazement, that the faster you drove them, the more solid they felt. The things they build seem to last forever.

My friend Jens Östmann, who designs everything but the hulls at Sweden Yachts, typifies my impression of this nation. He's soft-spoken but quick to laugh, pensive but full of deep passions, and he has astoundingly good taste and an artist's eye without the need to be showy. It was wonderful to see him after all this time and most reassuring, and rather astonishing, that his beautifully styled, impeccably built yachts, which were perfect when I wrote *Volume I*, had become even more perfect.

to be you went sailing to get wet, get bounced around, to have a good tussle with the sea, to pull ropes, haul sails, fold sails, change sails—to most people twenty years ago sailing was a very physical activity. Today many, if not most people want to stay dry and would rather not leave the cockpit. This makes for a very different approach in boatbuilding—from the opening transom, to make dinghy boarding and swimming easier, to having a dodger that's engineered into, not added onto, the boat. This search for comfort even affects the design of the head. People want a real bathroom on a boat, not a cramped closet where you do hand-to-hand combat with a beastly pump.

'They demand large and super-comfortable cockpits, which is actually going back to larger cockpits, which were common until Swan made little wells for your legs, and you went through a hole and down a long ladder into the cellar.

'Peter Norlin still designs all our hulls. And why we stay with his designs is that they are all very pure and beautiful. And just a little bit better every time. From the rail up, I do most of the design and I try to stay close to the spirit of the hull.

'One of the biggest changes over the years has been the abolishment of any remnants of the old IOR-rule influence on boat design. For a couple of decades, most boats were designed not to go as fast or be as comfortabe as possible, but to beat the loopholes in the IOR ratings. So you had these silly little mainsails, because big ones were penalized, and monstrous overlapping headsails, which were a nightmare to handle and gave you but a small percent of power for 50 percent more area. All because

'The transoms, of course, are opening. We were very slow in developing one because we wanted the best solution, while keeping our classic look. So it is an opening piece, operated either mechanically by a cable or by an electric motor. The big advantage of this over fixed steps in the transom is that the platform is a good few inches lower, making it much easier to get in and out of the dinghy or the water. The disadvantage is that it is a moving part.

'Then there is the gear. The things we put on a *45* today you would not have found on a 65-footer fifteen years ago. And I'm afraid I don't see a back-to-nature trend on the horizon. Gear and gadgets are wonderful as long as you realize that whatever moves eventually breaks. Generally, people get all this stuff without the faintest interest in maintaining them. That is fine

the overlap was not penalized. And of course you had to have three or four of them, because you cannot competitively reef a genoa. As a complete cure for the horrid genoa, look at our new headsail on the *45*—it is small and self-tacking, on a little track forward of the mast, arched forward to allow for good sail shape. The main, of course, is much bigger. It is typically bigger than the jib—about 30 percent more than it used to be.

'With the new sail fabrics, we can create a very-high-aspect jib with a lot of pull in it, a nice profile all the way up. We believe very strongly that the self-tacking jib is here to stay. It is amazing how much more people actually sail with it. You just set your sails once, and to tack back and forth, all you do is turn the wheel. You can do a tack, singlehanded, in 60 to 70 feet.

in Europe and North America, but not in far-away places. The sad thing is that with all these mechanical and electrical systems to maintain and repair, people tend to sail not from one beautiful, quiet anchorage to another, but from service yard to service yard. We can see it even here in Sweden, in coastal cruising; people sail from one marina to the next. Very few seek out serenity or solitude; they need services.

'So, having said all that, our *45* is really the Sweden Yacht of today. And we are working on a *42* on exactly the same lines. No extreme beam in the center; a boat that moves easily through the water with better tracking characteristics and of course more power, more speed. And, oddly enough, more volume below.

'The 80-footer that Germán Frers designed, of which we have built two, certainly reflects the desire for more speed and space. The nice thing about doing the big boats is that it widened our horizon dramatically. We are using elements of them in our small boats; for example, we are now very seriously beginning to use carbon spars. The biggest thing you learn in building a carbon mast is to *unlearn* everything you knew about aluminum mast building. You have to think *fiber* all the time. We are learning what the best things are to do, but mostly we see what not to do, with relation to the local stresses in mast cranes, spreader fixings, where the engineering is vastly different from aluminum. For example, aluminum has the same strength in all directions, but fiber strength depends entirely on which direction the fiber is going. If the piece is designed to take pressure, you want to run your fibers straight all the time. But if you just concentrate on that, you might forget the other stresses, so you might not put in enough of plus-minus 45-degree directional fibers to take twistings, pulling, etc. This might seem pretty obvious, but when you look at the record of carbon-fiber masts, their standup-to-breakup ratio is very high. But getting better every day. The people who have been building in carbon for the last ten years have gone through their learning period—they have had enough masts fall down to see what caused the failures; by now, they know how to remedy them. So we feel confident enough in the process at this point that many of our new 45s have carbon-fiber masts.

'Much the same change applies to going to swept spreaders instead of straight ones. Straight spreaders have only one loading—compression, straight into the mast. If you sweep the spreaders and change the bend in the mast, you also change the loading on the spreaders, adding a pretty drastic bend into them. So, all of a sudden, the mast tube is subject to pull in the front and pressure in the back, and it wants to change shape. You have to look at all new things with a very new eye and new thinking.

'Now, taking the mast as an example of how we approach things at Sweden Yachts, it is all those small details that we want to perfect, so we don't give our owners big headaches by rushing out something new just because other builders are doing it, or because it looks fresh and exciting.

'Fortunately, the people who have been laying up our hulls for twenty years are—like us—very keen on new technology as long as it has a reason *and* has been well tested. The layup of the hull has developed, as you know, from woven to knitted biaxial roving for its better strength. And we reinforce in many areas with a much higher use of unidirectional fibers. We still use balsa core for stiffness, along with a longitudinal beam to stiffen the hull even more.

'Below the water, we have come up with some good new ideas—such as flaring the top of the keel to give a wider sealing surface to avoid leaks. And of course shifting the ballast much lower by having the bulb begin 2 feet below the top of the keel.'

So their 45, shallow draft, has a magnificently shaped bulb; it looks very organic, swept and rounded like a sea mammal—or as Jens said, 'It wants to make love to a dolphin. We needed more weight well down to have the same stability. We have managed to maintain the lead weight so the boat is no heavier, and it has the same depth of center of gravity, so the boat is exactly as stable as the fin-keeled boat. In order to reduce turbulence at the exit, we have put on small wings. So when the boat makes leeway, wanting to create a vortex, which in turn takes energy, thus speed, from the boat, the wings prevent that. Upwind, it's very close in performance to the standard keel.

'The skeg is gone, but we have oversized the solid rudderstock. The base, where the rudder is attached, has a diameter of 6 inches. Then there is a sacrificial area where the solid becomes a tube, so that if you hit something at a great speed with the bottom of the rudder, the lower end breaks off without bending the whole structure in the hull. You would then have a smaller surface, of course, but quite sufficient for an emergency.

'Oh, yes, you noticed we have abandoned the broad sheer stripe and gone to the more elegant fine cove. Now that is a good example of the pace of change here; it took us three years to decide on that one.'

This kind of attitude might raise eyebrows in an industry where the annual razzle-dazzle, brand-new gizmo is the norm much too often, to the neglect of the vital, unseen details that in the end separate a well-found, first-class yacht from a giant, endless, and very costly headache.

At Sweden Yachts, I watched two shipwrights installing the genoa track—carefully, slowly, at great expense, but to absolute perfection. It went something like this. The track was fit dry, the holes drilled, then the track was removed. The holes in the deck were countersunk to create a hollow where a sealant ring can form. If this step is left out, as the bolts are torqued down, most of the sealant is squeezed out, leaving you with a micron of stuff, which seals about as well as tissue paper. Next, the bolts were slipped into the freestanding track, then each and every bolt was *wrapped* with spaghetti-shaped caulking, so that every thread would become an O-ring as well. You can imagine what a slow and careful process this is. Then the track was maneuvered with great care into position, the caulked bolts pressed home, the nuts and washers installed below and torqued. Simply the very best way to build a yacht.

Their teak decks are laid in PM-polymere. A plethora of well-distributed weights are used, to apply the correct pressure to achieve the proper thickness of adhesive.

The interior work has gone from very fine to very beautiful. As examples, the searails are wonderfully sculpted and heavy, with a concave interior for very good grip. And there is an astounding round piece of solid wood worked into a louver to put over Dorade-vent holes and heater outlets. And if that were not enough, they have even more complex oval versions of these over the stereo speakers. These are light years ahead of the horrible plastic fittings that mar most boats—ours included. I learned in their woodshop how these boats become as excellent as they do: A cabinetmaker was using a sanding block with as much care as if he were creating a rocket component instead of a trim piece for the sink.

So overall, Sweden Yachts is still the absolutely first-class yard it always was, plus a lot more. Their very steady crew of thirty-five turns out works of modern art second to none. And they manage to keep their costs well below others by a relentless application of creativity and intelligence. They sell without dealers, direct from the yard—not only to have fewer mouths to feed but also because they sincerely believe that getting a boat of this class should be a very personal experience. They want each owner to have the opportunity of coming to the yard, talking to the designers, and seeing the boats being built, to get clear ideas of what they would like to have on their own boats.

As the Michelin Green Guide would say, 'Well worth the detour.' To the tenth power.

It's difficult to cease being complimentary about Sweden Yachts in general, and their new *45* (top and bottom of this page) in particular. The handling and speed are excellent, the design lines perfect, and the innovations almost without end. One of the most striking is the rig and self-tacking jib of the *45*. You have to have eagle eyes to see in the bottom photo (better in the deck illustration, page 210) the curved track directly forward of the mast, which allows you, miraculously, to tack without touching a sheet. The forward curve is to ensure proper sail-setting at any sheeting angle.

Paradise. It's so quick and efficient, you could practically tack up a creek. Their swept-back spreaders preclude the need for running backstays in normal sea conditions. In the stern, note the opening, hinge-down portion, which in fact creates a walk-through transom. It has steps inside of it for swimming and easy boarding. This opening portion can be either mechanically or hydraulically operated. On this page is their majestic 70-foot cutter, with its dual cockpit. Note, in the small photo below, the perfect solution for a secondary companionway—a hermetic aluminum-and-Plexiglas hatch with a similar drop-board. In the deck photo to its left is a rail around a forward hatch, which allows the mounting of a small dodger—a priceless commodity in rain or the tropics, providing bow-to-stern ventilation below, even under sail.

Swoontime. There simply are no interiors more pure, practical, or sophisticated than those of Sweden Yachts. They are, one and all, architectural masterpieces. The detailing is so integral that the interiors seem not to be assembled out of pieces, but rather hewn out of a solid chunk. From the eminently grippable, perfectly ergonomic searails that double as handrails, to the flush-fitting vertical corner pieces (in the photos above and below), finishing with the trim pieces above and below the portlights that also house the blinds, everything seems to grow out of the mass around it. Note also the housing around the microwave oven (opposite, top right) and the trim under the companionway in the same photo. In the photo below, apart from the corner pieces that create a solid column, there is the small grille over a speaker. It is routed out of a solid piece of wood. You might say, 'So what?' but you must realize that anyone who puts so much thought and effort into

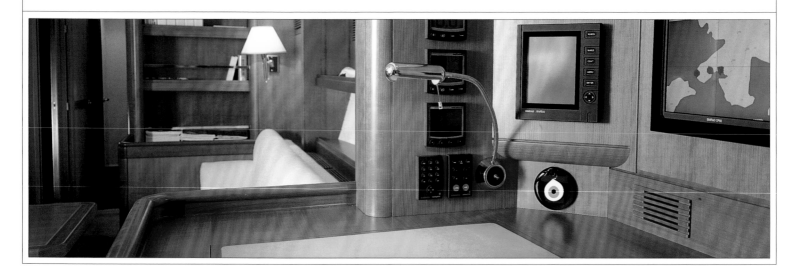

such small details inevitably ends up building a perfect yacht. While all these interior photos are of the *70*, the mentality and the craftsmanship carry over into the smaller boats as well. Most builders would do well to take lessons in creativity from the calm, aesthetically sophisticated designers at Sweden Yachts.

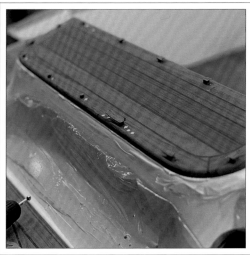

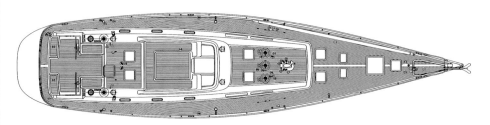

Nowhere do you get more luxury boat for your money than at Sweden Yachts. The engineering is superb and the execution flawless. The purity of design is evident in their 80-footer with the double cockpit, top left. To its right is the genoa track installation that I described in the text, while next to it is the super-protected topsides during construction. The photo to its right shows the most spectacular keel in boatbuilding—it belongs in the Museum of Modern Art, and it works like a dream. Next is the tooling for the backbone grid, then, the bow of the *70*. Below it, the move-

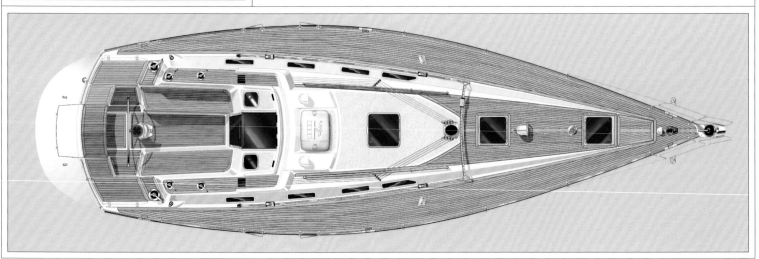

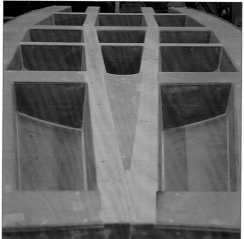

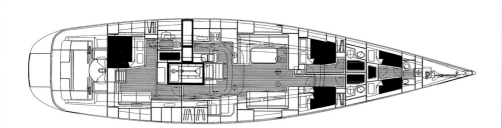

able navigator's chair (used in the smaller boats) gets my 'Genius' award. It slides fore and aft—locking securely— depending on whether you want to sit or proceed to the aft cabin. In the photo below that, and the deck illustration of the new *45*, left page, note the tooled set-in for the life raft. It is in an excellent location, safe and up high, where it's accessible and most likely to remain above water. Next, the bronze through-hull for the refrigerator has a built-in coil, cooled by seawater, and the complex corner trim piece above it is among the best yacht joinery anywhere. *Bravissimo!*

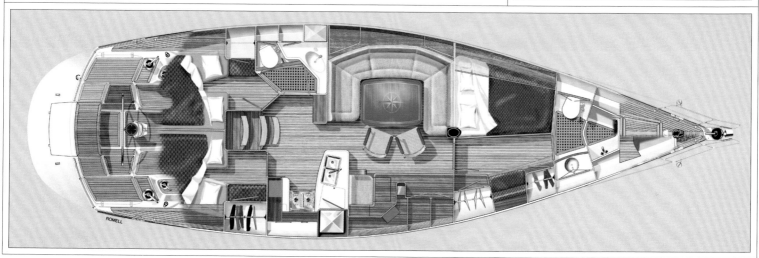

'We are even fanatical about having a very deep gloss on the wood-work, so we use old-fashioned, one-component, penetrating oil varnish, which dries slowly. We sand five or six times. While most builders do a multicoat process in one day, it takes us a week. But then you'll be look-ing at it for a long time, so we think it's worth the extra effort.'

TURNER YACHTS

Turner Yachts, set in the beautiful wine region of Ontario, Canada, is one of the most consistently innovative and avant-garde sailboat builders in the world. With carbon fiber and Kevlar, pre-pregs and large-scale oven post-curing, they are well into the category of 'extreme' boat-building. Some call it, 'High Tech.' I would call it 'Best Tech.'

My first question to Rob Turner—known as one of the nicest guys in the boatbuilding industry—was, How on earth did you have the courage to get started in a market awash with sailboat builders, many of whom have to build powerboats as well to put meat on the Sunday table?

'Well, I was sort of talked into it. I had been at C&C in product development until the fire in 1995. A bit later, someone who had bought a number of boats from us couldn't find the boat he wanted, so he came to me for advice. Based on his requirements, I sent him to Bill Tripp for the design and suggested a builder who could eventually suit his needs. He got the design, talked to the builder, got a price, but he just wasn't thrilled. So he asked me if I would build the boat. After a lot of discussion and convincing, I agreed. At that time, C&C was closing, so we grabbed their ten best boatbuilders and also acquired some of their really sophisticated equipment.

'When I was at C&C, we had a contract with DuPont to develop some new materials for us. Through this, I met a brilliant engineer of theirs who helped us greatly, establishing relationships in the industry, so we could learn about the very newest and best materials, and processes, as fast as possible.

'We built our first 46-footer. Since then we've built two 56s and we're working on a 66. The people we build for have all been racers. They are now in their fifties and want to go cruising, but they want to cruise fast. Plus they want to do pickup races as they go—Newport-to-Bermuda, the Jamaica Race, things of that kind. The first 56 owner did the New York Yacht Club's Spring Series and came in second overall. He honestly feels that the 56 is a breakthrough boat. He was beaten only by a super Grand Prix racer. In the Boothbay Regatta, he was first, with a pickup crew, and second at the Monhegan Island Race.

'To help racing and cruising, we have a hydraulic lifting keel, which gives you a 12-foot 6-inch draft that allows you to go to windward like a Grand Prix boat. But such a draft precludes you from visiting a lot of areas, so it retracts—straight up—to 7 feet 6 inches, which is pretty darn good for a 56-footer.

'But we don't just build the boats for speed. No one who goes sailing wants a boat that is uncomfortable in a seaway; comfortable handling comes first. And a performance boat is simply more comfortable in a seaway because it has better drive, less windage, a taller spar, so it can reach above the crest of the waves and catch the wind and keep moving. In a slow sailboat, you can get caught in weather you just can't get out of. With a faster, more powerful boat, you often can.

'It seems that more and more, people want boats that are rigid, that can withstand the elements, that are intelligent in the manner in which they are put together. In the past, we always talked about displacement as a single factor. A light boat was instantly dismissed as not being any good in a seaway. Similar discussions centered on the full keel as being best in a seaway; but the fact that the full keel has all but disappeared—and at the same time a hell of a lot more people are crossing oceans safely and fast—pretty much disproved that theory.

'As for the tracking issue, if you look at rudder designs today, rudders are less steering devices and more foils. The reason is that these boats are simply much easier to drive. They don't have tracking problems. Design, certainly aided by computers, has changed dramatically. It's true that some of the old fin-keel IOR boats, with their enormous beam and sucked-in, weird stern sections, were asymmetrical, out of balance, and skittish. But in terms of design, the problem was not tracking, but balance.

'The big difference today is that the new boats tend to sail on top of the water, not just through it. That is what Bill Tripp does best; he gets the boat up for better boat speed and better motion.

'What was absent in the old discussion about boats being lightweight, was the structure of the boat. And, most important, how big panel sizes were—that is to say, unsupported areas of the hull. So you could have a very lightweight boat without any structure in it, and yes, there could be oil-canning, rudders binding, and on and on. But if you build the boat to be lightweight, with lots of internal structure for support, like we do, with beams both longitudinal and athwartships—apart from the core, which already has great stiffness—then the boat will be the best kind of boat one can build. We break down the panel sizes so that the largest is less than 3 feet across, then those problems do not exist.

'We use Core-Cell in the hull and balsa in the deck. If you execute the process correctly, either core is a good core. I think there is a stigma in the market about balsa getting wet. But if you engineer your boats well, there will be no core—only solid material—where the penetrations are. Then how is it going to get wet? Unless, of course, you have a catastrophic event, in which case the core you have is of minor consequence.'

Then, smiling, Rob holds up a sample piece of the outer skin of their hull. There are eleven layers of laminates in it, of Kevlar and carbon fiber—the Kevlar for impact, the carbon for stiffness—which, bonded, vacuum-bagged, and cooked, together make up a thickness of just over a communion wafer. Okay so maybe it's more. It might even be close to an eighth of an inch. It has zero air in it. Next to this outer skin comes the core, then the inner skin, which is almost identical to the outer skin. They're balanced. That's important for the same reason that in an I-beam the top and the base of the I need to be the same thickness to work well. The resultant finished hull in the 66 has a thickness of about 38 millimeters, very close to 1 1/2 inches.

The panel he showed me was about 2 feet long, weighed next to nothing, and was absolutely unbendable. To stiffen the unbendable panel, Rob adds longitudinal and athwartships beams. If you're impressed so far with the Turner boats, just wait until you read the rest. The building of the hull goes like this:

'We buy our carbon fiber from Japan. It is shipped to our Californian supplier, YLA, who supplies the aerospace industry. They impregnate it with resin, a low-temperature-cure resin. Impregnation means the resin, all catalyzed, is infused under pressure to a precise content of so much weight per area. That's the big advantage of pre-preg; you get a guaranteed fiber-to resin ratio. Then it, the pre-preg material, is shipped to us, rolled up in individual layers in refrigerated trucks. At this stage, the stuff is dry to the touch—well not dry, sort of like the taffy we used to buy as kids. A bit tacky. When we open these rolls, they are quite workable for some time, even months. What sets it off is heat. As we lay it up, we do all different orientations: 0-90, 45-45 to total eleven layers. But after each four layers, we de-bulk it: We vacuum-bag it—press it all down—to make sure there is no air in it. Then we lay up the next four layers. So we go through a series of vacuum bags. Then the core goes down and it is vacuum-bagged into place as well. What's interesting is that the foam core has tiny holes in it for the air to escape as you're vacuum-bagging, but you see what's happened—the resin itself has migrated into these holes so you

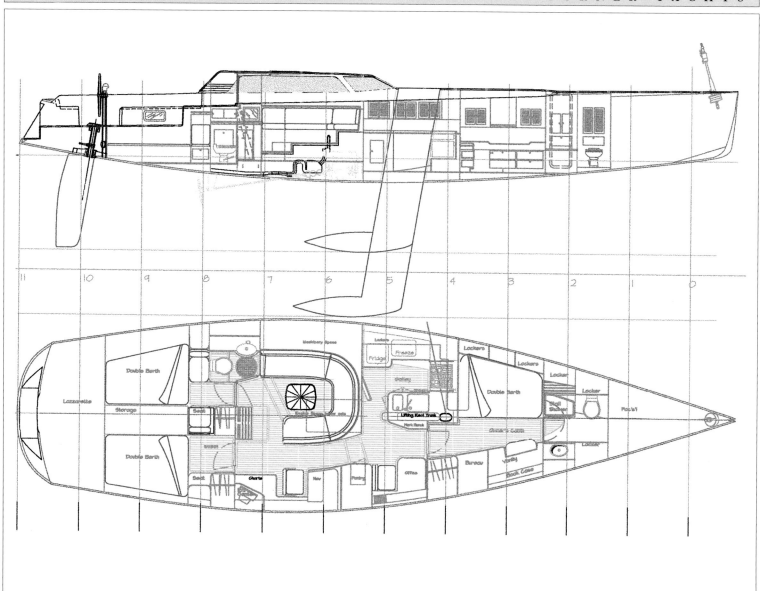

actually get a resin attachment between the two skins.

'After the core is vacuum-bagged in, we lay up the inner skin just like we did the outer. Then we actually cook the boat. The whole boat. In a giant oven. We put about 40 thermocouplet sensors on a hull so we can control the temperature of all areas to within plus or minus 2 degrees. On an IMS-rule boat, we have to, by the rule, cook it at 176 degrees Fahrenheit. On non-IMS racers, we go to 200 degrees. That extra temperature gives us about 10 percent more strength out of the materials.'

When I tell him in absolute sincerity that this is wonderful stuff, his eyes light up like a kid's and he says, 'Yes, it really is, isn't it? This is the ultimate achievable in hull construction to date. And we achieve it,' he says, without the slightest hint of boasting. 'That's why people come to us.

'There are three other similar builders in the U.S.— Goertz, New England Boatworks, and Westerly on the west coast—but they're basically one-off builders, while we're more production-oriented, so we have better prices.

'We also do a process called wet-preg, which is similar to pre-preg except we put the resins into a machine and roll the materials through it. It comes out resin-impregnated. We roll that onto another reel and lay up from it. What is interesting is that they are close to each other in quality. Pre-preg is very much an aerospace technology. We use nothing but epoxies with both systems.

'We wanted to bring to the market the best possible boat in terms of construction, in terms of materials, and in terms of finish. Design and seaworthiness of course go without saying. We did experiments with resin infusion, a very good process, but we found some shrinkage problems, uneven heating, things that made me worry. I am convinced we get better structures with more control, lighter weight, and a better finish, although there are many more steps with the process. Compared to a hand-laid-up hull, we put in twice the labor and about 15 percent more material cost.

'It's not just the weight-saving that counts, it's what you are getting out of the material—the best possible characteristics it possesses. If you want a carbon hull, the only way you can do it, and have it worth anything, is to heat it. By heating it, you get a 50 percent increase in strength. That's huge. Tap this panel here. It sounds like aluminum. It's so dense it's almost metallic. And, as I said, now we have this tremendous hull, and we're going to go and reinforce it with beams. If anyone knows a better way to build a boat, I'd love to hear about it.'

Well, Rob won't hear it from me, because it's not just the hulls he does so well, it's every structural piece and then well beyond that; it's every sophisticated super-yacht finishing detail.

Structurally, the 56 is built to encounter any sea condition anywhere and survive. It has, in the forefoot, a secondary skin, so you can destroy part of the bow and keep on sailing. The decks are as 'Best Tech' as the hulls. They have an inner and outer skin of Kevlar, with balsa coring. And deck hardware is not just installed the way of mere mortals.

'There's a right way and a wrong way,' Rob enlightens, 'to put deck hardware on a boat. We take the outer surface and drill an oversized hole into it, *to* the bottom skin, *but not through* the bottom skin. Then we fill the drilled hole with epoxy and immerse a G10 tube—which is a military spec, solid epoxy and E-glass tube. The bonding of epoxy to epoxy is the ultimate. Then we drill and tap into that G10. So there is absolutely no

possibility for a deck leak. For the winches and handrails, aluminum plates are laid into the laminate. Then we drill through the composite tube that butts up to the aluminum, then in turn drill and tap the aluminum and bolt into it. The inner skin remains unbroken. No chance for leaks.'

All holes—portlights, hatches, vents—are laid up in the mold, as opposed to being cut later. This allows not only for pretty recessed edges with flush-fitting installations, but, of even greater importance, it prevents any water penetration into the core of the deck. It is also a structural factor, in that it allows the layup to have continuous fibers for strength, instead of cut, thus weakened, ones.

The reinforcing longitudinal stiffeners for the hull and deck are all E-glass and carbon. They are laminated over pieces of foam and vacuum-bagged. There are four longitudinals in the cabintop itself. The chainplates are all Kevlar—about ninety-six layers of it—laminated with the hull to form an integral part. The bulkheads are all composite and so is the cabin sole.

The hydraulic lifting keel is normally all the way down, regardless of heading. The nice thing about it is the absence of keel bolts. The keel itself is made of manganese bronze, but the bulb is lead. Inside the keel is a stainless steel hydraulic cylinder, which means when they cast the keel, they have to have a void inside to allow for that. That cylinder attaches down low in the void, and then it comes up and another big pin goes through the cylinder, so everything is interlocked.

The rudderpost comes up in a watertight compartment, so if there are any leaks around the bearings, or even damage to them, the water cannot enter the boat itself.

For the exhaust system, instead of running hoses, they run composite tubes, all glassed together—no hose clamps, no vibration. And it's half the weight. On a boat the size of the 56, with the engine close to the center, the exhaust hose can be a significant length and an equally significant weight.

The stanchions forward are works of art. They are split halfway up, and hinge—inward only—so when the spinnaker sheets or guys lean against the stanchions, they bend in.

And of course their 56 has a furling jib, but the drum and the gear are not on deck like they are on every other boat on this planet; they are below the deck. The publicized reason for this is to get a longer luff, hence more power on your genny. But privately, they'll tell you that it's to make the boat look cleaner, less cluttered, more sophisticated. Of course. Why didn't we think of that?

These kinds of minor miracles are nearly impossible to farm out, so at Turner they have their own magician—a modest, super-patient man called Jack who worked at C&C for twenty-seven years. They have beautiful metal lathes, and they do a lot of machine work both in metals and that God-sent G10 stuff. Some of the pieces Jack makes—'If the owner wants something that doesn't exist, I have to invent it'—are the stanchion bases. They are of G10, drilled and tapped—'It's as strong as aluminum. They are bonded into the deck and the stanchions slip into them. To prevent any water going into this dead-end slot, we use a rubber O-ring.'

We are poking about in the engine room, where all the mechanical systems are located, when Rob points to a wonderful little machine. 'See this little guy here?' he says. 'What is it?' I say. 'A compressor,' Rob says, almost confidentially. And then he adds, with as much pride as if his dad had just been voted King of the Universe, 'Jack made that from scratch.'

R ob Turner's boats, designed by Bill Tripp Design, are without doubt some of the most daring cruiser/racers of recent times, both in concept and in the methods of construction. Above is the unmistakably audacious 56, with the best raised saloon in the world in a boat under 60 feet; from it, you get a perfect view all around while sitting at the dinner table. Note the plumb bow in the same photo, and the beautifully tooled transom (left and below). In spite of its size, the 56 is a super-light—but super-strong—racer that can benefit from some rail squatting (below). In the

same photo, note the Park Avenue boom, into which the mainsail flakes with surprising ease. On this page are two shots of the 46, certainly the prettiest boat of its type. Not only are the hull and deck a match made in heaven, but the tooling and detailing are perfect. The excellent aft cabin (see layout drawing, page 221), with an immensely accessible double berth, is achieved by having the companionway well forward. Access to it is made secure by double, elk-hide-covered handrails. To the right, the bow of the 56 says one thing: 'Out of my way, please,' with a friendly smile.

Turner Yachts has created some of the most original concepts in sailboat interiors. With fearless bravura, and a very European sensibility, they have made boats as visually exciting and as comfortable as the best architect-designed, ultramodern house. The main cabin of the 46 (bottom right on opposite page) is as inviting and as luxuriously at ease as any saloon anywhere. Beside it is the forward ensuite cabin of the 56. Above it is the raised saloon of the 56, with its

wraparound views, infinite light, and beautifully inlaid table. A couple of steps down is the galley (opposite page, top). It is so well laid out that two people can work securely even in a seaway. The stainless steel splashboard with molded Corian countertop ensures longevity. The two photos at bottom left show the unique concept of a double nav station. The station facing forward (and nearest the companionway) is for pure navigation, while the part facing aft is for communication. Pretty brilliant.

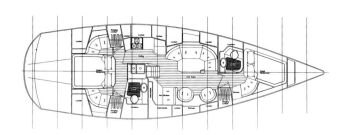

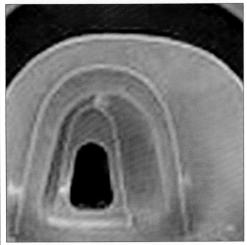

This is about as high-tech and high-creativity as boatbuilding gets. Top left—to increase the genny luff without increasing mast height, the furling drum is set belowdecks. The two white photos on this page are the Kevlar and carbon-fiber hull and deck 'post-cured' at about 180°F in the Turner ovens. On the opposite page, top, look past the twin carbon-fiber steering wheels, deep into that photo, and you'll see the most amazing cockpit table—it's hydraulic. Up, it's a table; down, it's flush into the cockpit sole, with only the two 'Toblerone' wedges sticking up to

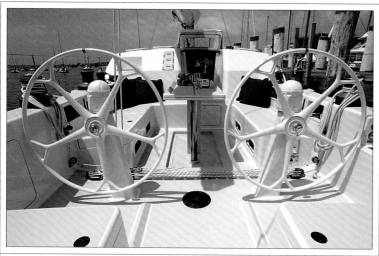

brace feet on a heel. To the right, the ultra-secure, composite companionway ladder weighs but a few pounds. And below is the *coup de grâce*. The plug on the right is a heavy hand-laid-up hull. Beside it is the foam-cored, double-skinned, Turner hull. The triangle (about the thickness of a wafer) is one of the skins, made of eleven layers of carbon fiber and Kevlar. Thank you, Rob Turner (smiling man with mustache). You make sailboats—and writing about sailboats—one of life's most exciting joys.

Few builders that I have run across in my travels seem to be having as much fun building boats as does Rob Turner. His eyes literally blaze with enthusiasm as he shows you around his shop of modern miracles. When someone has this depth of technical knowledge, and enjoys his work so totally, it's easy to see why he builds some of the very, very best sailboats in the world.

SPECIFICATIONS

for

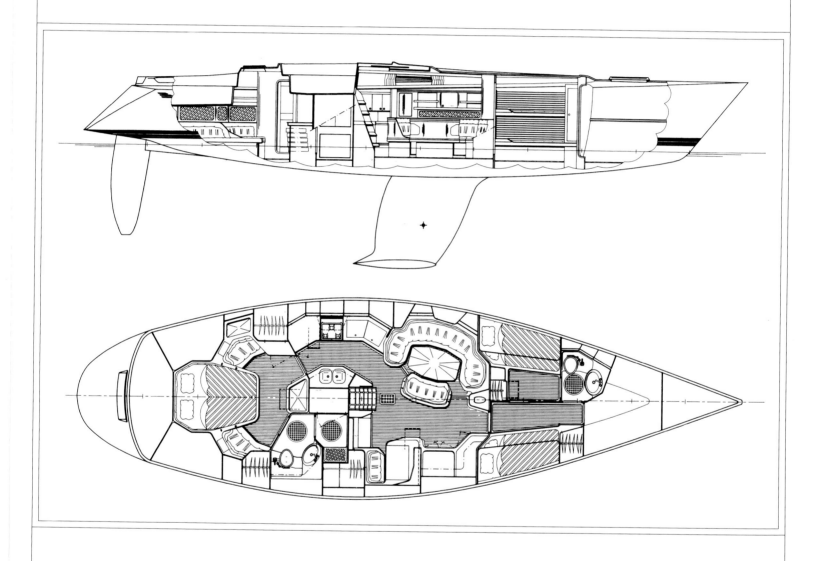

75

SAILBOATS

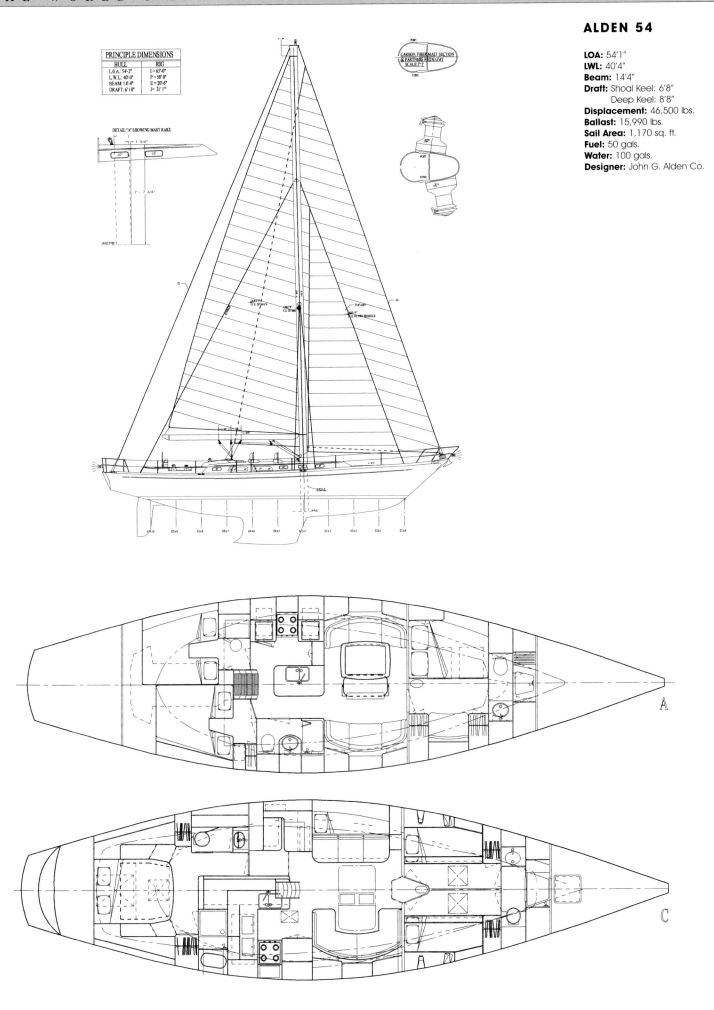

PRINCIPLE DIMENSIONS

HULL	RIG
L.O.A.: 54'-2"	I = 65'-0"
L.W.L.: 40'-0"	P = 58'-0"
BEAM: 14'-4"	E = 20'-6"
DRAFT: 6'10"	J= 21'1"

DETAIL "A" SHOWING MAST RAKE

CARBON FIBER MAST SECTION
@ PARTNERS FROM GMT
SCALE 3"=1'

ALDEN 54

LOA: 54'1"
LWL: 40'4"
Beam: 14'4"
Draft: Shoal Keel: 6'8"
　　　　Deep Keel: 8'8"
Displacement: 46,500 lbs.
Ballast: 15,990 lbs.
Sail Area: 1,170 sq. ft.
Fuel: 50 gals.
Water: 100 gals.
Designer: John G. Alden Co.

ALDEN 54

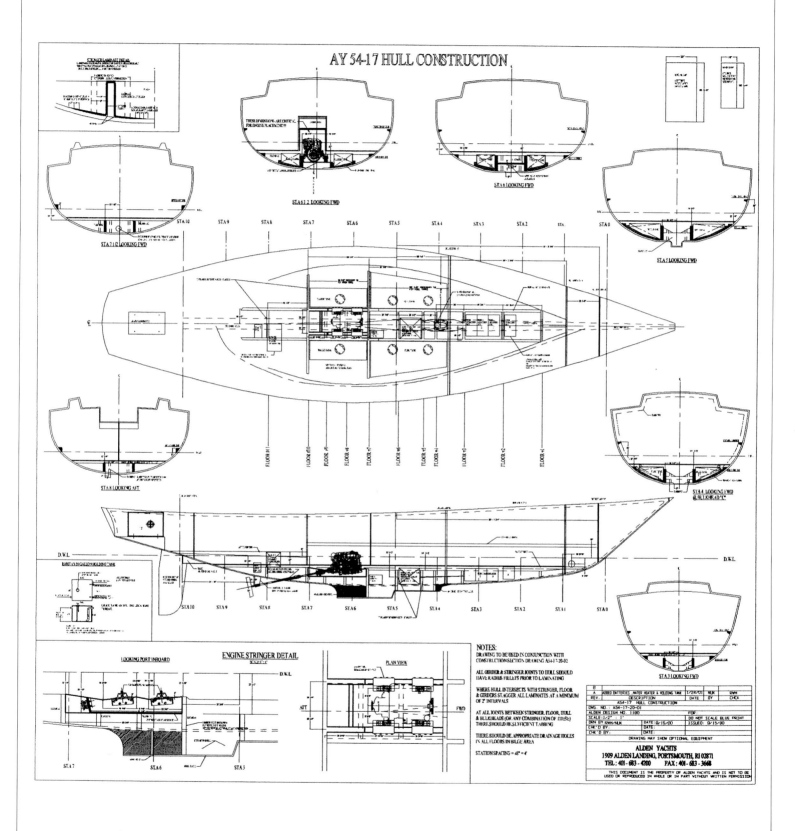

BALTIC 52

LOA: 53'5"
LWL: 43'2"
Beam: 15'5"
Draft: 9'11"
Displacement: 31,967 lbs.
Ballast: 13,228 lbs.
IM: 75.44'
J: 20.34'
P: 67.47'
E: 20.43'
Designer: Sparkman & Stephens
Layout and Styling: R & J Design/
Baltic Yachts

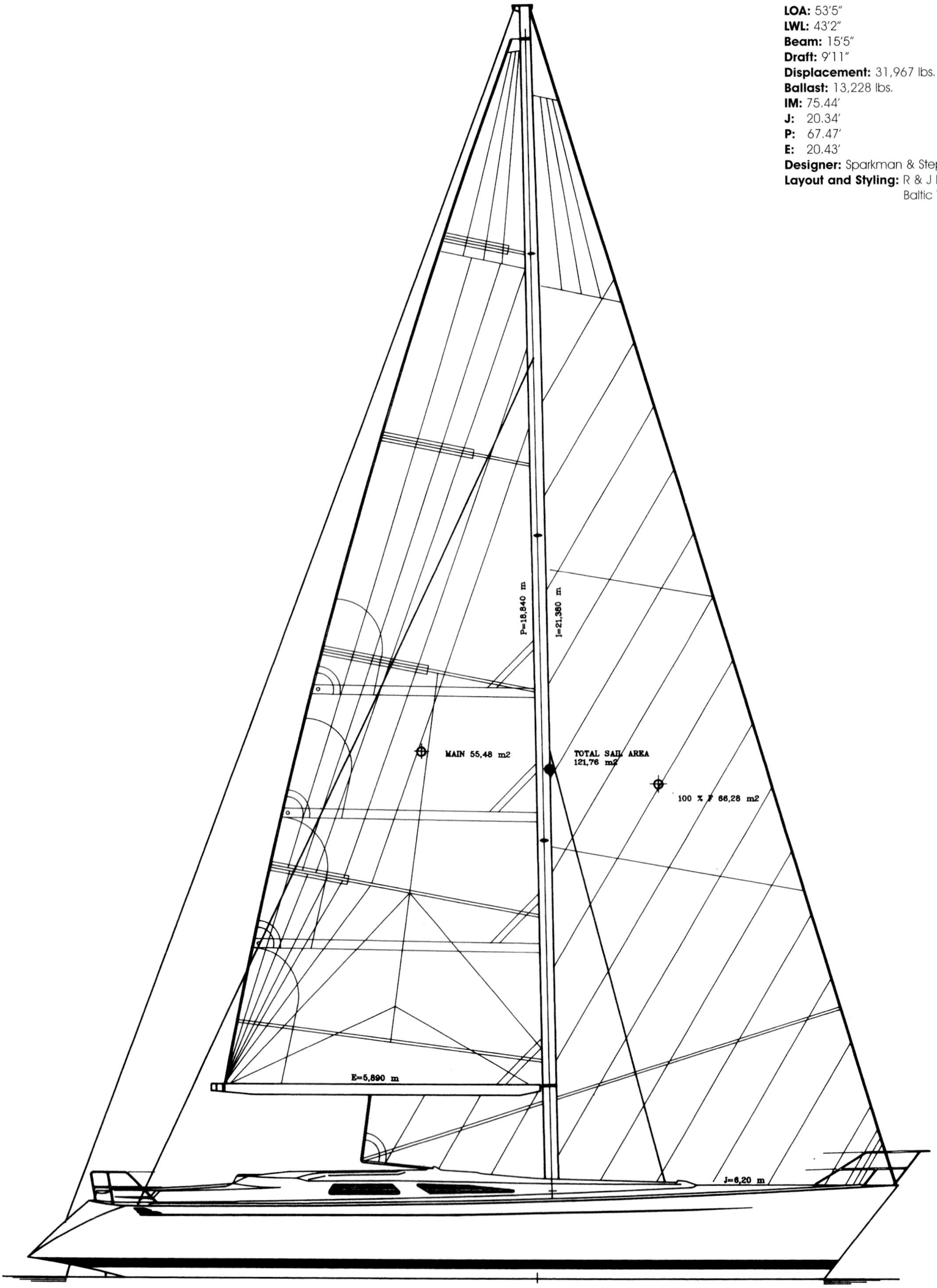

P=18,840 m

I=21,380 m

MAIN 55,48 m2

TOTAL SAIL AREA
121,76 m2

100 % I 66,28 m2

E=5,890 m

J=6,20 m

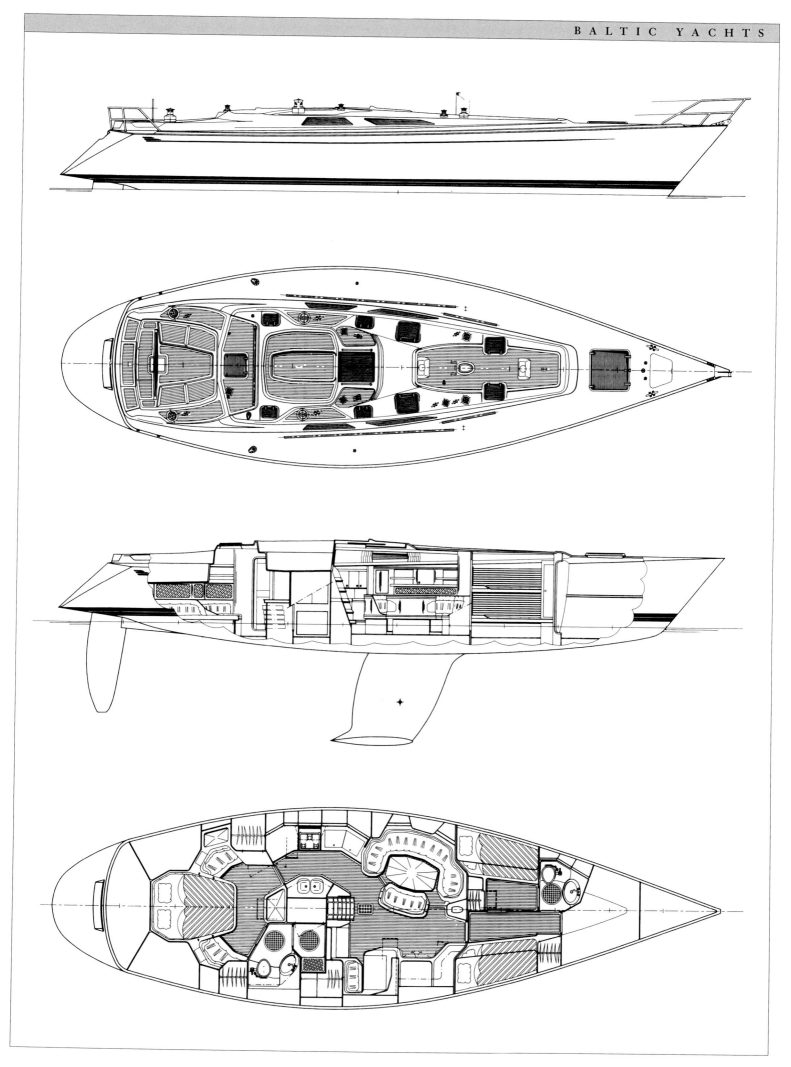

HALLBERG-RASSY 43

LOA: 44'6"
LWL: 38'2"
Beam: 13'5"
Draft: 6'7"
Displacement: 28,000 lbs.
Ballast: 10,500 lbs.
Sail Area: 1,000 sq. ft.
Fuel: 105 gals.
Water: 174 gals.
Designer: Germán Frers

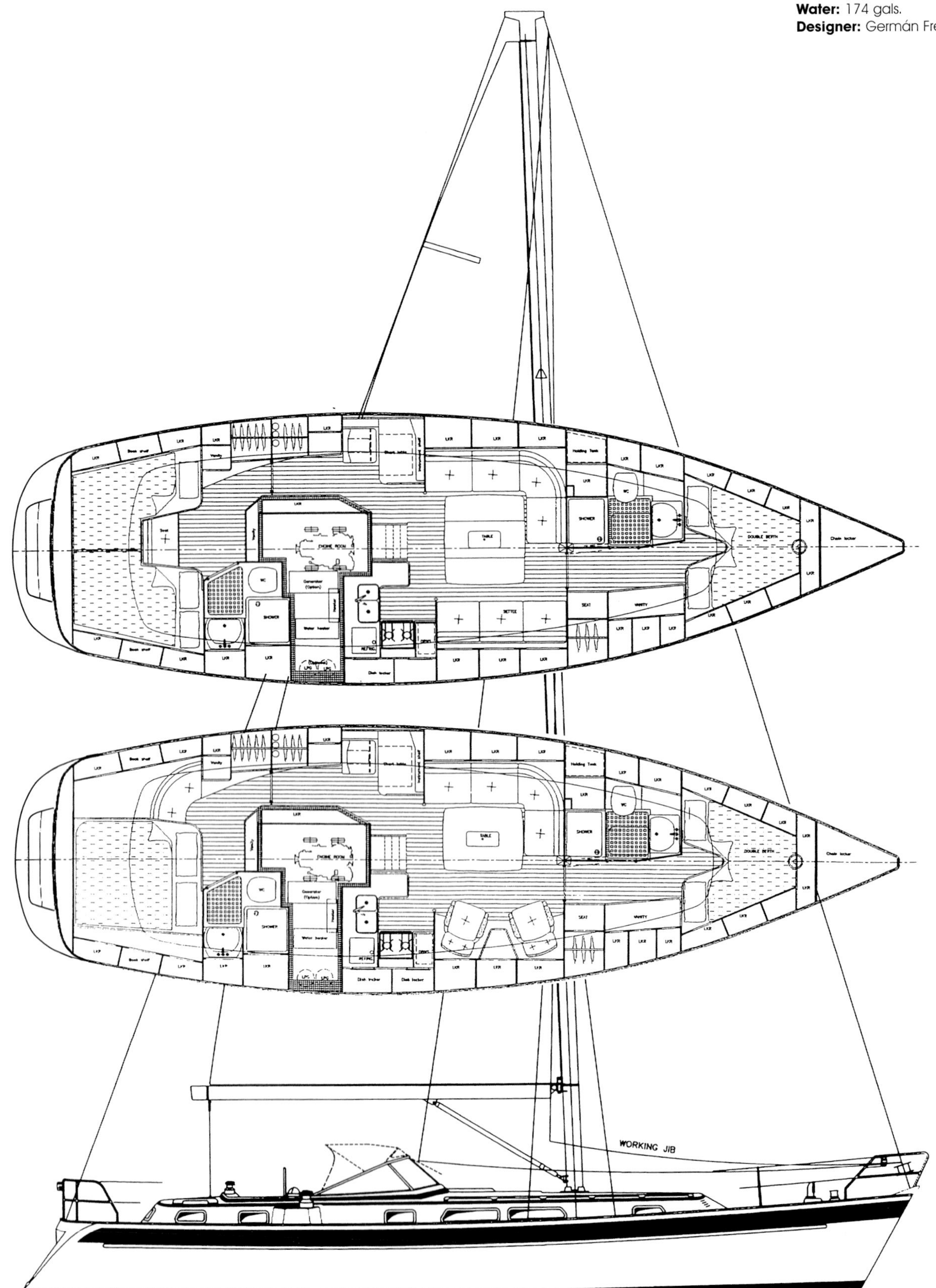

HALLBERG-RASSY 46

LOA: 48'6"
LWL: 38'8"
Beam: 14'3"
Draft: 6'2"
Displacement: 36,300 lbs.
Ballast: 14,550 lbs.
Sail Area: 1,076 sq. ft.
Fuel: 175 gals.
Water: 243 gals.
Designer: Germán Frers

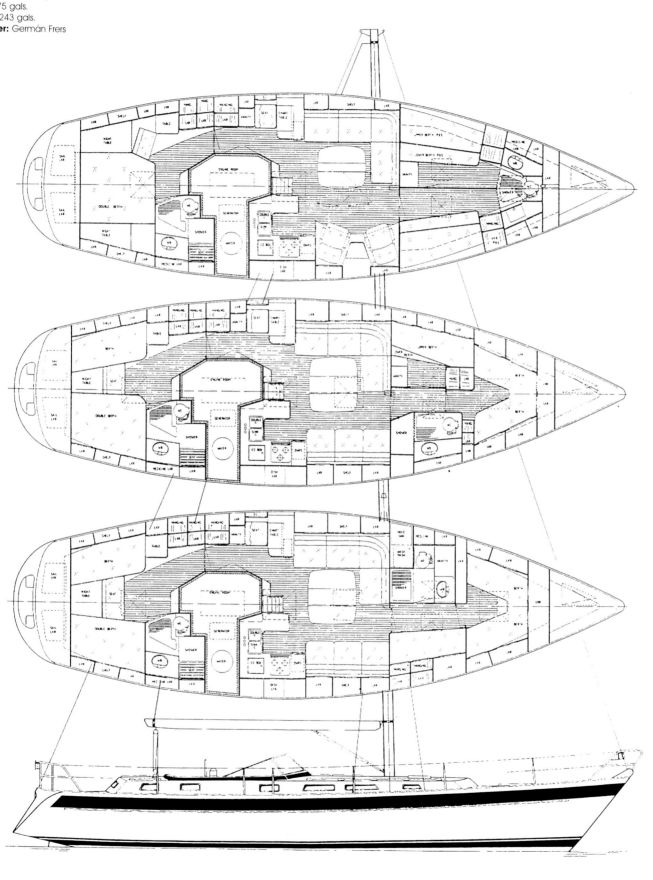

CHERUBINI 44

LOA: 50'
LOD: 44'
LWL: 40'
Beam: 12'
Draft: 4'10"
Displacement: 28,000 lbs.
Ballast: 12,000 lbs.
Sail Area: 1,133 sq. ft.
S.A./Disp: 19.67
Fuel: 75 gals.
Water: 165 gals.
Designer: John Cherubini
Builder:
Independence-Cherubini
51 Norman Ave
Delran, N.J. 08075
Tel: (856)764-1112

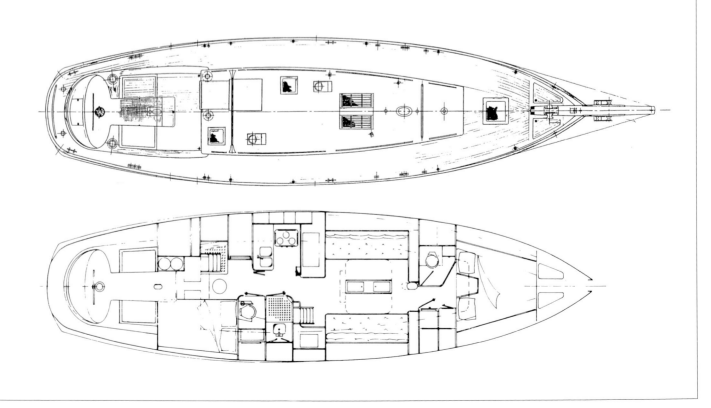

CHERUBINI 48

LOA: 56'8"
LOD: 48'9"
LWL: 44'0"
Beam: 13'0"
Draft: 5'0"
Displacement: 37,000 lbs.
Ballast: 16,900 lbs.
Sail Area: 1,218 sq. ft.
S.A./Disp: 17.2
Fuel: 100 gals.
Water: 200 gals.
Designer: John Cherubini

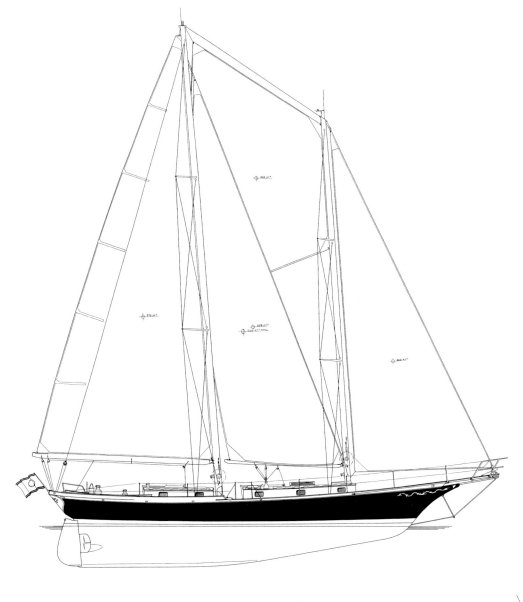

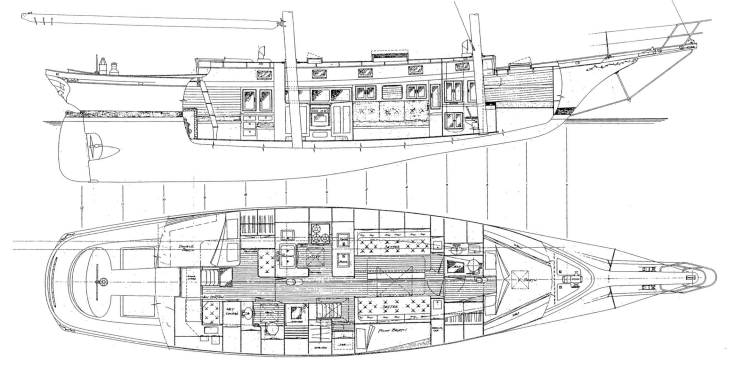

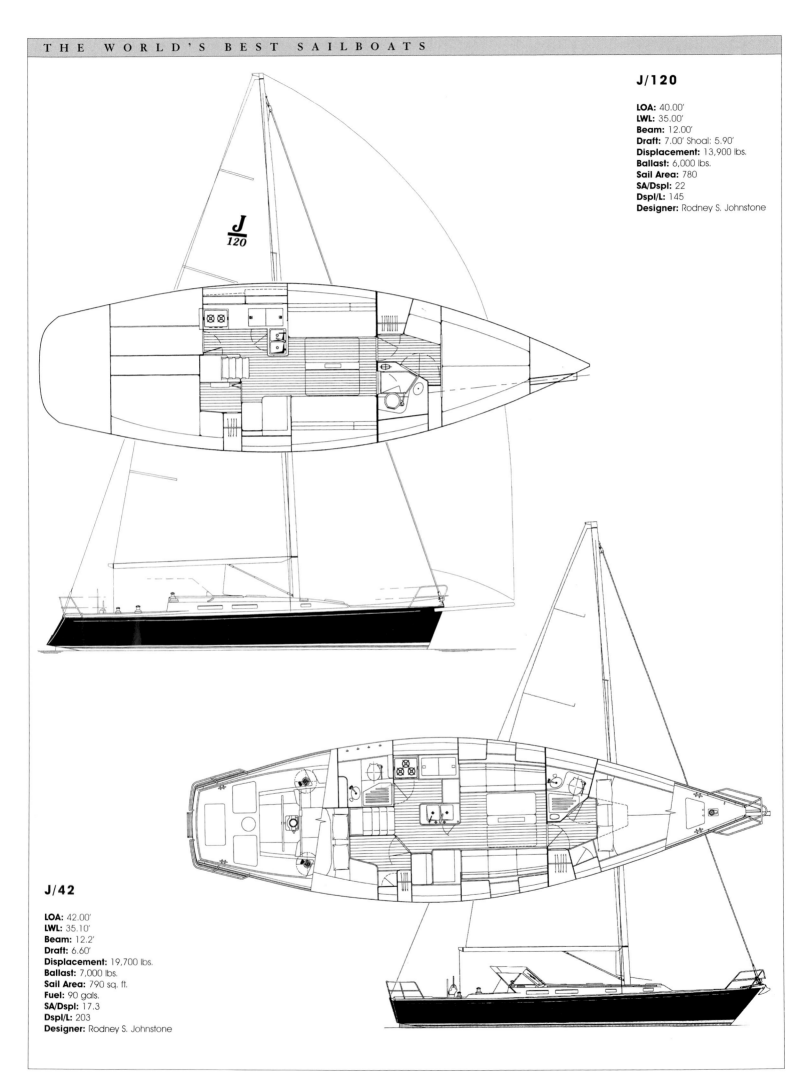

J/120

LOA: 40.00'
LWL: 35.00'
Beam: 12.00'
Draft: 7.00' Shoal: 5.90'
Displacement: 13,900 lbs.
Ballast: 6,000 lbs.
Sail Area: 780
SA/Dspl: 22
Dspl/L: 145
Designer: Rodney S. Johnstone

J/42

LOA: 42.00'
LWL: 35.10'
Beam: 12.2'
Draft: 6.60'
Displacement: 19,700 lbs.
Ballast: 7,000 lbs.
Sail Area: 790 sq. ft.
Fuel: 90 gals.
SA/Dspl: 17.3
Dspl/L: 203
Designer: Rodney S. Johnstone

J/46

LOA: 46.00'
LWL: 40.50'
Beam: 13.80'
Draft: 6.10' Deep: 7.50'
Displacement: 24,400 lbs.
Ballast: 9,400 lbs.
Sail Area: 1,021 sq. ft.
Fuel: 90 gals.
Water: 117 gals.
SA/Dspl: 19
Dspl/L: 164
Designer: Rodney S. Johnstone

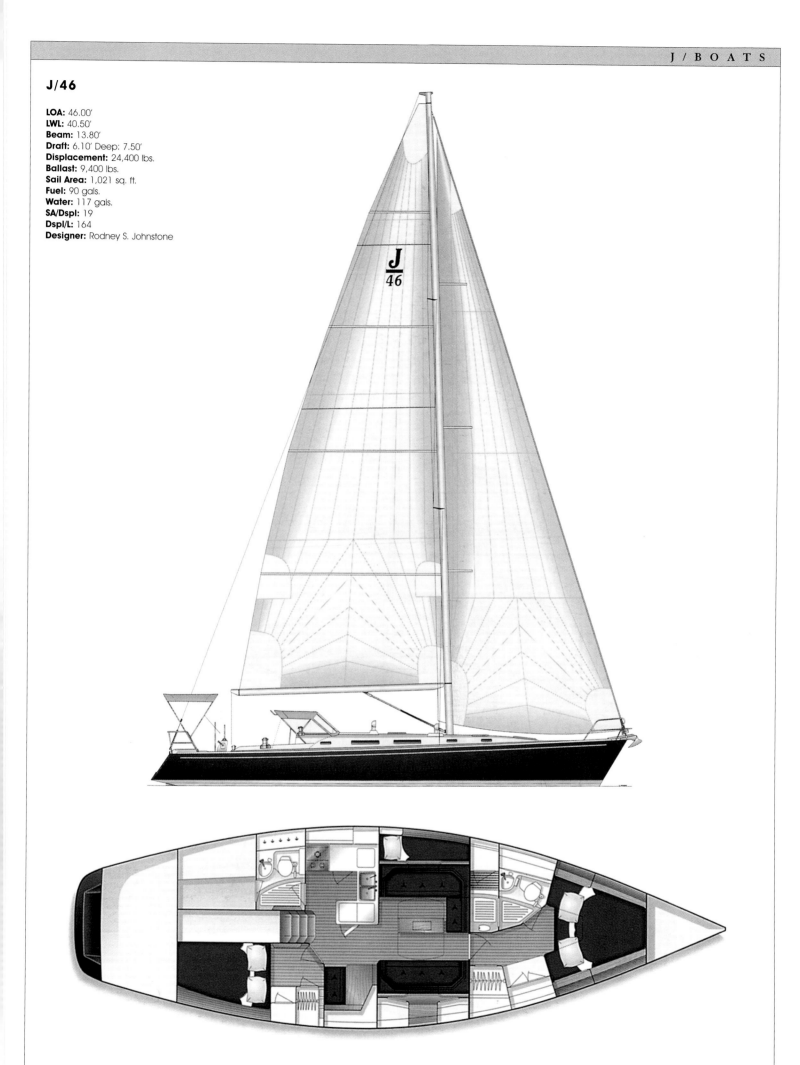

MORRIS 454

LOA: 45'4"
LWL: 39'7"
Beam: 13'3"
Draft: 8'0"
Displacement: 20,500 lbs.
Ballast: 8,600 lbs.
Sail Area: 1,000 sq. ft.
Disp/L: 148
SA/Disp: 21.36
Fuel: 60 gals.
Water: 82 gals.
Designer: Chuck Paine

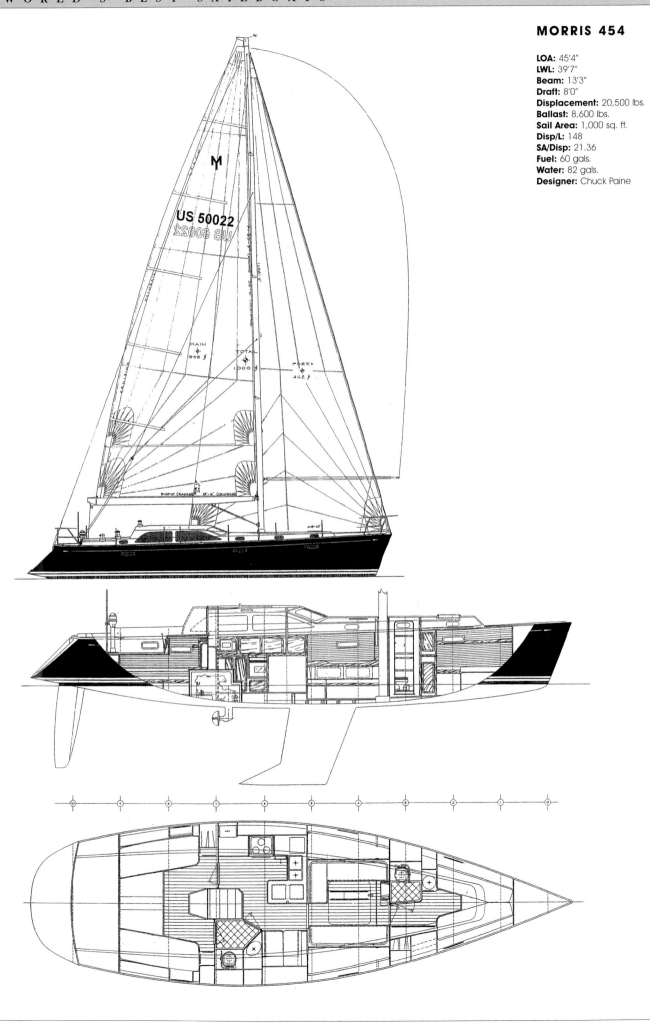

MORRIS 486

LOA: 48'6"
LWL: 41'8"
Beam: 13'9"
Draft: 6'6"
Displacement: 24,458 lbs.
Ballast: 10,700 lbs.
Sail Area: 1,080 sq. ft.
Disp/L: 151
SA/Disp: 20.51
Designer: Chuck Paine

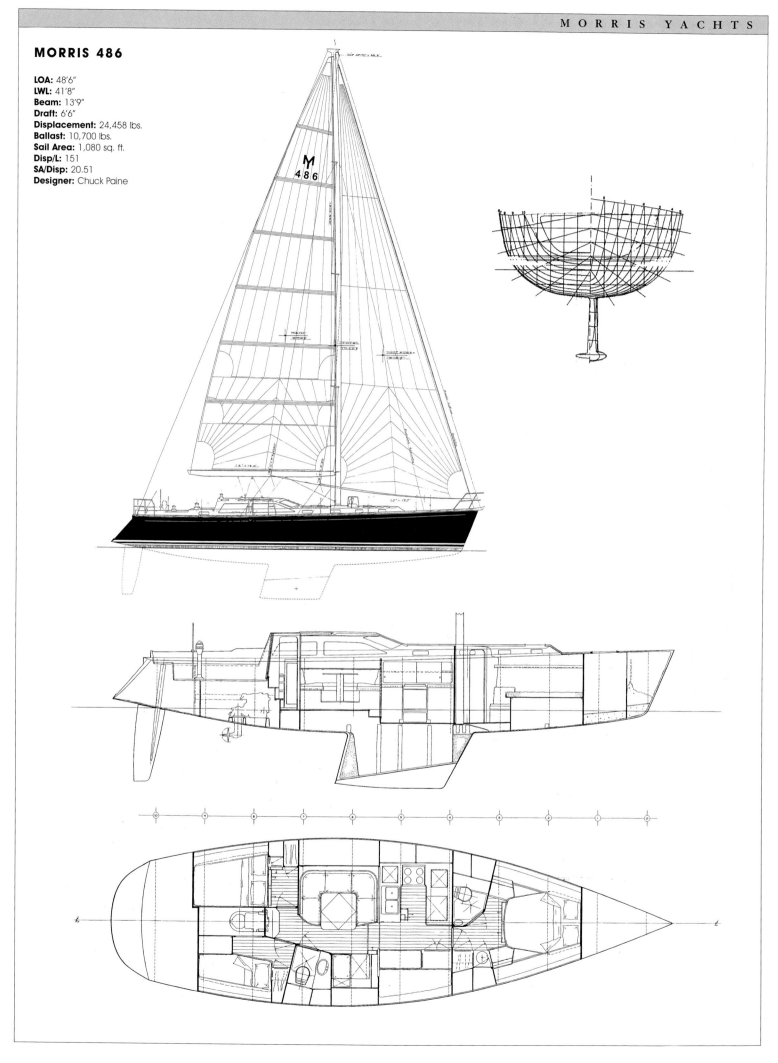

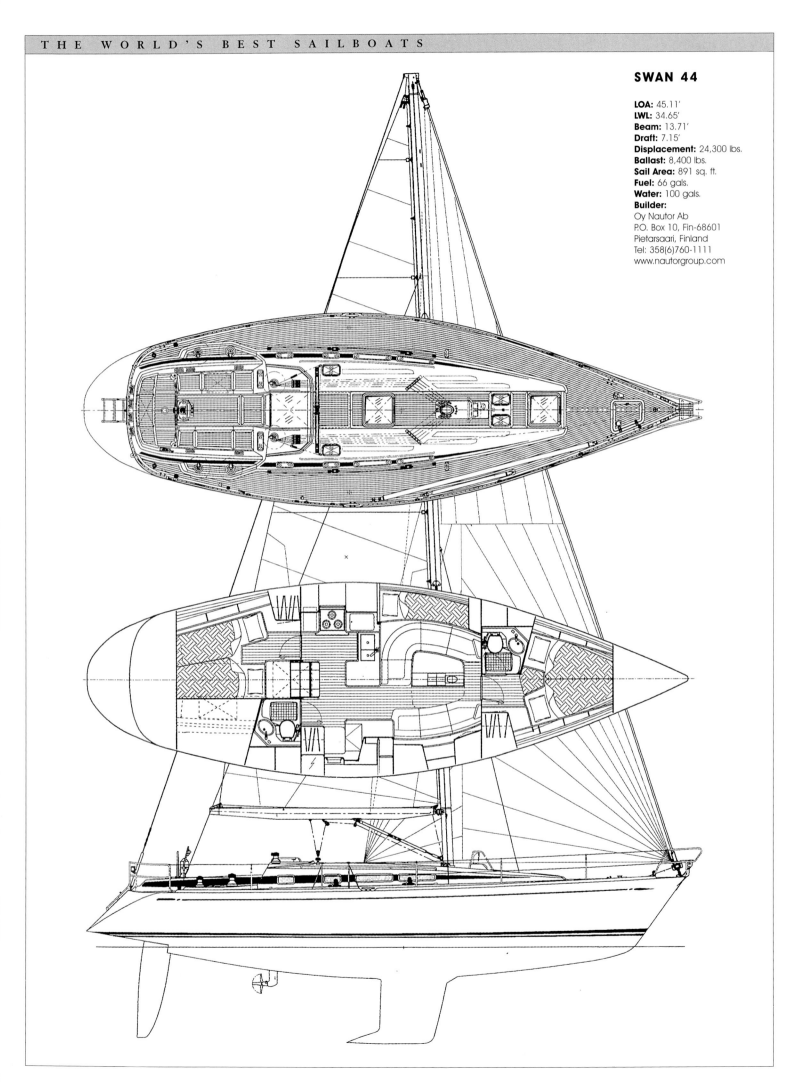

SWAN 44

LOA: 45.11'
LWL: 34.65'
Beam: 13.71'
Draft: 7.15'
Displacement: 24,300 lbs.
Ballast: 8,400 lbs.
Sail Area: 891 sq. ft.
Fuel: 66 gals.
Water: 100 gals.
Builder:
Oy Nautor Ab
P.O. Box 10, Fin-68601
Pietarsaari, Finland
Tel: 358(6)760-1111
www.nautorgroup.com

SWAN 45

LOA: 45.37'
LWL: 39.60'
Beam: 12.86'
Draft: 9.19'
Displacement: 19,510 lbs.
Ballast: 8,820 lbs.
Sail Area: 1,366 sq. ft.
Fuel: 39.6 gals.
Water: 92.5 gals
Designer: Germán Frers

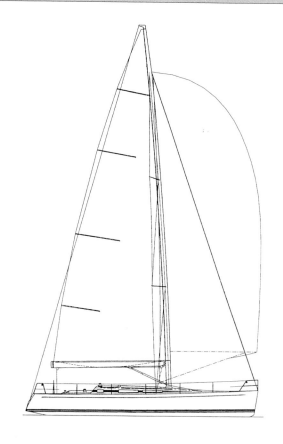

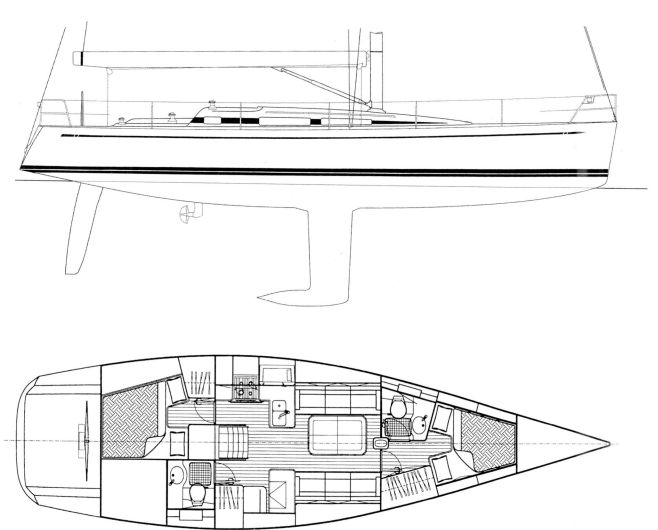

OYSTER 42

LOA: 43'6"
LWL: 33'9"
Beam: 12'10"
Draft: 6'0"
Displacement: 26,600 lbs.
Ballast: Bulb
Sail Area: 150% foretriangle:
972 sq. ft.
Fuel: 120 gals.
Water: 156 gals.
Disp/L: 309
Designer: Rob Humphreys
Builder:
Oyster Marine Ltd.
Fox's Marina
Ipswich, Suffolk, IP2 8SA
England
Tel: 44(0)1473-688-8888
www.oystermarine.com

OYSTER 49

LOA: 50'6"
LWL: 43'9.5"
Beam: 15'0"
Draft: 7'3" Shoal: 6'0"
Displacement: 45,745 lbs.
Ballast: Bulb (HPB)
Sail Area: 150% foretriangle:
        1,460 sq. ft.
Fuel: 210 gals.
Water: 156 gals.
Disp/L: 243
Designer: Rob Humphreys

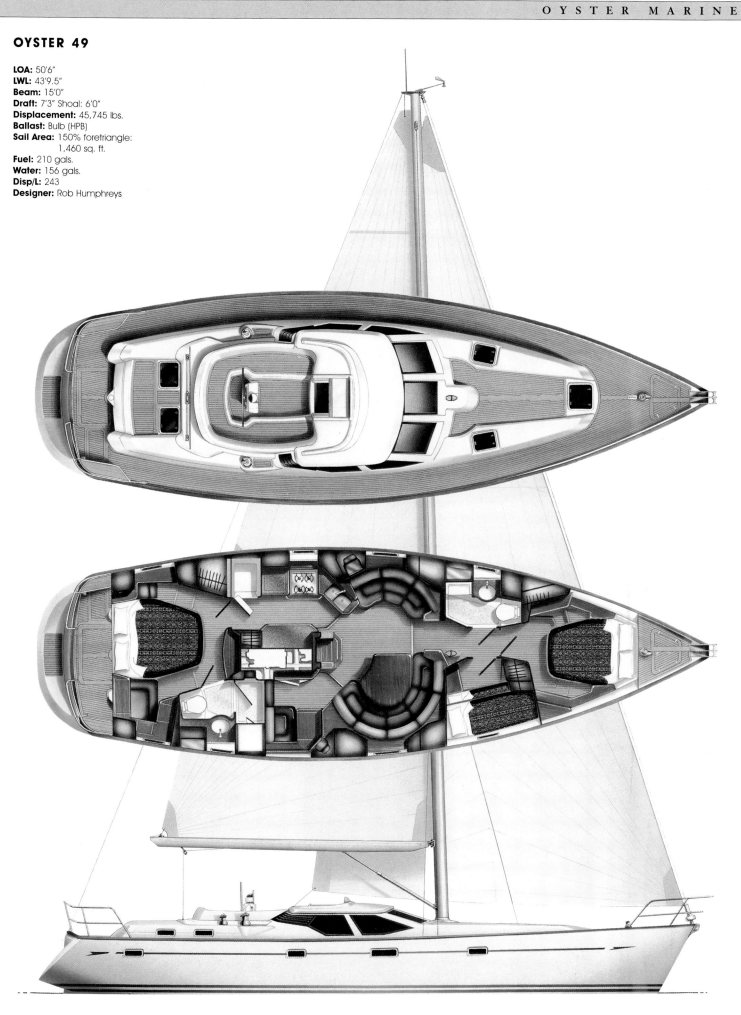

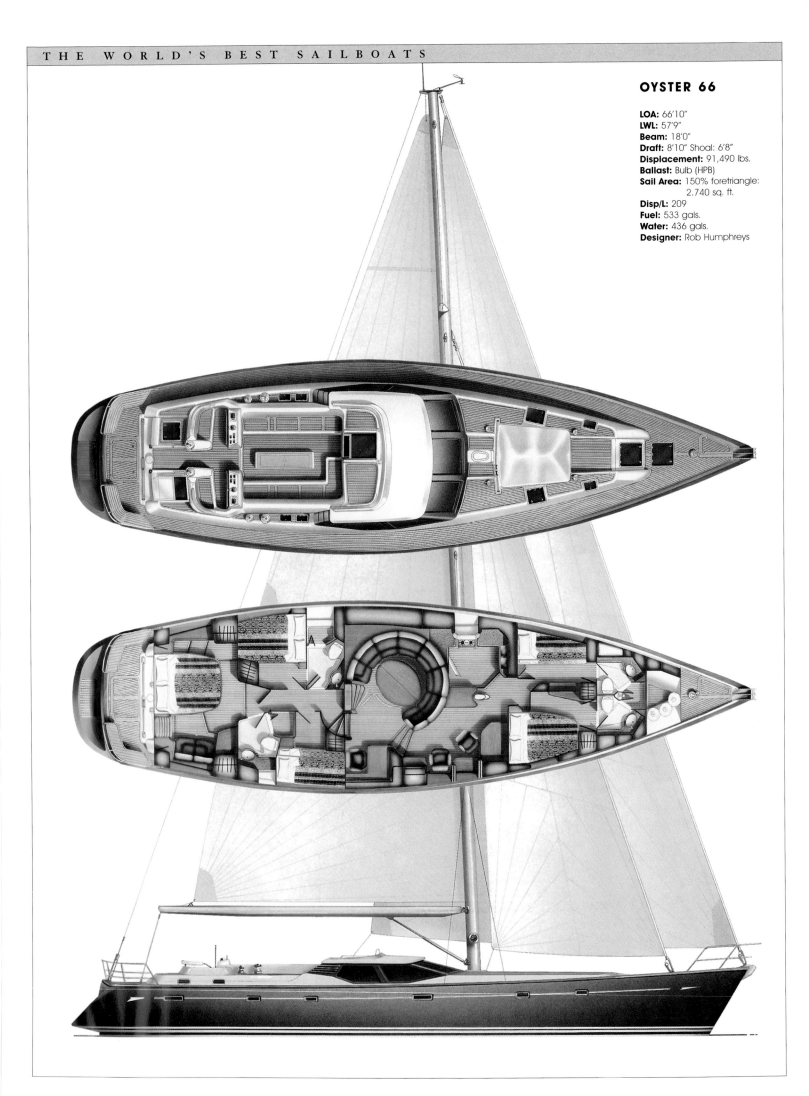

OYSTER 66

LOA: 66'10"
LWL: 57'9"
Beam: 18'0"
Draft: 8'10" Shoal: 6'8"
Displacement: 91,490 lbs.
Ballast: Bulb (HPB)
Sail Area: 150% foretriangle:
     2.740 sq. ft.
Disp/L: 209
Fuel: 533 gals.
Water: 436 gals.
Designer: Rob Humphreys

OYSTER 82

LOA: 81'11"
LOH: 79'11"
LWL: 70'6"
Beam: 20'9"
Draft: 10'4"
Displacement: 134,481 lbs.
Sail Area: 150% Foretriangle:
3,966 sq. ft.
Fuel: 925 gals.
Water: 793 gals.
Designer: Rob Humphreys

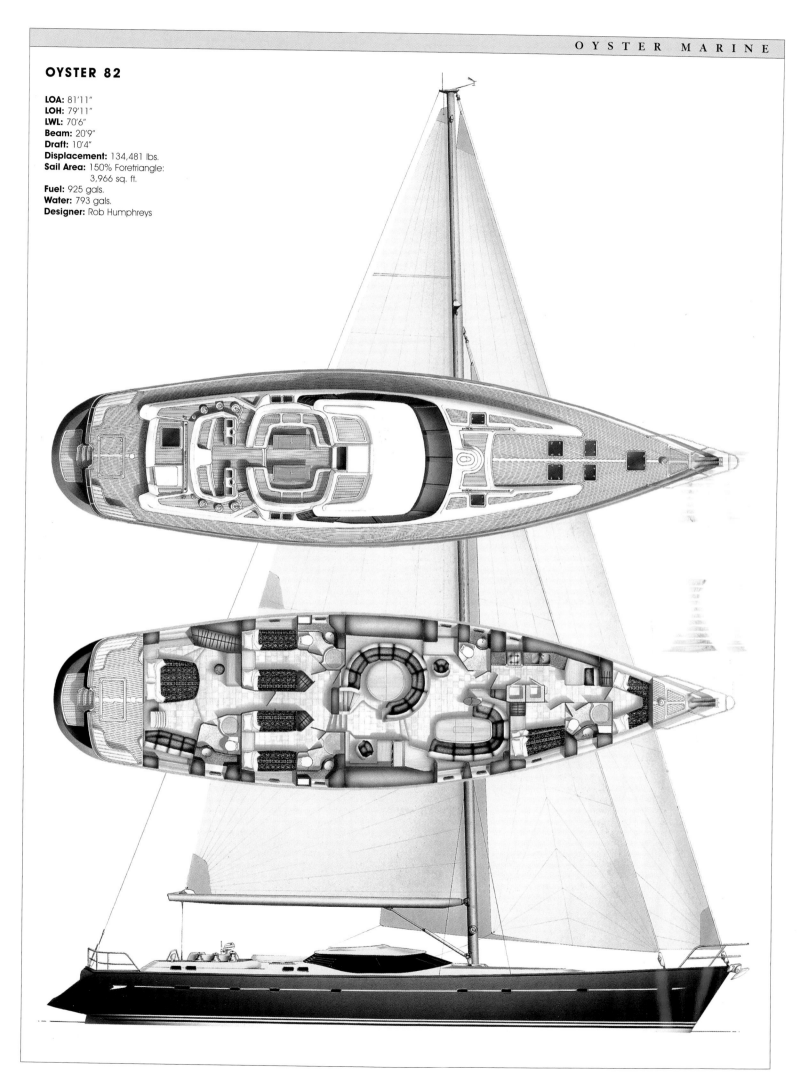

CREALOCK 34

LOA: 34'1"
LWL: 26'2.5"
Beam: 10'0"
Draft: 4'11" Shoal: 4'1"
Displacement: 13,200 lbs.
Ballast: 4,800 lbs.
Sail Area: Sloop: 534 sq. ft.
Cutter: 649 sq. ft.
Fuel: 38 gals.
Water: 75 gals.
Designer: W.I.B. Crealock, N.A.
Builder:
Pacific Seacraft Corp.
1301 E. Orangethorpe
Fullerton, CA 92831
Tel: (714)879-1610
www.pacificseacraft.com

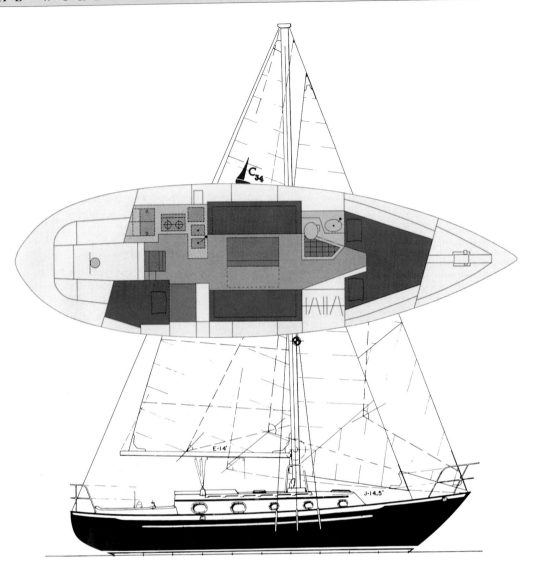

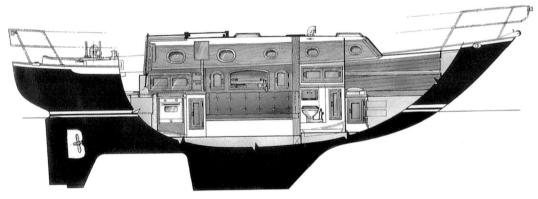

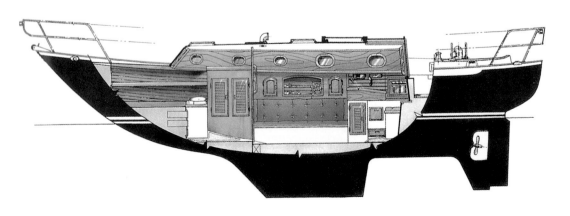

CREALOCK 37

LOA: 36'11"
LWL: 27'9"
Beam: 10'10"
Draft: 5'5" Shoal: 4'5"
Displacement: 16,000 lbs.
Ballast: 6,200 lbs. Shoal: 6,400 lbs.
Sail Area: Sloop: 619 sq. ft.
            Cutter: 758 sq. ft.
Engine: Yanmar 51 hp
Designer: W.I.B. Crealock, N.A.

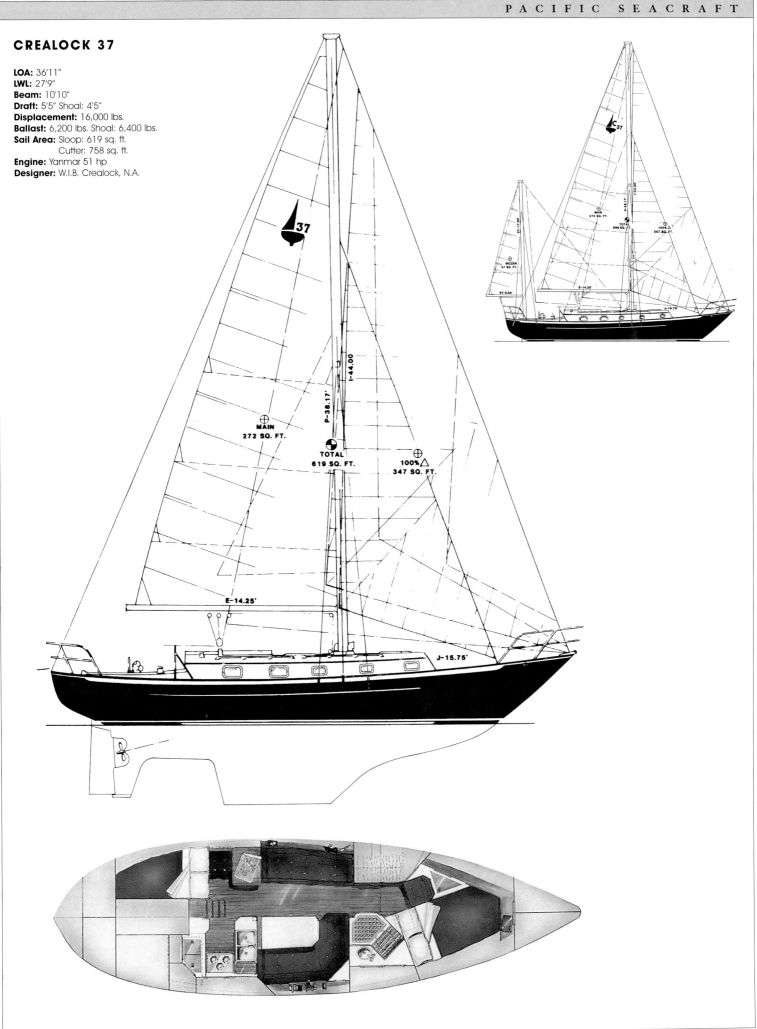

CREALOCK 40

LOA: 42'2"
LWL: 31'3"
Beam: 12'5"
Draft: 6'0" Shoal: 5'1"
Displacement: 23,600 lbs.
Ballast: 8,800 lbs.
  Shoal: 9,100 lbs.
Sail Area: 847 sq. ft.
  With Staysail: 1,032 sq. ft.
Fuel: 70 gals.
Water: 150 gals.
Designer: W.I.B. Crealock, N.A.

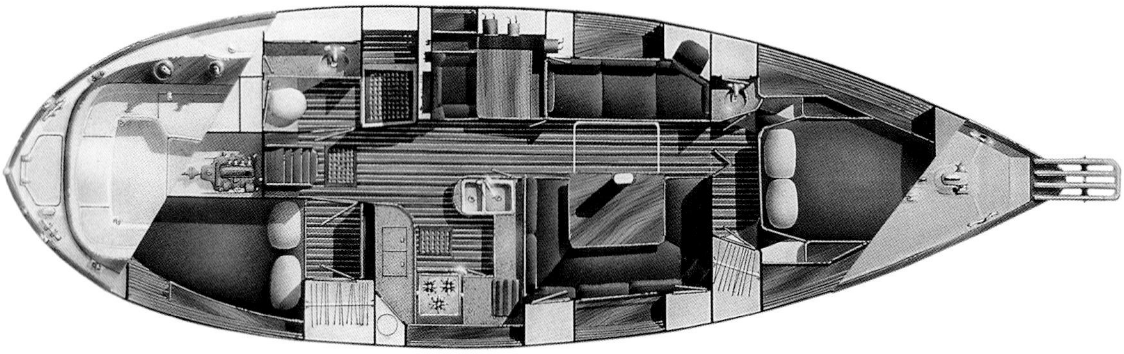

CREALOCK 44

LOA: 44'1"
LOD: 44'1"
LWL: 33'6.5"
Beam: 12'8"
Draft: 6'3" Shoal: 5'3"
Displacement: 27,500 lbs.
Ballast: 11,000 lbs.
Sail Area: 971 sq. ft.
Designer: W.I.B. Crealock, N.A.

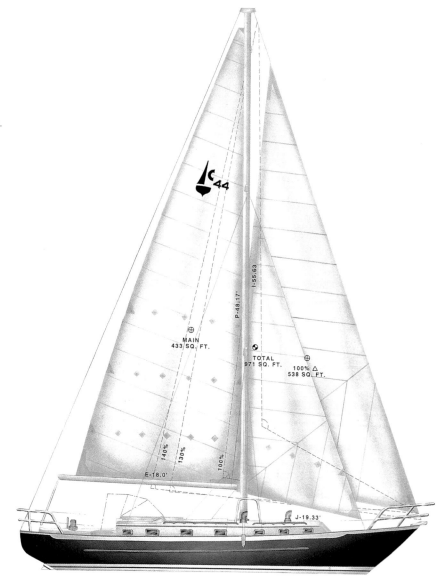

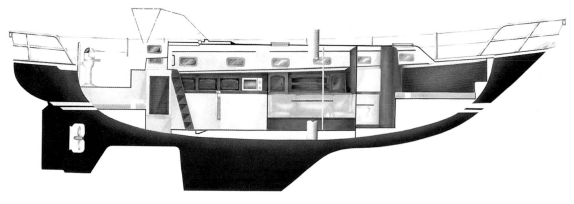

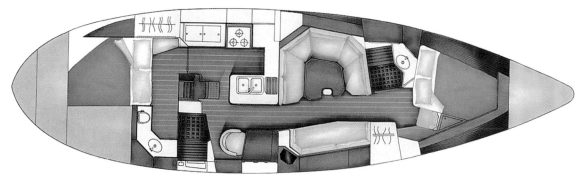

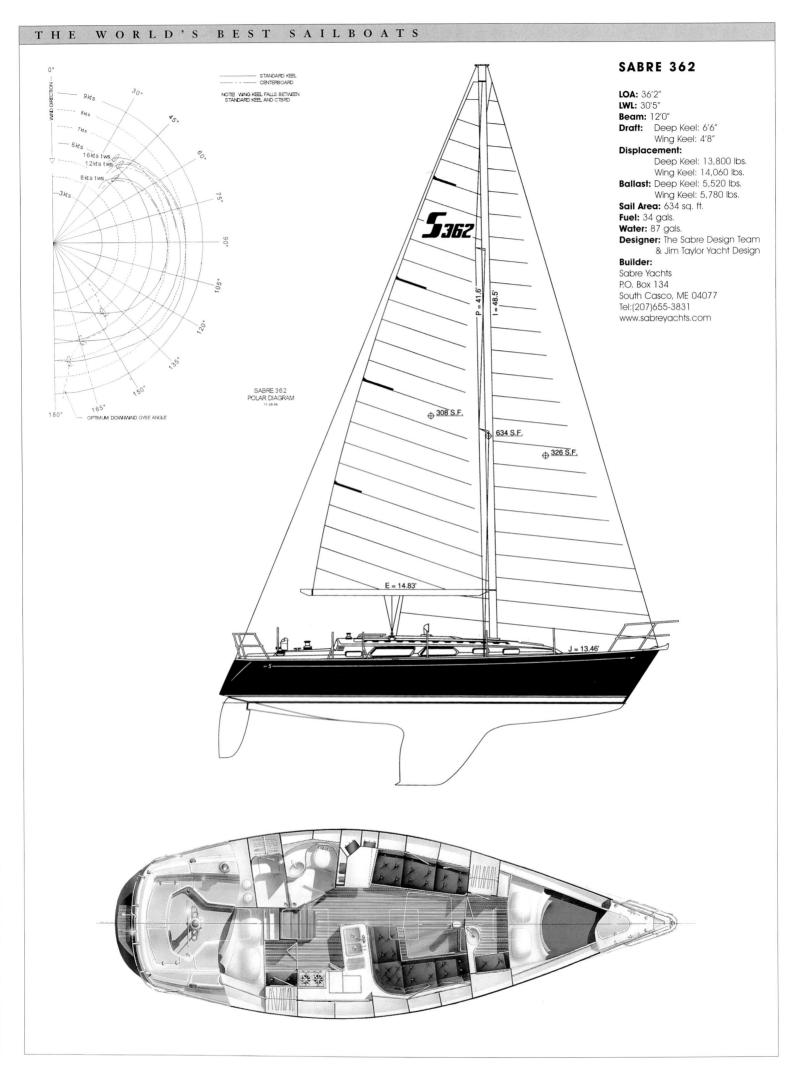

SABRE 362

LOA: 36'2"
LWL: 30'5"
Beam: 12'0"
Draft: Deep Keel: 6'6"
      Wing Keel: 4'8"
Displacement:
      Deep Keel: 13,800 lbs.
      Wing Keel: 14,060 lbs.
Ballast: Deep Keel: 5,520 lbs.
      Wing Keel: 5,780 lbs.
Sail Area: 634 sq. ft.
Fuel: 34 gals.
Water: 87 gals.
Designer: The Sabre Design Team
      & Jim Taylor Yacht Design
Builder:
Sabre Yachts
P.O. Box 134
South Casco, ME 04077
Tel:(207)655-3831
www.sabreyachts.com

SABRE 362
POLAR DIAGRAM
11.20.96

SABRE 402

LOA: 40'2"
LWL: 34'0"
Beam: 13'4"
Draft: Fin Keel: 6'3"
Bulb/Wing: 4'11"
Displacement:
Fin Keel: 19,300 lbs
Bulb/Wing: 20,000 lbs.
Ballast: Fin Keel: 7,300 lbs.
Bulb/Wing: 8,000 lbs.
Sail Area:
100% Foretriangle: 822 sq. ft.
Fuel: 50 gals.
Water: 100 gals.
Designer: Jim Taylor Yacht Design

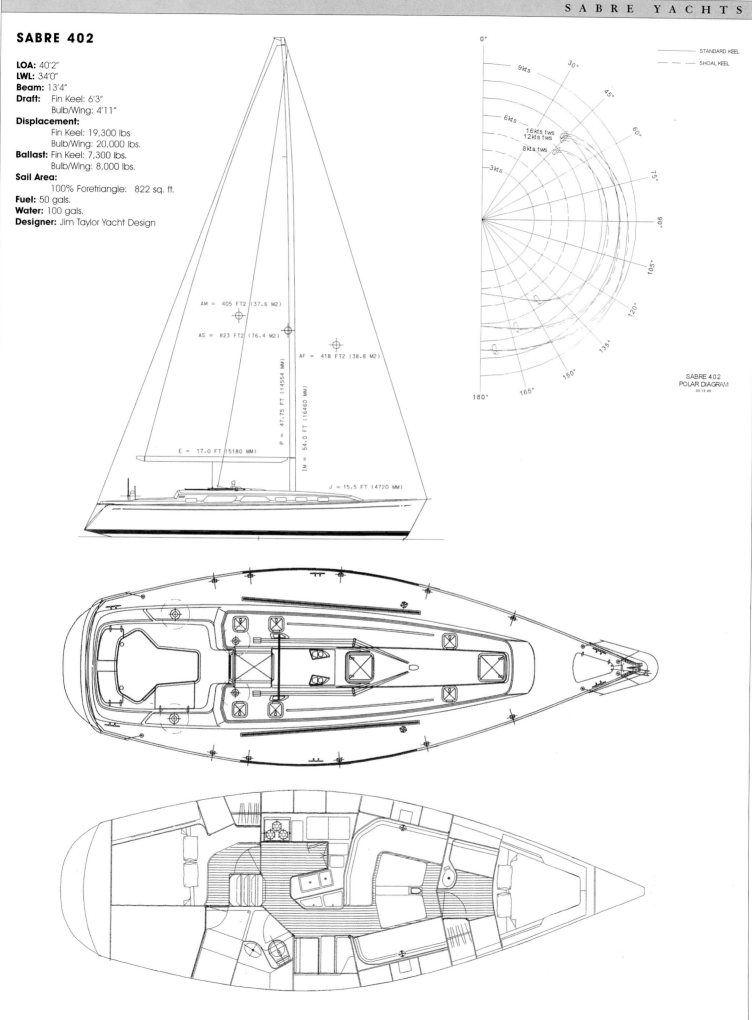

STANDARD KEEL
SHOAL KEEL

AM = 405 FT2 (37.6 M2)

AS = 823 FT2 (76.4 M2)

AF = 418 FT2 (38.8 M2)

P = 47.75 FT (14554 MM)

IM = 54.0 FT (16460 MM)

E = 17.0 FT (5180 MM)

J = 15.5 FT (4720 MM)

0°
9kts
30°
45°
6kts
16kts tws
12kts tws
60°
8kts tws
3kts
75°
90°
105°
120°
135°
150°
165°
180°

SABRE 402
POLAR DIAGRAM
03.13.98

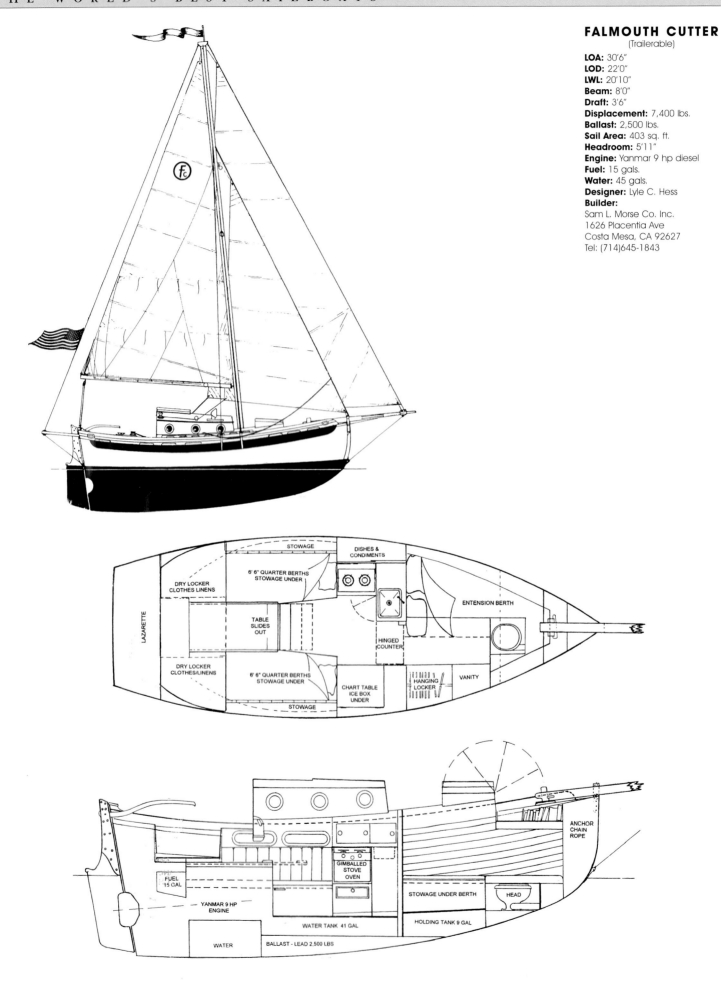

FALMOUTH CUTTER
(Trailerable)

LOA: 30'6"
LOD: 22'0"
LWL: 20'10"
Beam: 8'0"
Draft: 3'6"
Displacement: 7,400 lbs.
Ballast: 2,500 lbs.
Sail Area: 403 sq. ft.
Headroom: 5'11"
Engine: Yanmar 9 hp diesel
Fuel: 15 gals.
Water: 45 gals.
Designer: Lyle C. Hess
Builder:
Sam L. Morse Co. Inc.
1626 Placentia Ave
Costa Mesa, CA 92627
Tel: (714)645-1843

BRISTOL CHANNEL CUTTER

LOA: 37'9"
LOD: 28'1"
LWL: 26'3"
Beam: 10'1"
Draft: 4'10"
Displacement: 14,000 lbs.
Ballast: 4,600 lbs.
Sail Area: 673 sq. ft.
Headroom: 6'1"
Engine: Yanmar 27 hp diesel
Fuel: 32 gals.
Water: 74 gals.
Designer: Lyle C. Hess

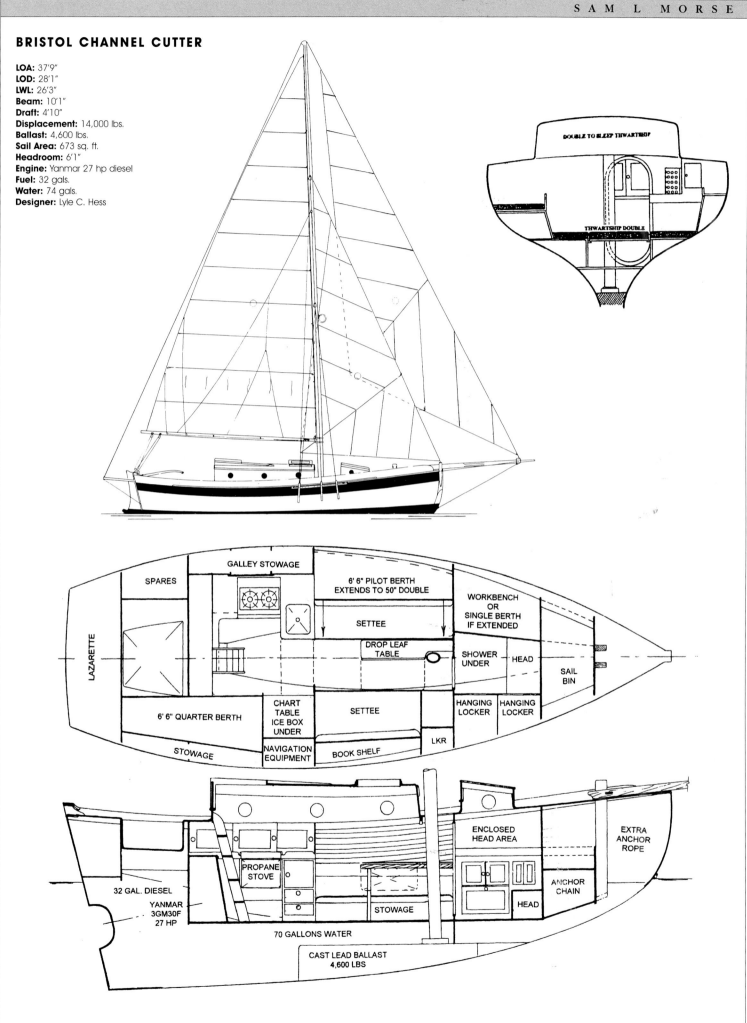

SHOALSAILER 32

LOA: 32'5"
LWL: 30'0"
Beam: 12'9"
Draft: 2'6"
Displacement: 9,532 lbs.
Sail Area: 540 sq. ft.
Headroom: 6'4"
Designer: Schulz, Carter & Assoc.
Builder:
Shannon Yachts
19 Broad Common Road
Bristol, RI 02809
Tel: (401)253-2441
www.shannonyachts.com

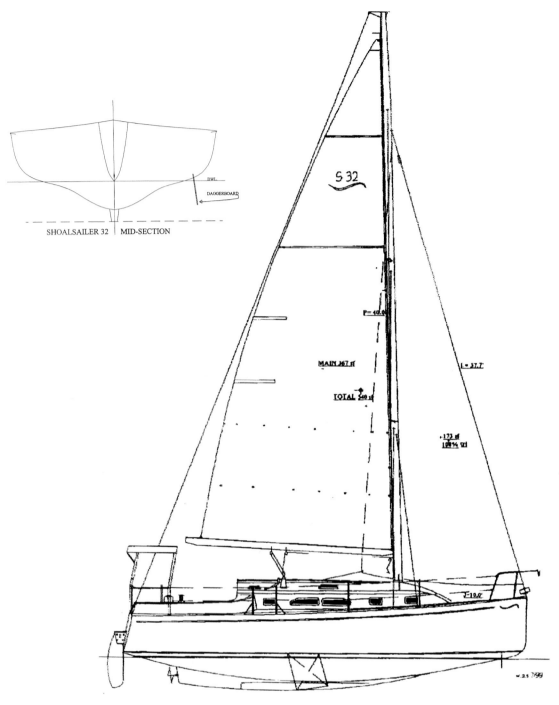

SHOALSAILER 32 | MID-SECTION

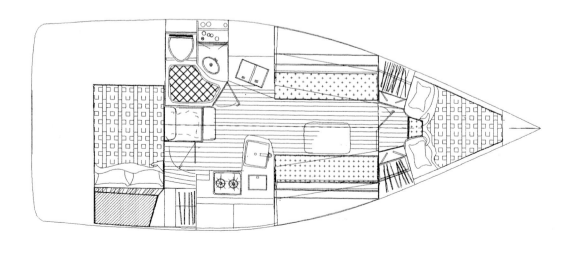

SHANNON 39

LOA: 41'7"
LOD: 38'7"
LWL: 32'10"
Beam: 12'0"
Draft: Fixed Keel: 5'6"
 Centerboard: 4'5"/7'8"
Displacement: 18,700 lbs.
Ballast: 6,900 lbs.
Sail Area: Cutter Rig: 705 sq. ft.
 Scutter Rig: 749 sq. ft.
 S'ketch Rig: 795 sq. ft.
Disp/L: 243
SA/Disp: 17
Fuel: 60 gals.
Water: 100 gals.
Designer: Walter Schulz & Assoc.

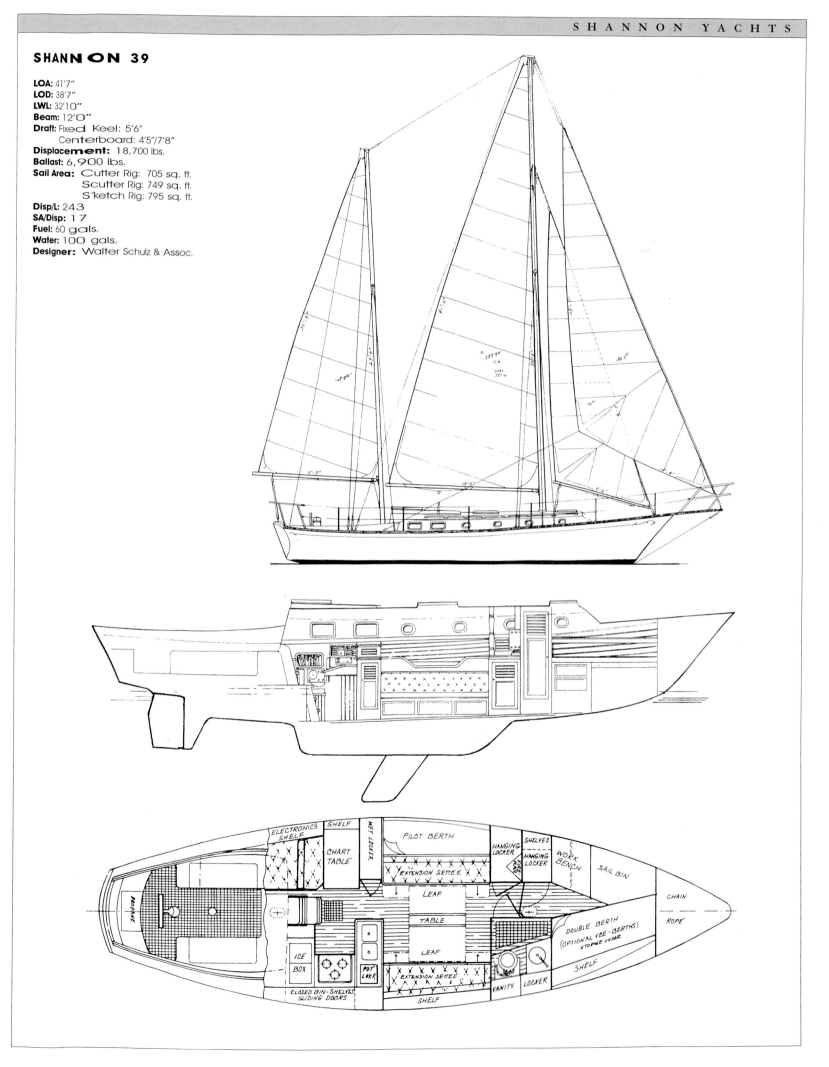

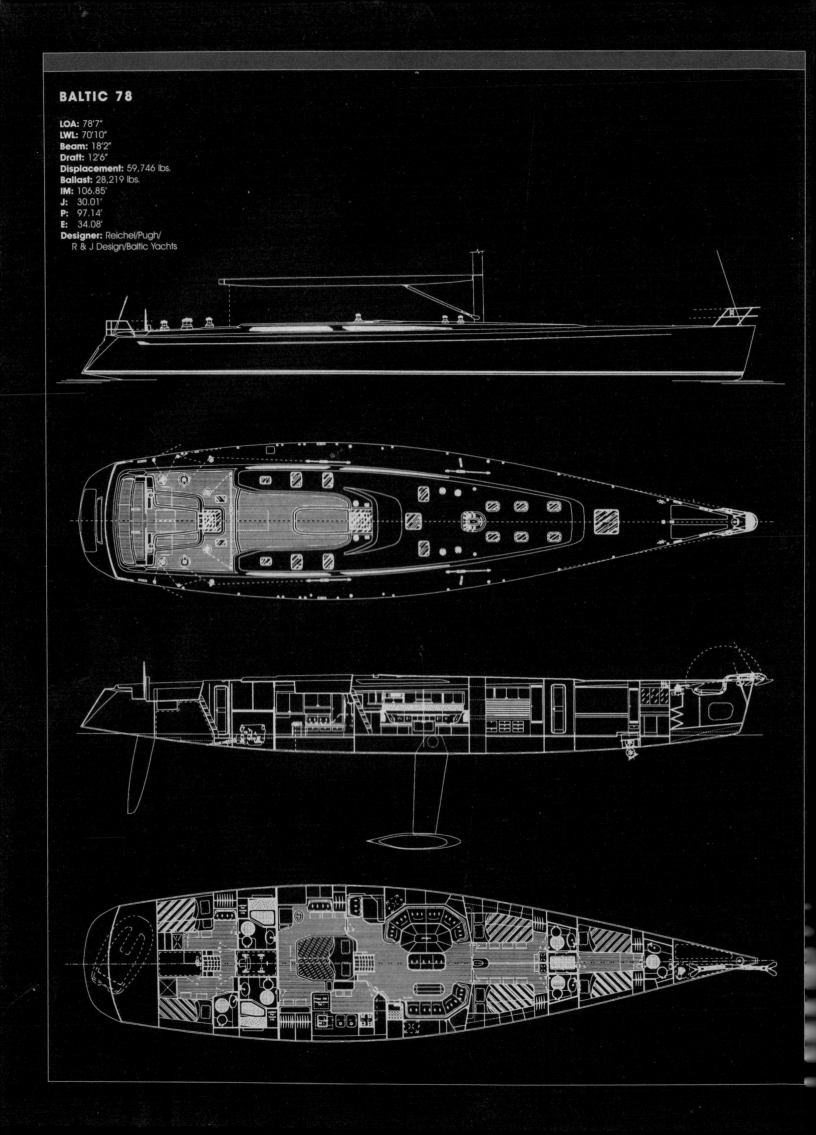

BALTIC 78

LOA: 78'7"
LWL: 70'10"
Beam: 18'2"
Draft: 12'6"
Displacement: 59,746 lbs.
Ballast: 28,219 lbs.
IM: 106.85'
J: 30.01'
P: 97.14'
E: 34.08'
Designer: Reichel/Pugh/
R & J Design/Baltic Yachts